Turkish German Muslims and Comedy Entertainment

CURRENT ISSUES IN ISLAM

Editiorial Board

Baderin, Mashood, *SOAS, University of London*
Fadil, Nadia, *KU Leuven*
Goddeeris, Idesbald, *KU Leuven*
Hashemi, Nader, *University of Denver*
Leman, Johan, *GCIS, emeritus, KU Leuven*
Nicaise, Ides, *KU Leuven*
Pang, Ching Lin, *University of Antwerp and KU Leuven*
Platti, Emilio, *emeritus, KU Leuven*
Tayob, Abdulkader, *University of Cape Town*
Stallaert, Christiane, *University of Antwerp and KU Leuven*
Toğuşlu, Erkan, *GCIS, KU Leuven*
Zemni, Sami, *Universiteit Gent*

Turkish German Muslims and Comedy Entertainment

Settling into Mainstream Culture in the 21st Century

Benjamin Nickl

LEUVEN UNIVERSITY PRESS

Published with the support of the

Popular Culture Association of Australia and New Zealand
University of Sydney
and
KU Leuven Fund for Fair Open Access

Published in 2020 by Leuven University Press / Presses Universitaires de Louvain / Universitaire Pers Leuven. Minderbroedersstraat 4, B-3000 Leuven (Belgium).
© Benjamin Nickl, 2020

This book is published under a Creative Commons Attribution Non-Commercial Non-Derivative 4.0 Licence.

The licence allows you to share, copy, distribute and transmit the work for personal and non-commercial use providing author and publisher attribution is clearly stated. Attribution should include the following information:
B. Nickl. 2019. *Turkish German Muslims and Comedy Entertainment: Settling into Mainstream Culture in the 21st Century*. Leuven, Leuven University Press. (CC BY-NC-ND 4.0)
Further details about Creative Commons licences are available at http://creativecommons.org/licenses/

ISBN 978 94 6270 238 7 (Paperback)
ISBN 978 94 6166 341 2 (ePDF)
ISBN 978 94 6166 342 9 (ePUB)
https://doi.org/10.11116/9789461663412

D / 2020 / 1869 / 57
NUR: 717, 732

Layout: Coco Bookmedia
Cover design: Paul Verrept

Contents

Preface 7

INTRODUCTION
Finding a Voice of Their Own 13

CHAPTER I
Germanness, Othering and Ethnic Comedy 41

CHAPTER II
Clash Films 61

CHAPTER III
Television Narratives of Ottoman Invasion and Cohabitation 93

CHAPTER IV
Bridget Jones's Halal Diary 119

CHAPTER V
Funny Online Kanakism 149

CHAPTER VI
Settling into "Post-Migrant" Mainstream Culture 173

CONCLUSION
European Muslims' Issues: Turkish German Comedy in a Global
Entertainment and Identity Politics Framework 183

Notes 191

References 201

Preface

My sincere gratitude goes to Leuven University Press for making this book available through their Open Access scheme. I also thank Dr Erkan Toğuşlu and the *Current Issues in Islam* series editors for including this discussion of Turkish German comedy in their series of scholarly, peer-reviewed publications initiated by the Gülen Chair for Intercultural Studies (GCIS). Thanks go to the Popular Culture Association of Australia and New Zealand (POPCAANZ) for supporting this book with a publication grant. I am grateful to the School of Languages and Cultures (SLC), located in The University of Sydney's Faculty of Arts and Social Sciences, for providing financial support for the Open Access publication of *Turkish German Muslims and Comedy Entertainment: Settling into Mainstream Culture in the 21st Century*.

This book is the result of many conversations with colleagues and friends, and students, about what funny means in the face of a resurgence of racism and ethnic, anti-Muslim bias in German society and across the globe. And how Turkish Germans can use cultural comedy practices to counter this bias.[1]

There has been an ongoing series of events causing majority societies in non-Muslim countries to question the place of Muslim minority communities in their nation states.[2] After 9/11 and the rise of ISIS, and fundamentalist terror attacks on European capital cities, the discourses of Islamist fanatism and militant Jihadism have surged. This has been playing out in newspapers, books, on television and in online contexts. The negative stereotyping of Muslimness was highly effective in its influence on public opinion.

In the 21st century in Germany, right-wing movements like the German PEGIDA have formed around the idea of Muslimness as a global threat. Supporters of this movement have argued that the Muslim threat would never go away. They have said that Muslims could not possibly be integrated into the Western model of democratic liberalism. How could they, if those Muslims cannot even laugh at Danish cartoons and French caricatures of the Prophet or acts of brownfaced comedy sketches? Even Muslim majority communities who had lived in their host countries for generations, as is the case with Turkish Germans in Germany, were suddenly suspicious if they did not find humour in the derision of certain cultural values or community lifestyles.

This meant that humour associated with an ethnic community and jokes about its origins, beliefs and community characteristics turned into a pop cultural litmus test. Being on one or the other side of ethnicity-themed humour, so held majority opinion, became a clear indicator for liberal attitudes in liberal societies. Even with its Holocaust history and working through its separation of East and West, German society was not exempt from this reductive thinking. Allegedly, laughing at certain jokes or rejecting them measured one's stance on the relationship between Islam and the cultural tolerance discourse of modern nation states. Socially speaking, having to laugh at one's derision to be accepted as part of the in-group is problematic. It is an essentialist practice to regulate expression of identity. It demands conformity. Most importantly, it is undemocratic where it others and excludes members of an ethnic group from fully participating as themselves in daily life in their own homeland and country of legal and permanent residence with or without German passports.

I have written this book to engage with this discriminatory practice and add a new depth and new dimensions to our understanding of the social function of comedy entertainment in German culture. I deliver a case study of Turkish German Muslims and how some of their funniest, wittiest and somewhat provocative community members use comedy entertainment to settle into German mainstream culture in the 21st century as who they are, not who they should be. These creative minds use comedy in different mass media types to entertain all of Germany with a popular culture viewpoint on the issue of Turkish Germans' ability ever truly to belong—while several generations of the community have already lived for decades in the country and made it their home regardless of their nationality. I acknowledge here the achievement of a diverse community in laughing about a mindset that wants to keep Turkish Germans and Islam out of Germany, or at least keep Muslimness and Germanness separate.

Professor Alison Lewis has guided my thinking along the way, and I thank her for that. I also extend my gratitude to the reviewers of my manuscript. I owe them a great deal of appreciation for their insightful suggestions.

Most of all, I would like to thank my family and friends for their continuous support. And here is to Oma Lennerl, who undoubtedly has the best sense of humour one could hope for. It truly makes the world go round.

*Dude, Turks here start out young with their jobs.
I was an interpreter at the age of eight.
My dad pushed letters from the German authorities
into my hands, asking me what they said.
At eight, I was still doing my ABC song in school, you know?!
And he goes, "what the hell you, you learn no German in school?"
And I go, no idea what it says in those letters.
When I was ten, I was an interpreter. I was interpreting for my mom at
the doctor's. And then he blabs for half an hour about patella, labella,
yadda yadda. What do I know what the hell he said?!
And she goes, "what did he say?"'
And I go: all looking good!
Folks, I really had so many jobs when I
was young. Interpreter, barkeeper, doctor, dentist's assistant;
oh boy, I really worked a lot back then.*

—Özcan Coşar, second-generation, Turkish German stand-up comedian
Excerpt transcribed and translated from his 2017
comedy tour programme *Generation Aldi*

---

*It's not easy being an Afghan. You know, because, when I go to Afghanistan,
I'm a German. And when I'm here, I'm a Turk. Can just nobody tell us apart.
A German woman walks up to me. And so she asks me: "Are you a Turk?"
And I go: "Nope, I'm Afghan." Says her: "Same difference really!"
Or a Turkish guy walks up to me and says: "Why aren't you a Turk?"
I said: "Well I thought being a Turk is so mainstream."
But there's one thing we have in common with the Turks.
We're just as hairy as they are. We're really hairy.
I mean, if you see us naked, you'd believe that we're wearing black leggings.*

—Faisal Kawusi, second-generation, Afghan German stand-up comedian
Excerpt transcribed and translated from his *NightWash live*
Finals 2015 performance *Being a Turk is Mainstream*

In die Augen, in den Sinn	*In your eyes, in your mind*
Der Kopf spuckt alte Speicher hin	*Your head spews out what's been stored behind*
In die Augen, in den Sinn	*In your eyes, in your mind*
Im geschlossenen System ist kein Platz für alte Fragen	*Closed systems don't have room for old questions*
Die dümmsten Ideen kommen durch die Hintertür	*The dumbest ideas get in through the back door*
Wenn wir Angst haben dann raschelt's überall	*Everything is scary if we are afraid*
Und das alte Gift fängt an zu wirken	*And the old poison takes effect*
Alle Türken heißen Ali, typisch Zigeuner	*All Turks are called Ali, gypsies as usual,*
Wo ein Bart ist, ist die Bombe nicht weit	*Where there is a beard, a bomb ain't far off,*
Tanzen können die alle gut,	*They can dance well, all of them,*
Tanzen können die alle gut,	*They can dance well, all of them,*
Aber das Boot ist voll	*But the boat is full*
[8 Euro?	*[8 Euros?*
In die Augen, in den Sinn	*In your eyes, in your mind*
Der Kopf spuckt alte Speicher hin	*Your head spews out what's been stored behind*
In die Augen, in den Sinn	*In your eyes, in your mind*
Der Blick wird verbogen durch die Kruste im Hinterkopf	*Your view clouded by what's sitting deep*
Uralte Knoten sind kaum noch zu lösen	*and immobile in your head,*
Deutschland, Deutschland, über alles —	*Ancient knots are so hard to untie*
gibt's im braunen Sumpf	*Germany, Germany, above all else —*
Flüssiger Strom der da durch Schläfen pumpt	*it's there in the brown swamp*
	Liquid current pumping through your brain
Alle Türken heißen Ali	*All Turks are called Ali*
Ach ja, alle Polen klauen	*Oh yeah, all Poles are thieves*
Klau ja alle außer uns!...	*Steal anything but us!...*
...unterdrücken ihre Frauen	*...oppress their women*
Tanzen können die alle gut,	*They can dance well, all of them,*
Tanzen können die alle gut,	*They can dance well, all of them,*
Doch abgesehen von Disco Fox herrscht hier Tanzverbot	*But there's no dancing to be done here, save for Disco Fox*

—"Alle Türken heißen Ali"/"All Turks are called Ali",
song by German band *Jupiter Jones*, released in 2016

Figure 1: "Dschihad!-Gesundheit!", Achim Greser and Heribert Lenz, political newspaper cartoon, first published in the Frankfurter Allgemeine Zeitung, 2005. The perspective of two prominent German cartoonists on issues of Muslim integration plays on the denial of the broader public and its perception of the Muslim Other. Western fears of Islamic terrorism, which has become a well-rehearsed trope in Western media, are lost in translation during a subway ride. This mocks the neglect of the Muslim community's lived realities after years of coexistence in German society. Credit: Greser & Lenz/F.A.Z., reprint with permission by the artists.

INTRODUCTION
Finding a Voice of Their Own

Turkish German Muslims and Comedy Entertainment

If it is not the Jews, it is the Muslims. And if it is not the Muslims, it is the Gay, the Lesbian, or the Transsexual community. The list could continue, as there is plenty of discrimination in Europe to go around when it comes to minority groups. The realities of their lives do not matter. In fact, knowing more about them has traditionally made it harder for mainstream audiences to find amusement in jokes which come at the minority community's expense. Muslims of Turkish German descent have been prime targets in that sense since male and female Turkish migrant labourers arrived in the 1960s to fill the demand for a cheap workforce in a booming post-war economy in West Germany (Herbert, 1990; Chin, 2009). German majority society for decades ignored the spectrum of Turkish German migrant identities, relegating their cultural representation mainly to reductive myths of sensationalist dramas and tragedy. Screens and books were filled with stories about honour killings and domestic abuse (Weber, 2016). They coded Turkish Germans as incongruent with German social values and helped to consolidate certain stereotypes around the physical appearance of Turkish Germans, their behaviour, clothing items like the headscarf, and the alleged lack of ethno-social diversity in the community. After 9/11 a profound sense of Islamophobia came to the fore and Turkish Germans became part of the global threat of radical Islamist terror (Ramm, 2010: 183). The essentialist conceits, then, all fed back into the imaginative construct of cliché Turkishness:

first, it was low-skilled manual labourers taking advantage of the German welfare state. They oppressed their Turkish housewives and forced them to wear headscarves; later, it became about religious extremism.

It is emblematic for these developments that the exoticist logic of Oriental Otherness around Turkish German culture could endure for so long (Berman, 2011). *Türkenwitze* or jokes about Turks as being lazy, uneducated, low-class, religious zealots or unable to master the German language are still readily available in German society. A popular meme making the rounds online for years now reads, "What's *Alice in Wonderland* in Turkish?—Ayse in Aldi! [a popular German food discount store]". Another meme shows two men laying out carpets neatly next to each other in several rows to ready the prayer room in a mosque for worship. The caption atop the image says, "Turkish air force". However, humour has also worked well to address anti-Turkish and, after the events of 11 September in 2001, anti-Muslim attitudes in Germany, with a cultural narrative to support the social narrative of Turkish German integration. This book describes how this happened: how the Turkish German community, grown from thousands to millions over half a century, managed to settle into the cultural mainstream on its own terms and with its own voices and stories; and how Turkish German comedy entertainment came to shape a new conception of inclusive Germanness and cultural diversity in society in the 21st century in spite of anti-immigration sentiments.

Over the past two decades, from roughly the late 1990s to today, Turkish German filmmakers, screenwriters, book authors and stand-up comedians have developed a novel form of funny entertainment culture through a series of broad-ranging multimedia and commercially successful productions. This funny entertainment culture did not begin at the turn of the new century, but it did take on a distinctive form and quality after it, as I explain here and in the main chapters. Its swirling aesthetic emphasises variety of identity. Its broad repertoire of styles, media types and genre elements reflects an abundance of culture through the mixing of languages, belief systems and national heritage.

Turkish German comedy entertainment in the new millennium is an expression of cultural diversity. It is also reflective of a longer history of Turkish German migration (Göktürk, 1999). It revisits historical and more current tropes of both Germanness and Turkishness. They are connected to notions of societal centre and social periphery, and the willingness of communities to embrace cultural change. There are elements of majority and minority culture discourse which have a role to play in developing intersectional dialogue across communal differences and the discrimination against one's ethnicity, religion, gender or sexuality. The emphasis on social strata and the playful engagement of identity politics in this newer kind of Turkish German comedy entertainment is one of its defining features. Its innovative formulation functions as a public arena, whether the comedy screens in cinemas, gets broadcast on television, is published in books, streams online or goes viral on social media. Its narratives illustrate multi-layered connections which link the seriousness of Islamophobia and ethnic bias against German Others to the lived realities and intergenerational memories of Turkish Germans either born in Germany or socialised in the country.[1]

That this new formulation could crack the entertainment culture code in Germany explains in part the lack of mainstream visibility for earlier comedy made by Turkish Germans, mainly those of the so-called first generation. This is despite Turkish German comedy culture's rich history and critical acclaim. Boran details how Turkish German humour culture begins in the early 1970s. There was humorous cartoon art closely related to newspaper lampooning and Turkish German *Kabarett* acts, overtly political satire performances leading up to the creation of popular troupes like Şinasi Dikmen's and Muhsin Omurca's *Knobi Bonbon-Garlic Candy* in 1985 (Boran, 2004). In 1990, Nursel Köse, who later starred in Fatih Akin's critically acclaimed film, *Auf der anderen Seite-The Edge of Heaven* (2007), and Günay Köse were among the founding members of the first female-led Turkish German comedy troupe. Their act, the *Putzfrauenkabinett*, was a play on the German compound noun for *cleaning ladies' supply closet*. It connoted *a political cabinet made up of cleaning ladies*. In 1992, the Köses also co-founded another Turkish German satire act named *Die Bodenkosmetikerinnen-The floor beauticians*. The name was to hint at the economic identity attached to Turkish German women in working-class service roles (Boran, 2004).

Culture critics in Germany praised the heavy political satire of these troupes for the political messaging of the comedy and its ingenuity. It attracted both German and Turkish German audiences with its niche character and cosmopolitan expression. Yet, it failed to gain the same traction in German mainstream popular culture as lighter, Anglophonic comedy entertainment genres. Those genres got directly imported to Germany from America and Great Britain in the late 1980s and early 1990s after German reunification. This prompted younger Turkish Germans to build on the imported genres' mainstream culture appeal and to merge them with local content and formats. The new amalgams achieved what earlier forms of Turkish German comedy culture could not: they became part of popular mainstream culture, attracting millions of viewers domestically and abroad, garnered staggering numbers of likes and clicks, and continuously topped German book bestseller charts.

Approaching Turkish German Narratives: Social Hierarchies and Status of Ethnic Comedy

Two crucial pieces of the puzzle that is the success of Turkish German comedy culture in the 21st century are the social mechanics of German society and the status of humour and ethnic comedy genres.[2] The newer Turkish German comedy entertainment employs ethnicised, or *Turked*,[3] versions of popular international entertainment media and forms of popular mainstream humour. They had come to Germany with stories built around Anglo-American multiculturalism which German audiences would readily watch or read with a sense of frivolous, guilty pleasure (Halle, 2009). Those entertainment items rose to popularity in Germany because they were untainted by the unease of German mainstream culture in confronting on screens or in books the repercussions of the country's Nazi past. There were also tremendous social problems in reunified Germany. One was a surge in xenophobic sentiments against asylum seekers and people of colour during the unemployment crisis of the 1990s. The avoidance of these issues in real life and in the German mainstream media had German newspaper feuilleton columnists declare the 1990s as the decade of German *Spaßgesellschaft*. It meant a hedonistic fun society, driven by shameless embrace of easy consumer culture. Its members desired supranational brand identities, especially Americana pop culture productions and consumer goods, with which they could substitute the burdensome label of Germanness (Biendarra, 2012). By the end of the decade, Germany's so-called literary brat-pack, a group of young pop literature authors, had already picked up on this "wilful superficiality and disdain for history and politics" (McCarthy, 2015) in bestselling novels by Christian Kracht, Benjamin von Stuckrad-Barre, Alexa Hennig von Lange and Florian Illies.

This context matters because two cultural caesuras in Germany add vital cornerstones to my scholarship on the country's ethnic identity politics and its cultural consumption. One is WWII. The other is the post-reunification period of the 1990s. Connecting the social history of Turkish Germans to that of Jewish Germans and East Germans is a critical intervention to shift attention to similarity instead of assumed difference in the history of Germany's ethnic identity discourse. A focus on similarity highlights certain parallels between the cultural prestige of alleged pure Germanness and the ideological striving for Western capitalism in the German *Heimat* or home, and its mediated depictions in popular culture. As I explain here and in chapter one, next to 9/11, WWII and German *Wende* or reunification had a tremendous impact on the cultural dynamics of inclusion and exclusion around Turkish German identities and other forms of Germanness, Jewish German as well as East German. The new Turkish German comedy entertainment conquered Germany's mainstream culture at a time of massive change and profound cultural reorientation in the German body social.[4] The wider public did not necessarily consider its productions as German. The different media types through which German and German-speaking audiences consumed these Turkish German productions also had a transnational flair. To borrow a principle from El-Tayeb's critical scholarship on ethno-cultural discourse in German society, Germans who cannot properly be German cannot be makers of German mainstream culture (El-Tayeb, 2011). In the case of Turkish German comedy entertainment, this was true before Turkish Germans became desirable in the German mainstream for their Otherness and, later ironically, were accepted as Germans for their contributions to it. The Turkish German works of comedy I have assembled here demonstrate this process. They were the beneficiaries of a transnational charisma, which first allowed them entry to and later confirmed their place in mainstream culture in Germany.

Herein lies the specificity of the materials I have selected for this book. Their origins are international, and their core is hybrid. Yeşilada confirms that "they do not operate with traditional binary oppositions, but with transcultural characters and storylines. [...] Cultural boundaries have been gradually blurred, and the former guest worker figure [in more political comedy acts like Garlic Candy] has been substituted by protagonists with transnational features" (Yeşilada, 2008: 74).[5] The extended creative vocabulary has enabled Turkish German creatives to define a new-fangled form of cultural self-representation in sound (Hilman and Silvey, 2012), image (Halle, 2009), and in the plot of literary fictions (Gramling, 2011). Branded by its makers as cosmopolitan comedy entertainment about identity issues, all audience segments can relish in the development of ethno-social consciousness from a safe distance.[6] There is no accusatory tone or blame. Instead, the new phase of Turkish German comedy culture thematises social tensions between and in certain ethnic communities in Germany, suggesting that the same storylines and forms of humour could just as easily take place in New York, London or Istanbul. Its productions revolve around the global consequences of migration and multi-ethnic coexistence.

Without dwelling on the dark side of the social issues they represent, Gueneli shows that the affiliation with transnational comedy culture offered Turkish German filmmakers such as Fatih Akin an increased repertoire of creative choices and styles beyond Turkish and German (Gueneli, 2019). Turkish German filmmakers like Akin derived it for films like *Im Juli-In July* (2000) and *Solino* (2002) from multicultural clash film comedies such as Richard Benjamin's *Made in America* (1993). The interracial clash comedy romance between Whoopi Goldberg's and Ted Danson's characters was among the 15 most successful cinematic releases in Germany in 1993. The funny plotline of this American comedy blockbuster closely resembles the clash comedy film plotlines under critical review in chapter two. And like those Turkish German clash comedies, *Made in America*'s entertaining message is not that the idea of diverse, modern multiculture is broken. Rather, the playful mix and fusion of identity markers indicates that any hostile relationship between clashing ethnic and other identities can be salvaged if the underlying prejudiced viewpoint is addressed. Optimistic viewpoints abound, probing new ways of co-existing in this world as a diverse community. It is a comedy around a cosmopolitan, positive concept of ethnicity explicitly designed to compete in the international commercial mainstream.

The humour at play in all the cultural synergies and skilful adaptations of mass entertainment genres and popular media types I write about in this book turns on social variables. Who and what gets made fun of or is turned into the butt of a joke or the punchline of a humorous scenario implies the potential importance of recognising the constructedness of such positions as Self and Other. It is a cultural commentary on the unfixedness of Germanness and German society, which we should think of as the remedy to the ills alleged by anti-immigrant right-wingers: social instability, the loss of German *Leitkultur* or guiding culture, authentic ways of being Turkish or German, and having to decide that one can be only one or the other. Turkish German comedy culture in the 21st century offers with its variety of genres and media types an arsenal of tools, each exquisitely applied to a unique social purpose. It is to reflect on the datedness of certain societal norms and their persistence. As the bitter-sweet ending of *Almanya-Willkommen in Deutschland-Almanya-Welcome to Germany* reveals, it is about looking ahead with an appreciation for a difficult past.[7] However, we should not get lost in the latter or deny it. This would only reify the notion that Turkish German migration is a failed project and that Islam is and always will be un-German.

Questioning cultural impenetrability and the segregation of ethnic communities is the central tenet of the ethnic situation comedy *Türkisch für*

Anfänger-Turkish for Beginners, on which I elaborate in chapter three. It shows how Turkish Germans who were steeped in the comedy genres they fused their perspectives and issues with could add to these genres' existing mainstream allure. To the lived realities of their Turkishness they added the association of being German Other, being international, being cosmopolitical and being non-white, Turkish or Muslim. In chapter four, I detail how a gender angle adds even more potency to Turkish German mainstream comedy's subversion of reductive perceptions of multifaceted identities in Turkish German chick-lit and Turkish German dick-lit. To test whether this hopeful outlook on social change has endured not only in more traditional media-type formats of film, television and literature, I put in dialogue Turkish German stand-up comedians and the social media reception of their performances in chapter five. In this respect, *Turkish German Muslims and Comedy Entertainment* answers the question posed by the suggestive title of Şinasi Dikmen's 2002 comedy routine *Quo vadis, Türke?-Where are you going, Turk?* Where indeed have Turkish German comedy producers and artists been going, and in what direction has humour taken some of them since the turn of the century? I engage with this question with a brief, German-specific synthesis of post-migration culture in chapter six, before ending the book with a perspective on Muslim issues in a European comedy context.

A Word on Ethnic Humour and Its Social Pragmatics

I apply the social pragmatics of humour through close readings to the narratives of Turkish German entertainment comedy, contextualised by a short explanation of specific production styles or genre conventions and distinct historical developments. One may think of it as a way to explain how Turkish German culture has mastered the change from ventriloquised object of German entertainment to designing active voices with real influence on German mainstream culture in little more than half a century. Turkish German comedians, filmmakers, authors and screenwriters have brokered significant cultural standing for themselves by infusing mainstream comedy with alleged ethnic or minority issues. My aim, though, is to expand the field of Turkish German culture and comedy studies rather than to arrive at a definitive account of Turkish German comedy entertainment and its roles in the new century. This is partly because the study of humour with its many forms and functions in different societies and among and within groups is complex and contextual. Above all, it is perennial.

Moreover, interpretative analyses of humour and a cultural critique of its uses in mass-culture entertainment demand a narrow lens to illustrate the fine line between humour to divide and to include people who live in certain social and cultural frameworks. And since these two distinct uses of humour, pro-social and anti-social, are inextricably linked to the lived realities of Turkish German individuals, Turkishness, Germanness and mainstream comedy as discussed in this book, I address them with very specific historical reference and in light of certain media types and particular themes and methodology. The limitations of this strategy are as much acknowledged and present as they are specifically situated. So is my scholarly and personal identity as a white cultural studies researcher who is not Turkish German and received his postgraduate training mainly in America and Australia.

Humour is "an umbrella term to cover all categories of the funny" (Lippitt, 1994: 147), including comedy, wit, satire and jokes. It embraces many structures and types of funny material. There are, in fact, too many to list here for a purposeful overview. Directly relevant to the study of Turkish German comedy entertainment are such types as scripted jokes and dialogues, quick-witted repartees, wordplays or puns, and humorous modalities as described by Jorgensen (1996: 614-615) and Martin (2007: 5-10). Then there are the cardinal forms of mainstream comedy entertainment: sketches, parodies, long-prose fiction novels and comedy performances, both live-staged and recorded (Holmes, 2000: 165-166).

It is important to acknowledge the difficulty in using humour in the context of ethnic comedy as a critical approach to reflect on Turkish German issues and identities in contemporary Europe. Humour relating to community clashes and the co-existence of different ethnic groups in Germany presents a terrific challenge. When is it okay to laugh at a joke about religious bias? What marks the fine line between self-deprecation and sarcasm and a form of internalised Islamophobia and racist speech? When does comedy reproduce what it aims to subvert? Are the punchlines of mainstream comedy hefty enough to deliver critical messages about Turkish German women's experiences of misogyny? Or about Turkish German men's experiences of being labelled terrorists, religious fanatics, or camel fuckers? Precise correlations between forms, functions and effects of humour in mass mediated comedy entertainment can be hard to identify. They are even harder yet to discuss by attributing social messaging to them. Interpretations of comedy writing, dialogues or performances and audience reactions, as Roach and Milner Davis note, "are often culturally specific, subjective, context-dependent and variable" (Roach and Milner Davis, 2019: 2-3). Humour comes in many forms and its functions and effects are both intended and unintended. I am not going to claim otherwise in this book.

There is agreement though about a specific use of humour in ethnic contexts, which is based on ideas, assumptions or widely held stereotypes and clichés about national, racial or religious groups. The conflation of the latter two applies to the Turkish German community. As I discuss further in chapter one, ethnic humour, here in mass-cultural application to mainstream entertainment referred to as ethnic comedy, comes in two forms. One is derogative in nature and intended to vilify and to ridicule certain ethnic groups and/or communities. Its purpose is to segregate and to create a hierarchical distancing between Self and Other. This function reflects a politicisation of ethnic comedy in popular culture, which also goes back to a racialised worldview. The historical development of ethnic comedy is reflected in the systemic bio-politics of modern racism as borne out in American blackfaced minstrelcy (Mahar, 1999) and in Nazi Germany in anti-Jewish propaganda dressed up as funny newspapers cartoons (Luckert et al., 2009) and conveyed through film comedy (Weinstein, 2019).

The second form is the direct opposite. In a related manner of politicised usage, it subverts the former's intention to assign the ridiculed a lower place in society or to exclude them from the majority. It is governed by a sense of multicultural togetherness which undoes the fear of Others imposed on all members of society by cosmopolitan anxieties (Mandel, 2008: 14). One can liken those anxieties to a competition for ethno-cultural supremacy and the fear of losing out on power in society as if it were a limited good. It is an agenda which harks back to a neo-liberal doctrine in Western capitalism of resource scarcity and ideological dominance. The Cold War's stand-off between America and the Soviet Bloc has foregrounded the underlying scare tactics of this development globally since the early 1980s. Both forms of ethnic comedy, however, need to be acknowledged as a duality of action and reaction. One is successful if it triumphs over its twin adversary.

Studying ethnic comedy requires consideration of what is funny and at whose expense, "firstly from the [imagined] audience or perceiver's cognitive experience of 'getting' the humour and secondly from the affective response—which may or may not be one of enjoyment and pleasure" (Roach and Milner Davis: 3). Ethnic comedy in favour of creating homogeneity in modern multicultures may be unsuccessful if it amounts to little more than a personal attack on proponents of derogatory ethnic comedy. It fails where it is used as a tool to retaliate. The imagined audience or actual observers or readers may not comprehend pro-multicultural criticism as a critique of systemic racism if they feel directly attacked. The inherent danger is to turn pro-multiculturalism into a social wedge issue (Gillota, 2013: 6). This assessment is consistent with Sollors' provision that "laughing at others is a form of boundary construction" (Sollors, 1986: 132). This book sets out to present the undoing of these boundaries through the kind of ethnic comedy which punches up against a system of boundaries. When ethnicity-generated humour blurs the out-group/in-group line, it becomes an intentional site for intercultural dialogue taking place in the public arena of popular culture (Lowe, 1986: 440). Forms of ethnic comedy which deconstruct boundaries and foster debate about the mixing of cultures are effectively aligned with the "enlightened and egalitarian values of Western liberal democracies" (Berghahn, 2014: 2). Any discussion of what I refer to here as pro-social ethnic comedy should help to illuminate this aspect.[8]

The pragmatic theorisation of humour in ethnic comedy to reflect on its intended functions in factual reality is another delicate matter. I present a more detailed discussion of this approach linked to Germany's long history with ethnic denigration of German minority identities during the Holocaust and around the time of reunification in the next chapter.

Politics of Religion and Muslim Representation

The right of Muslims to be represented in mass-culture narratives about Germany as an enrichment of rather than a burden on the country underpins all the ethnic comedies assembled in this book. It is the most prolific issue in a conversation about fears that "Germany does away with itself" (Sarrazin, 2010). This catchphrase, which was the much-cited title of Thilo Sarrazin's 2010 book on integration and immigration from Muslim majority countries to Germany, sparked a heated debate. Sarrazin's theses were overtly polemic. They held that immigration had adverse effects on German culture, economy, demographics and crime rates. However, to allege the failure of Muslim migrants to integrate stood out in the best-selling screed as a xenophobic rallying cry against Islam. Sarrazin indistinctly lumped together hundreds of thousands of individuals who identified with one of the many forms of Islam. He associated them with a certain genetic pool because of their non-Christian countries of origin and their migratory displacements from Muslim-majority societies outside Europe

(Gilman, 212: 48). Sarrazin's claims about this gene pool stipulated that it presented a concrete threat to social cohesion as Muslim birth rates in Germany were overtaking native-German rates. One threat to German society, as followed from this misconstrued logic and haphazard assemblage of decontextualised facts, was the tainting of the national genome. Another one was cultural colonisation. Sarrazin described in detail his refusal to have his grandchildren's daily routine determined by the Salat, the Muslim call to prayer five times per day. All this would lead to less economic productivity and a steady decline in German quality of life, he insisted.

Official statistics of Germans with a migration background tell a different and much less alarmist story. Of the 10.6 million people who have immigrated to Germany since 1950 70.6 per cent are from other European countries, including 32.3 per cent of intra-European migrants with European citizenship. 16.4 per cent come from Asia or Oceania. Only one quarter of German residents with a migration background are Muslim. Their largest group, 2.9 million, is of Turkish descent. Individuals of Arab origin, who gained worldwide attention in 2015 and 2016 during the European refugee crisis in their daily media portrayal both in and outside Germany, amount to barely more than 800,000 residents; this is less than one per cent of the total population (Foroutan, 2013: 4; Holmes and Castaneda, 2016: 159). In European comparisons, Germany comes second to France in Muslim population size. It comes in fifth in the Muslim to total population ratio after France, Belgium, Austria and the Netherlands. Many more examples exist to point out the gap between imagined crisis and factual reality. The ones cited here, though, show in illuminating essence that transnational mobility, both forced and voluntary, and ethnic diversity are at the centre of public and political debates about the future of Germanness in the new century. It is no coincidence that Sarrazin entitled the follow-ups to *Germany Does Away with Itself* in an equally provocative manner. *The New Terror on Virtue: On the Limits of Free Speech in Germany* and *Hostile Takeover: How Islam Hinders Progress and Threatens Society*. The two books came out in 2014 and 2018, respectively. The latest book, one may find hardly surprising, has been used by German right-wing parties such as the Alternative for Germany, the AfD, as reference material for their nationalist party platforms.

In its broader sense, Muslimness is a term now used in German public and scholarly discourse to mean cultural difference. With Islam, Muslim identities are the subject of considerable academic inquiry and empirical research, particularly in cultural studies of everyday-life communication and identities. The fear of being swamped or outnumbered by Muslims is of course not entirely new in German society. For instance, abundant flows of Iranian refugees to West Germany in the 1970s and 1980s were met with the stigma of being incongruent with German liberal values. Rainer Werner Fassbinder's much-decorated melodrama from 1974, *Ali: Fear Eats Soul*, for which an earlier working title was *All Turks are Called Ali*, centres on this social context. Being a danger while Muslim in German society resurfaced as an omnipresent talking point in 2001 in the wake of 9/11. German media reports revealed that some of the religious terrorists involved in the attacks on the Twin Towers and other sites in the United States had lived undercover for many years in Germany. The fallout of these circumstances was enough to create public reaction against Muslim Germans as irrevocably different and Other. Now, two decades into the 21st century, current thinking about violence against Muslim women again impedes circumspect intellectual discussion about Islam in the West (Berghahn, 2014: 2; Weber, 2013: 2-5). As Weber, an expert on Islam and gender in Germany and Europe, notes, "modern humanity has been constructed as both European and as universal; the racialized 'Other' against whom the 'modern human' [is pitted] disturbs this construction by laying claim to human rights from the very heart of Europe" (Weber, 2016: 68).

Muslims in German society find themselves in a complex dilemma in the new millennium. They risk appearing averse to majority society's dominant values if they proudly emphasise their minority culture. Other minority members or groups call them spineless assimilationists if Muslims open their mosques or appear frequently on popular television chat shows and on radio to talk about everyday Muslimness. The ways in which cultural representations of an alleged liberal multiculturalism are implicated in this dilemma are more expansive than one would like to admit. It is, after all, in no small measure that popular culture and majority culture texts about Germanness and Otherness have contributed to the circulation and replication of the Muslim Other in Germany and Islam in Western Europe (Matthes, 2007). How these texts have fictionalised or tried to imitate reality is documented in many works on the poetics of German culture and thought, as described in influential studies by Cheesman (2007) or newer, transnational discussions by Gezen (2018). However, those texts are less frequently questioned for being complicit in replacing actual lived reality with virtual lives or fictitious experiences and memories.

Tragedy versus Comedy

The fictional representation of reality in literature has spawned productive theories for readings of texts as codes of social reality. These theories, some of which are more and some less equipped to handle the extraction of social meanings from fictional entanglements, are of course not definitive. I say so specifically as I go here beyond the meaning of literary texts to include an armoury of popular culture fictions about Turkish German identities in several mass media types: literature as well as film, television, digital online video and recorded live-stage performance. Within this constitutive limit though, one can claim that literary-based criticism does not usually dictate any particular adherence to form. It is also fitting to argue that the idea of textual reception of different cultural entertainment formats is widely accepted today. Much of this development owes its success to the politics of feminism. Second-wave feminism was a driving force in the readings of texts across media types and genres predicated on their popularity (Radway, 2006: 4). Feminist theorems about feminine values and behaviour have shaped the study of popular culture narratives. Two intersecting tenets in feminist and popular culture studies are that the personal is political and that valid knowledge about social inequality can come from any cultural object or practice (Hollows, 2000: 20-21). Feminist cultural analysis, informed by wider debates about culture studies such as work at the Centre for Contemporary Cultural Studies in Birmingham, is therefore invaluable. It has freed contemporary narrative analysis from the firm grip of traditional historical criticism and rear-guard structuralism, and even the hard-nosed claim of new criticism's academic disciplinarity in the 1960s and 1970s in Northern America and Western Europe.

Yet, gender is only one of many crucial dimensions in considerations of mass culture representation. Both the nation and the national are another. Research into the political economy of culture, cultural policy and lived realities of Turkish German communities suggests that Germany's cultural canon systematically marginalised their Muslim Otherness (Mani, 2007: 33; Berman, 2011: 1-4). This process has become more understandable following the publication of Edward Said's seminal work, *Orientalism*, in 1978, which has been productively challenged and critically reworked for German cultural studies scholarship (Murti, 2001; Jenkins, 2004; Marchand, 2009). Most researchers in transnational German cultural studies have already absorbed a central claim associated with post-colonial theory, which underpinned Adelson's study, *The Turkish Turn in*

Contemporary German Literature, published in 2005. It is the belief that literary and other cultural fictions are not divorced from reality.

Fictional representations exert a direct influence on readers and viewers. Hence, fictions deeply immersed in the national and meant to convey a nation's imagined identity contribute to oppressive structures such as colonialism and ethnic bias. The resulting displacement from actual reality through fictions about allegedly real Germans and supposedly authentic Germanness was the bane of Turkish Germans claiming Germany as their home with or without German passports. Adelson's assessment of Turkish German cultural production alludes to this issue in light of German reunification in 1989, when political and imagined worlds clashed in the new Germany. Once the political East-West binary had disappeared with the iron curtain, German culture had to confront the complex entanglements of its own national, and formerly divided, cultures in myriad ways. The realisation, as the makers of Turkish German culture had suggested all along, was that the simplistic "between-two-worlds" paradigm no longer sufficed to explain similar entanglements of Turkish German culture beyond the German national archive. Adelson's summary is poignant: Germany as "the center of Europe [was and] is no longer Eurocentric" (Adelson, 2005: 13). All this is not to suggest that any and all fiction about Turkish Germans living in Germany should be read as historical corrective owing to majority society's ideological prejudice. Collectively though these earlier Turkish German fictions, and those discussed in this book, participate in grounding Turkishness and Muslimness in Germany as a permanent home, not a transient "host country" (Mushaben, 2008: 3) for Germans of migrant descent.

Turkish German identities have contributed to an evolution. They have forced key figures and industry giants in Germany's cultural establishment to find a new meaning for the national between the traditionally nationalist affiliation with German soil and German "Heimat" or home, and new ways of diasporic attachments to multiple communities in different places and non-Western countries. It was a laborious effort. The creative labour entailed in this arduous project and the work of inclusive community formation are far from complete, as Gezen's work on the reception of Bertolt Brecht in Turkish theatre reveals (Gezen, 2018: 10-14). In this respect, Turkish German comedy confirms the close link between humour and transnational sociability, as it "serves to enhance group cohesion and solidarity and reduce social distance" (Roach Anleu and Milner Davis, 2018: 11).

One important fact, though long disregarded, is that German culture norms counteracted the positive attraction to comedy and to new forms of transnational Germanness expressed through it. Like the attitude and intended outcome of anti-social ethnic humour I elaborate on further in chapter one, the status of tragedy as German culture's preferred representational mode has been instrumental when ousting Muslim characters and identities from the national imaginary. Why attend to this point? The conflation of tragedy and national Germanness, and comedy and the transnational ethnic Other, sheds light on problematic notions of inclusive thinking in German society related to Turkish Germans. It dates back centuries. Many works in the German canon are connected to the mode of tragedy as the only acceptable form in which to represent the nation truthfully. This link is how Germanness, based on a uniform native culture and the resulting national character of highbrow tragedies, informed the exclusive ethno-cultural architecture of "Kulturstaat" (see Eckart and Rohe, 1999, on the German culture nation; Pautz, 2005: 40). It is no coincidence that the German nation state endured for so long on principles of cultural uniformity, which would later inform a concept of ethnic purity by referring to Bismarck's successful drive towards national unification in the 19th century. It was based on the rallying of German-speaking communities around the idea of excluding non-Germanness and the economic and social benefits of the unification of German states. German-speaking communities had caught a glimpse of this mechanism through their economic and military collaboration during the Napoleonic Wars from 1803 to 1815.

German-speaking communities realised that there was tangible power in uniformity at the same time as Goethe's *Faust. A Tragedy* elevated the tragic mode to a national German artform, a uniform value in German culture. The text, written in standardised German, catapulted tragic German literature onto the world literature stage, adding to its desirability. Although "cultural hybridity and cross-cultural exchange were always the norm" (Kontje, 2018: 2) in Germany, the most celebrated works are tragedies by authors, poets and playwrights such as Goethe and Schiller. Why? Because these German-language texts revolve around a cohesive, German monoculture. This monoculture was desired internally by Germans and validated externally by non-German communities around them. As Pirro suggests, the stronghold of tragedy in German culture has also dominated academic thinking and critical scholarship: "[e]pisodes of radical political discontinuity, of which Germany has experienced its share, have often led German intellectuals to generate theories of works of tragedy as a means for rethinking the nature of German and identity and community" (Pirro, 2011: 148). By considering tragedy's twin pole, I suggest here that comedy is equally effective in rethinking the nature of German multiculture in the 21st century.[9]

The concept of tragic Germanness as national narrative has an uneasy relationship with the ideal of multicultural inclusion. Skolnik explains that classical literature in pre-modern Germany inscribed minority cultures in the margins and not the centre. The "historical drama above all" (Skolnik, 2014: 79), according to Skolnik, fused minorities like the German Jews through its status as intertext with an emerging national culture of the German canon. Yet, this fusion served mainly to write Jews superficially into the German culture nation rather than fully integrating them in real life. It was so that Jewishness could harmonise on paper with "a liberal conception of a universal bourgeois culture" (Skolnik, 2014: 78). In real life, however, the price of Jewish German minority integration into German majority society was often conversion. The reception history of works such as Lessing's historical drama, *Nathan der Weise-Nathan the Wise* (1779), and its famed ring parable points to this development. The historical drama forged a connection between popular German majority society and the enlightened Jew, which fused Enlightenment and Judaism to create a German-Jewish fantasy. Nathan upheld his Jewish identity on stage while Jews in everyday life struggled for what Moses Mendelssohn called civic acceptance or civic incorporation of German Jews as full citizens (Meir, 2001: 251).

The tragic mode did lead to similar token inclusions and de facto exclusions of Turkish German identities in fictions and actual reality. Books, articles and conference papers on Turkish German comedy have abounded in recent years to study humour as a strategy of counter-discursive inclusion (Bower, 2011: 2014; Berghahn, 2012; Androutsopoulos, 2012; Spielhaus, 2013). This did not happen unexpectedly. As the mode of comedy is overwhelmingly set in the representation of social realities of society, the comedic is well equipped to disrupt imagined national cultural traditions, especially where the tragic mode of artistic expression is tied up with ideology, ethnicity and nation building. Of course, sometimes, there is a deliberate blurring of the line between highbrow tragedy and lowbrow comedy to keep the readers or viewers interested. There are twists and turns to remind audiences that they are the arbiters of unconventional plot actions or sudden turns in the depiction of stock characters. For instance, the television sitcom, *Türkisch für Anfänger-Turkish for Beginners*, regularly plays on the fourth-wall illusion of viewers as silent observers of what is happening on screen. At other times, Turkish German filmmakers tease genre conventions to display a creative transnational originality free from Germany's established tragic or comedic habitus. Comedy films such as *Almanya: Willkommen in Deutschland-Almanya: Welcome to Germany* depend upon obviously tragic elements to precipitate a mid-film tragedy; but at heart they are a comedic works about social realities.

One persistent point I make in this book is that German majority culture is easily weaponised if, as in its canonised tragedies, it idealises a cultural ideal of uniform Germanness and assimilationist inclusivity which simply never existed. For Zambon, transnational Turkish German identities and ethnic comedy necessarily contradict the use of any exclusionary representational mode as control mechanism for the image of German culture (Zambon, 2017: 552). I, too, argue here that pro-social ethnic comedy, unlike tragedy, supports communal interchange with its positive attitude towards inter-ethnic interactions.

Close Reading Comedy: The Proof Is in the Plot

Emplotment and narrative are important variables in this discussion. Contemporary accounts of understanding and misunderstanding comedy, particularly those from scholars and practitioners of ethnic comedy, have learned to treat them as if style and substance were not always the most convivial bedfellows (Brummet, 2010; Gray, 2004: Haggins, 1995; Hall, 1997). Comedy texts with their plots based on race or ethnicity ceaselessly invite nuanced explication. They explore complex issues of community and allegiance in society. Mainstream comedy entertainment does so most famously, according to Mather, by starting to draw during the 1990s upon some of the culturally contentious comic paradigms and attitudes associated with that era, like stereotyping of ethnic identities and larger-than-life plot development (Mather, 2005). It was commonplace for the so-called "easy multi-culture" comedies of the 1990s to feature more extensive representations of race, gender and ethnicity with regard to issues of nationality and cultural nuances within minorities' own communities. The American sitcom's privileging of black women characters in its narratives (e.g. *Family Matters*, 1989-1998) and the export of those formats globally were also something of a riposte to the television dominion of family-friendly comedy featuring male desires, social roles and aspirations (e.g. *Happy Days*, 1974-1984). In Great Britain mainstream comedy films set in diverse neighbourhoods showed first- and second-generation Asian female figures in a mosaic pattern of intertwined stories. Even popular British film dramas like *My Son the Fanatic* (1997), written by Hanif Kureishi, based their plots around comic clashes of generations and cultures, "exploring the lack of common ground between Muslim fundamentalism and liberal Western values" (Mather, 2005: 86). This kind of ethnic comedy is one defined by recurring themes: the multi-faceted nature of home for first-, second- and third-generation immigrant families; the complex structures between one's roots, origins and visions of the future; the immense difficulty of reconciling inherited cultural traditions with personal choices in life; the positioning of the Other as outsider in the national culture or in one's own community. Continuously, though, it left audiences with feelings of mixed emotions when they could not decide whether a situation or series of events was dramatic or comedic in aesthetic potency of form and intent. At whose expense did the laughter come? And what, if any, was the social function of this comedy?

Consumers of comedy have their work cut out for them when encountering ethnicity-based humour. Its practices at once solicit and endlessly rephrase contexts for understanding and interpreting what a comedy text or a comedian means by funny or setting up something or someone as the butt of a joke. In this way the dominant strategies of modern ethnic mainstream comedy have themselves become iconic for legitimating the reading practice which "[now] throws into relief [text-immanent] genealogies and analytical opportunities against the backdrop of transnational expansion, postcritial self-reflexivity, and interdisciplinary collaboration" (James, 2020: 2): close reading. No matter how much new and nuanced forms of comedy entertainment based on ethnicity or race seem to thwart and evade the job of interpretation; they re-energise in the process humour scholars' critical attention to form for understanding comedy's social, philosophical, ethnic and geopolitical work. And while close reading and formalism are in no way identical, nor do they always engender each other, the surge of debates about what is funny and what is politically correct sustains a formal analysis which in turn confirms close reading's persistence, adaptability and suitability in comedy research—even if this discussion has been getting somewhat lost in recent debates about so-called cancel culture outrage to comedy and comedy artists.

To determine the critical currency of this approach is to determine the questions which are key to interrogating a comedy genre. How does its plot engage the generic expectations for a certain kind of text? What sort of situation, wording or action or textual world is created by a filmmaker, author, screenwriter or stand-up comedian to deliver their comedy with its intended purpose, be it pro-social or anti-social?[10] A close reading can answer these questions.

The Turkish German Comedy Wave: Screen, Stage and Page Power

This leaves the matter of aesthetic taste in relation to ethnic enfranchisement. Besides differences in use of mode of representation, there is a distinct appreciation of mainstream entertainment in Turkish German comedy texts, films, videos and performances. The highbrow, lowbrow, middlebrow debate in cultural studies is long-lasting and ongoing. One would be ill advised to claim that even a short summary here could do it justice. However, these categories mean something specific in relation to Turkish German comedy entertainment because they stand for access to majority society through accessible art and lucrative entertainment forms on the minority's own creative terms.

For Turkish German entertainment culture in the 1990s, as described by Yeşilada, cinematic lowbrows became a platform which reached millions of Germans without migration background (Yeşilada, 2008: 75). More precisely, it was the politically incorrect satire in certain films luring audiences to the box office. These films, though varying in visual styles and formats, were informed by an easy overcoming of transnational boundaries and transcultural awareness, thematic features otherwise known as "Turkish Light or Lite-as in light-weight" (Yeşilada, 2008: 75). The significance of this refocussing stands out for earning Turkish German filmmakers unprecedented profits and for consolidating aesthetic purpose around social goals. Ownership of image was one watchword. Not being the ethnic drag costume for "Bio-Deutsche", that means organically grown Germans (Taberner, 2017: 330; Nouripour, 2014) or German-born citizens, by a *ius sanguis,* lineage of blood, was another. Bio-Deutsche entertainment culture from the 1960s to the mid-1980s in the main either produced highbrow tragedies of first-generation migrants from Turkey or mocked their plight as low-skilled labourers (e.g. *Shirins Hochzeit-Shirin's Wedding,* 1976; *40 Quadratmeter Deutschland-40 Square Metres of Germany,* 1986). Günter Wallraff's ludicrous brownfaced undercover stories suffice as contemporaneous proof of a sensationalist taste in gutter-press productions about Turkish German Alis. That his clichéd performance as Ali was as ill-informed as his choice of a floppy-haired wig and glue-on moustache in *Ganz Unten-Lowest of the Low* (1985) turned into a running gag among more serious journalists and scholars (Fachinger, 2001). General audiences and the wider majority society still embraced this skewed image of Turkish Germans despite Wallraff's wild collage of disparate cultural meanings and visual cues of Muslim Otherness as well as Turkishness. Turkish Light, essentially, had to meet the stereotypes at least to some degree at this level.

It was the second generation of Turkish German film artists with migration background who engaged the architecture of knowledge about Turkish Germans in mainstream culture like a brand. These artists had grown up in Germany or were born in the country; hence, they had full command of German and knew how to navigate the country's cultural landscape. An empowered Turkish German cinema was the first locus for Turkish German films about modern urban life. They were telling neither "'tales of poor guestworkers', nor the story of how 'Leyla gets liberated by Hans'" (Yeşilada, 2008: 77). Turkish Light, despite its alleged taint by Hollywood commercialism, was the breakout star of an internationalising entertainment culture in Germany during the 1990s. It took only a couple of years for the genre's producers to turn their work into mainstream staples of German entertainment on the big screen and on television. Out of all these artists, Hussi Kutlucan made the biggest comedic name for himself, merging popular styles of the US lowbrow comedy wave of the 1990s with multicultural storylines (Hake and Mennel, 2012: 6).

The early success of Turkish German comedy film and later also other forms of Turkish German comedy later falls in line with the minority's increasing power to say no to its spectatorial objectification. Göktürk has written at length about this turn in humorous entertainment culture. Her work tells of the role Turkish German identities played in a pseudo-liberal discourse around Germans' pop cultural pleasures and how that began to change when Turkish Germans wrote their own scripts (Göktürk, 1999: 1). Lischke confirms that the close link between Turkish German comedy, Anglophone mainstream humour and America's self-purported melting-pot multiculturalism in the 1990s also supported the rise of Turkish German comedy culture (Lischke, 2014: 97). Moreover, Turkish German comedy was a highly desirable escapism for Germans during most of the 1990s. The country experienced a rapid rise in xenophobia after reunification, with newspapers feeding almost daily into the fear of "Überfremdung" or over-foreignisation. In the 21st century, as discussed in the main chapters, all this evolved into a form of middlebrow comedy entertainment now considered part of German mainstream culture (Burns, 2007; Hake and Mennel, 2012).

Previous Scholarship

In the larger context of Turkish German cultural production, my work builds on critical scholarship about cultural compatibility: Turkey and Germany, East and West, niche and mainstream culture, and Islam and secular Europe. Without the contributions of scholars in the field of Turkish German studies and other essential scholarship on lived realities of diverse identities in German society, minority communities and ethnic or religious bias against Muslims, this book would not be possible. Cited frequently in this book for their pivotal contribution are the works by researchers such as Adelson. Her analytical thinking makes evident how much German society relied on representations of Turkish German culture to define its own identity in the 1990s, "a dizzying decade of structural transformations affecting Germany, Europe, and what many might call the world at large" (Adelson, 2005, 1). Her rejection of the "between-two-worlds" paradigm in *The Turkish Turn* situates Turkish German culture in a position of cultural authenticity instead of a minor German culture which was neither German nor Turkish. It addressed the status of Turkish German identities as the plaything of German elites' debates about socio-cultural progress in Germany as a migration nation.

This intervention emerged in line with Mani's (2007) and Brunow's (2011) calls to mind the gap left by German historians' refusal to write Turkish German history into the national memory of German society. They also showed that German studies scholars' practice of thinking of Turkish German squarely within the national dimensions of German culture widened the perceived rift between Germanness and Muslimness. Meanwhile, Burns (2013: 1) stressed that neither the majority nor the minority community wanted to gloss over cultural difference and see only bland forms of Turkish German assimilation in German mainstream entertainment. In this vein, it is useful to refer outside the realm of scholarship to audiences' consumption of mainstream culture entertainment. Halle's study of transnational film scholarship on European film in the 1990s found that its programming left younger audiences across the European Union with a feeling of dissatisfaction when faced with an array of "Euro-pudding" productions—a phrase to denounce often well-intentioned yet artificially sweet and harmonious film productions. Their multicultural casting choices and stilted scripts replaced the foregrounding of national conflicts in Europe with sucrose and overly bland narratives "that can only appeal to a least common denominator of culture" (Halle, 2008: 48). In this case Turkish German comedy also delivers more substantial "Turkish delights" (Göktürk, 1999).

Responding to the calls for thinking about Turkish German culture in transnational networks and with a resistance to assimilationist rhetoric, or discounting it as non-German Other as pointed out by El-Tayeb's (2016) discussion of the so-called "historic Turk" problem I discuss in chapter one, I turn to Turkish German comedy entertainment in the 21st century. It is itself defined by stories about Muslimness in Germany as a site of productive conflict, to be represented as lived realities in relatable contexts rather than sugar-coated or disproportionally dramatised. In the past decade, scholars like Bower (2011; 2011; 2014) and Bilici (2010) have already turned to newer Turkish German comedy to discuss political satirists like Serdar Somuncu or define the social functions of Muslim ethnic comedy in general.[11] They draw attention to a comedy which complicates Turkishness in Germany beyond its active construction as perpetual migrant Otherness and retrieves Muslimness in alleged Judeo-Christian societies from the perceived margins. Indicative of the potential to reformulate Turkish German Muslimness, by removing it from the stronghold of dramatic aesthetics, comedy performers such as Somuncu have added their own aesthetic influence and tradition. Affirming such notions of cultural empowerment and transformation, I bundle in this book several of these preceding scholars' distinct strands of critical thinking. This book extends their interventions to the field of comparative inter-media comedy and the social dimensions of mainstream entertainment in Germany in the 21st century.

Engaging the Terminology: Why the Problem is Bigger than "Just" Islamophobia

"German" Christianity, "Turkish" Islam—
Connected Histories, Parallel Societies

Ickstadt points out that Germany now has its third generation of immigrants with Turkish heritage and that Berlin is the largest Turkish city outside Turkey. The consequences of the Turkish German population's growth are signs of cultural assimilation, re-ethnicisation and the confrontation of Germans with social change across their country (Ickstadt, 1999: 573). Yet, it took decades before the German and Turkish German community did more to foster an acceptance of Muslimness as a permanent part of German society. The federal government's refusal to reform Germany's strict passport regulations until late into the 1990s fed into xenophobic attitudes of the majority population. And in most of the country's public schools educational administrators refused to accommodate Turkish German children with bilingual programmes offered nowadays in most of Berlin's primary and secondary schools (Ickstadt: 572-577). In particular the Christian Conservatives, who governed most of the federal states in the west, north and south of Germany, refused to acknowledge that the so-called Turkish German guest workers were in the country to stay. This was after the immediate need for blue-collar labour had waned during the recession of 1966 and with Germany formally ending its labour migration agreement with Turkey in 1973. Faas posits that the lack of governmental efforts to integrate Turks in Germany created uncertainty about the future in the Turkish German community. It also raised questions about the migrants' eventual return to Turkey (Faas, 2010: 59).

Indeed, parts of the Turkish German community, as well as members of the German Left, were dissatisfied with the Christian Conservatives' persistent refusal to acknowledge a diverse society. The frustration of non-natives and German liberals may help to explain the formation of political interest groups with a focus on Muslim integration. Sizeable communities of Muslims in Berlin, Munich and Cologne set out in the 1990s to form local organisations with a shared interest in incorporating Muslims better in German society. It was also then that the term "integration" quickly became the "new buzzword in political and education debates amidst a reform of the country's citizenship law (2000) which showed a new willingness of [rattled] German politicians, at least in principle, to grant citizenship" (Faas, 2010: 60) to Muslims in the country.

The efforts to rally Germany's Muslims around shared interests translated into six larger organisations. They are the Central Council of Muslims in Germany, the Association of Islamic Cultural Centres, the Council on Islam for the Federal Republic of Germany, the Islamic Community Milli Görüş, the Turkish-Islamic Union for Religious Affairs and the Alevi Movement. However, these organisations represent just a small part of the community as they cover the activities of only 800,000 Muslims in Germany (Faas, 2010: 59). The wider public's interest in their representative power is limited. This was exemplified by the disappointing reactions of Germans and Turkish Germans regarding the outcomes of the so-called integration summit series. The coalition government under German Chancellor Angela Merkel hosted the summits. The first one took place in July 2006, the second in July 2007 and the third in November 2008. The focus of the three events was the discussion of migration issues such as mandatory German language learning, higher education access, bilingual schooling and better job prospects (Gesemann and Roth, 2008: 11-14). Later summits also addressed the point of religious conflict. It soon became clear, though, that the larger public was not supportive of these summits and paid little, if any, attention to their outcomes. Crucial to the criticisms around Turkish German and Muslim integration was the assumption that Germanness would become unstable if the different ethnic communities remained isolated, a fear most commonly related in German and global media coverage to Angela Merkel's statement at the CSU/CDU's Berlin integration summit in 2010: "Der Ansatz für Multikulti ist gescheitert, absolut gescheitert [The idea of multiculturalism has failed, totally failed]" (Bizeul 2013, 1-2).

Public engagement had to emerge from a larger, cultural intersection. Kaya points out that the turning point came about for a growing number of both German and Turkish German filmmakers, television screenwriters and authors when they realised that additional actions were needed to involve the broader society in the debate about redefining Germanness in support of Muslim culture (Kaya, 2013: 5-6). This drew highly visible actions at the cultural level, covered by the national and international press, into the spotlight. Events such as the premier of *Almanya-Welcome to Germany* at the Berlinale Film Festival in 2011 have remained the largest force in pushing forward the debate about Muslim Germanness in modern German society (Emeis and Boog, 2011: 166).

Wessi, Ossi, Turk, and Jew—(Re)Integrated "Germans", Uneasy Alterity

"In looking at the ways migrants have appropriated multiple spaces [in Germany], it becomes evident that Turkish Germans continually reposition themselves as part of increasingly transnational networks" (Mandel, 2008: 9). So claims Mandel, a political anthropologist, by reflecting on Turkish German writer Emine Sevgi Özdamar's literary accounts of how Turkish Germans in Germany had to work through an emergent subjectivity, namely as Turks, German-Turks, Almancı or Turkish German. The Turkish German diaspora's coming of age, Mandel adds further, has not meant for it, "as many would have preferred, the peaceful 'bridging' of two distinct cultures. Rather, [integration meant] a coming to terms with both the consequences of deracination and the refashioning of assumptions about 'our *German* culture'" (Mandel, 2008: 1). The rejection of the ubiquitous leitmotif of the "bridge", engaged by prominent Turkish German culture theorists like Özdamar and Zafer Şenocak, reveals irreconcilable notions of different forms of Germanness at many levels of German social and historical discourse. This became even more apparent when the "bridge" was replaced by the notion of German "guiding culture". Though it cannot be reduced to just claims of ethnicity and authenticity, the dominant German narrative, that is, that of the West German or Wessi, has often homogenised and othered Jewish Germans, East Germans and Turkish Germans. It turned complex and diverse identities, regardless of shared national origins or language or even citizenship status, into a monolithic and mono-semantic epithet as Jews, Ossis and Turks. While Wessi denotes a more stable, linear and solidified progression in historical identity from post-WWII to modern German Federal Republic aligned with liberal politics of the Global North, Jew, Ossi and Turk are shown to have become signifiers of instability. They conjure up dichotomising views of Germanness through the lens of the Holocaust, the division of Germany, East German socialism and the continued denial of Islam's status as statutory body congruent with German law. This makes them "uneasy" monikers of German alterity, for they reject a neat tradition of homogenic German cosmopolitanism (Cheesman, 2007: 40-42; Twist, 2018).

All this, as I discuss in chapter one and the other main chapters in this book, is rooted in a normative identity politics in Germany. It is a pervasive, historical problem for many minority cultures in Germany, not just the Turkish German community. And it impacts on those who are not accepted as West, white and ethnically pure Germans. Also, it serves to reduce the fear of the Other by suggesting that its identity is easy to know and easier yet to fix, to "standardise" or West Germanise (Twist, 2018: 6). In this regard, Turkish German comedy entertainment represents in its fictions strategies to fear Muslim Others, and Otherness in Germany in general, less. It is possible by knowing more about the Self, asking why there is the obsessive need to fix the Other, and suggesting that understanding hybrid identities beyond readily available clichés offers freedom from thinking strictly in binary terms. In an excerpt from his prize-winning essay collection, *Wer ist Wir?: Deutschland und seine Muslim-Who is We?: Germany and its Muslims*, Navid Kermany argues that this complication of identity is necessary in contemporary Germany, as Germanness turns on a Western "we" and a Muslim "they". He points to the bounded notions of Muslimness in Germany, which were confirmed repeatedly by German culture's identitarian oppositions. These may encompass the conventional identity dichotomies: rural, urban; working class, elite; or, as I discuss in my work, German and Muslim:

And how many times have I heard in Germany that "we" don't have any issues with Muslims. Or all kinds of talk shows that bring up Islam: How can "we" deal with Islam, do "we" have to be afraid of Muslims? That this "We" also includes Muslims seems to be almost unthinkable for the talk show guests. It's not even meant to be offensive, at least not always. "We" Germans have to have a dialogue with the Muslims say those who mean well. While this is to be commended, it means that about 3 million people in this country would have to have that dialogue with themselves. (Kermani, 2009: 27)

"Turkish German", "Muslim"—Perennial Others in Germany
Germans as well as Turkish Germans have realised that Muslimness has become an integral part of German culture in the new century. That German society has changed profoundly is the central message of contemporary Turkish German comedy. However, the continued reference to Turkish Germans as non-Westerners has not stopped in the country's mainstream news media. The inherent dilemma is that a Muslim-German consciousness had already been established well before the 1960s. Berman argues that Germans have forgotten that Muslimness and Islamic culture had already been exposed to them in society long before the first labour migrants arrived from Turkey. She points to a general disregard for the impact of Muslim culture in Germany, and hence to its perception as foreign, which is simply wrong. Supported by the scholarship of the past two decades on German Orientalism, Berman illustrates that migratory relations between German-speaking countries and the Muslim Middle East date back as far as the Ottoman Empire (1350-1683). They continued into the imperial German state (1792-1930), the Third Reich (1931-1944) and into the first decades (1945-1989) after WWII (Berman, 2011: 12-13).

The extensive links between Germany and Muslim majority countries are largely unknown in the present day. This may have to do with Germany's majority population who tended to perceive Muslim identities as a threat to redefining its national identity as a Western one after WWII. Also, Germans have had a close interaction and frequent exchange with the Eastern world for centuries through trade and individual contact. But where there should today be a historical sense of European-Arab and European-Ottoman coexistence and contact with Islam there is only a "lack of knowledge about the history of contact [which] impedes a more nuanced comprehension of the [Muslim German] literary [and cultural] material" (Berman, 2011: 14).

The idea that Germans have refused to accept Muslims and the religion of Islam as part of their culture is not entirely new. Mani describes how the terms "Gastarbeiter"-guest worker, "Fremder"-stranger, "Ausländer"-foreigner, or "Inländer ausländischer Herkunft"-citizen of foreign origin, were common phrases used to refer to Turkish Germans during the 1960s, 1970s and for the most part of the 1980s until reunification. Mani's study of labour migration from Turkey to Germany provides further evidence that particularly West Germans lacked an intercultural awareness when they recruited the workers. He also concludes that West Germans tried to downplay their ties to Muslim culture when they were confronted with the integration of a community which they hardly knew after decades of neglect (Mani, 2007: 12). A widespread acceptance of the influence of Muslim culture on areas of German literary and cultural production, as the circumstances of contemporary Turkish German online comedy suggest in chapter four, thus feeds into a larger debate about what has changed since then.

Aims in the Study of Turkish German Comedy Entertainment

One could turn to many disciplines to identify the reasons for mainstream Germany's embrace of a transnational and cosmopolitan comedy culture aesthetic created by the country's largest Muslim community. Halle suggests an anthropological explanation. Turkish Light, and Turkish German comedy entertainment at large, sold so well because teens and young adolescents in reunified Germany could not be bothered with old separatist hats about East Germany and West Germany and neo-conservative Christianism (Halle, 2008: 13-16). Indeed, the monetary success of Turkish German comedy films such as *Kebab Connection* and Kaya Yanar's television sketch show, *Was guckst Du?!- Whatcha Looking At?!* (2001-2005), makes for terrific studies in cultural economics about the marketing of Muslim Otherness around the turn of the century. Though the transnational styles of Turkish German culture or stylistics of transnational comedy entertainment mean something different in areas of sociology or economics. They mean again something different altogether in historiographic terminology and media studies.

For those who study the transnational circulation of popular culture and comedy across the borders of nation states and the boundaries of certain communities, those stylistics are a matter of voice, of being heard, read and seen. This voice varies from Turkish German comedy artists like Somuncu being fiercely sarcastic on stage to culture creatives making light fun of shoes, shopping and dating, like Hatice Akyün in her chick-lit novels. Or, perhaps, it can be characterised by Sinan Akkus' circumspect use of American romcom cinema and elements of 1990s wedding comedies in the script for *Evet, ich will!-Evet, I do*.

Turkish German Muslims and Comedy Entertainment: Settling into Mainstream Culture in the 21st Century falls squarely in this diverse framework of interdisciplinary comedy, transnational media culture and Turkish German cultural studies. The aim of this book is to draw attention to many voices from many backgrounds, to what informs their comedy content and to the connection between Otherness and everyday life in German society in the 21st century. Research into Turkish German comedy has been flourishing for a little while now, especially in the context of film. Less attention has gone to television and stand-up, and less again to online media and user comments on re-published live content on digital video streaming platforms. An academic dialogue between all these different types of mass media is virtually non-existent. It is another aspect which this study seeks to remedy.

Muslims and Muslim identities, sadly because of their stigmatisation and appropriation by majority communities in the West, are going to stay a visible minority issue. In Europe, this issue has played out in stories about headscarves, burkas and more recently burkinis, veiled faces and domestic abuse. There is the persistent narrative of honour killings, of inhumane customs and rituals of a generalised Muslim world and a dangerously reductive perception of the religion of Islam, as Celik demonstrates (Celik, 2015). One hears of the Caliphate and the Islamist terrorist, the beheading of Christian infidels and the dangers of ISIS. Muslim refugees, more recently in Germany, are especially known for endangering the welfare state model. The scope of this book cannot encompass all these issues and how they feature in popular comedy entertainment in the new century. More studies, some of which have already started to appear and attract German comedy, humour and transnational culture studies scholars' attention, are needed to do this. While addressing how they play out in the Turkish German discourse, *Turkish German Muslims and Comedy Entertainment* can further the scope for contributions from other disciplines where lived realities of Muslim minorities hold productive insights into Europe's cultural embrace or rejection of Islam.

CHAPTER I
Germanness, Othering and Ethnic Comedy

"I was aware, of course, that Turkish and Arab pupils in German schools cause more (and other) problems than Italians, Russians, or Poles."
—Thilo Sarrazin (in *Hostile Takeover: How Islam Impedes Progress and Threatens Society*, 2018, English language edition, original title: *Feindliche Übernahme: Wie der Islam den Fortschritt behindert und die Gesellschaft bedroht*)

Summary

Ethnic comedy in Germany has a long and complex history. One can tell it in many ways. I give an account of it in this chapter in direct relationship to Germany's historical identity as a shrinking nation after WWII, and as a country in identity turmoil after 1989. Divisive ethnic humour, or more specifically anti-multicultural propaganda, has lent itself to German nationalism and cultural politics of Othering. It has allowed bio-Germans to expand and to keep united their imagined sphere of ethnically and racially pure Germanness while factually losing German territory after defeat in armed combat or struggling to redefine German national identity after reunification. Pro-social ethnic comedy, in turn, has enabled Turkish German comedy artists and producers of Turkish German comedy culture to carve out and widen a space for the depiction of their presence in this segregated and nationalist German imaginary.

In and Out of "Heimat" and Germanness: Historical Contexts of Turkish German Living

The history of Turkish German integration is testimony to a push-and-pull dynamic around the acceptance of ethnic Otherness in Germany. This has to do, as I have explained in the introduction, with German mainstream culture's preoccupation with German space as "Heimat", a home to belong to locally and at the same time nationally. It is inherently imbued with trans-historical Germanness and expansionist desires (Eigler and Kugele, 2012: 1-4; Blickle, 2004).[1] It is crucial to understand that "Heimat" links the definition of what is German to who can be German and hence may be allowed to reside in the country and call it their home. For this, Joseph Goebbels' invocation of "Heimat" through Nazi-sanctioned films in the late 1930s and Hermann Goering's propagandist call to arms to protect the German "Heim" as the last refuge of all German-speaking individuals are instructive. As Von Moltke has found, the Nazis' persistent uses of "Heimat", the German Home, on screen and in the mass media are revealing for their modern bio-politics. Nevertheless, they also relied heavily on anti-modernist sentiments around German homeland (Von Moltke, 2005: 58-62). The Third Reich's national-socialist agenda depended on proto-Fascist ideologies of national inclusion and expulsion, which were already deeply engrained in Germany's literary canon and mainstream culture (see the introduction). Turkish German comedy had and still has to go up against precisely this specific feature of German national culture. That is why Turkish German comedy makers and writers frequently employ the German Home as a shorthand. Whether it is a German neighbourhood, a German family home or the country's cultural institutions, landscapes and major cities, Turkish German comedy frequently starts out by showing Germany on film, in books and on the small screen or on stage as a restrictive and, ultimately, anti-Muslim space.

Nowhere has the German Home moved into greater prominence than in discussions about the suitability of non-traditional German Others to live in it as a national community. Islam, which offers an identity deeply embedded in religious beliefs and social practices and the language of the Quran, is therefore seen as a disturbance because it offers another, worldwide community of belonging: that is ummah, or Muslim community, a fundamental concept in Islam expressing the essential unity and theoretical equality of Muslims from diverse cultural and geographical settings (Roy, 2013). A vast diaspora of Muslim communities knows what it means to be part of Islam, which fosters an identity beyond a specific space or place or national culture. It is for this reason that German anti-immigration voices like that of Thilo Sarrazin try to frame Islam as anti-"Heimat" and anti-German. This segregationist identity discourse implies that the German Home and Islam cannot coexist or make for congruent, Muslim-German identities. The PEGIDA movement, which is short for Patriotic Europeans against the Islamisation of the Occident, made this thinly veiled form of anti-ethnic and anti-Muslim hate speech its mission when the organisation formed mob-like in October 2014 on the streets of Dresden in East Germany. Head of PEGIDA at the time, Lutz Bachmann, declared that Muslimness could not be separated from local regions in the Middle East or certain political domains, languages and ways of life diametrically opposed to "Heimat". Berman has proven that this divisive rhetoric is not new and in fact has a long history (Berman, 2014). "Heimat" in Germany can mean inclusive of difference, though it has consistently functioned as a perfidious identity marker in recent years (Vieten, 2016: 110). The German Home remains ridden with much polarising trepidation about being an ethnically open civil society. It is "one of the main elements in contemporary German renegotiations of what it means to be German and to live in a German-speaking environment" (Blickle, 2004: 154).

One implication of the regressive qualities of the German Home is that attitudes towards non-ethnic Germanness are fickle. The embrace of diasporic Muslimness, of ummah, can dissipate quickly if it is seen as a subversive, disruptive element outside the control of Germany's ethnocentric nationalism. The German and Austrian mainstream press and news media, for instance, were quick to talk about the fairy tale of September 2015. It relates to an immense wave of sympathy towards Syrian refugees arriving to the cheers of locals at Vienna and Munich central stations. A few months later, Vieten and Valentine note, management of those Muslim Others who came to Germany as refuges and asylum seekers in the new century took on quite a different tone. "Problems arise where structural asymmetry with respect to power and resources is underestimated. [...] Resentments—and even arson attacks—in some of the more rural areas of Germany, both in the east and west, remind us that cosmopolitanism(s) means plurality and complexity" (Vieten and Valentine, 2016: 2). Turkish German labour migrants found themselves in the same situation some few decades earlier. Coming to the country from several areas and different ethnic communities of Turkey to rebuild war-ravaged West Germany, many faced indiscriminate harassment in cross-cultural contexts and negative treatments at the workplace (Chin, 2009). However, the notion of working guest rather than permanent resident was even more consequential for the Turkish German community. Turkish Germans encountered a defensiveness after most of them chose to stay instead of returning to Turkey. In 1973, the number of Turkish Germans had risen to 605,000 in West Germany. It was at that time that the West German government introduced a total halt to all foreign labour recruitment. In 1974, the Turkish German community consisted of 60 per cent of working individuals and 20 per cent of non-working spouses, while another 20 per cent were second-generation children. German mainstream culture looked at these numbers with concern, as they meant that Turkish German families had replaced single labour migrant households. Turkish German population growth had become sustainable. The community would not leave.

In both these situations, the skewed fairy tale and the permanent guests' rejection point to the dilemma of the German Home. Otherness is welcomed until it threatens the established population's material, cultural and social interests. Political movements, or at least public demands, to oust Turkish and Muslim Others from Germany have grown in number and visibility over the past couple of years. This development suggests that the post-cosmopolitan narrative of "Heimat" is still as poorly understood in 2020 as it was 60 years ago when Turkish labourers were invited to come. As part of the efforts to understand, I discuss the discriminatory aspect of xenophobic thought in, and through, German "Heimat" around WWII and German reunification. Anti-immigration thinking and xenophobia were cultivated during the aftermath of one war and leading up to another, and after a split country was reunited. Whether essentialising ideas about Turkishness sit on the excessively racist or the subtle end of the spectrum, Turkish German comedy entertainment engages them through filmic, literary, performance-based or televised representations. It is bound up with the local and the national German Home, the present and the past, Self and Other, and so links to the specific as well as the general realities of life in multi-ethnic German society.

Ethnic Bias in Jewish German and Turkish German Lives: WWII and "Wende"

An Important Historical Continuity
It is essential to understand that the discrimination against Turkish Germans is no isolated phenomenon in German culture's historical dealings with ethno-nationalism. WWII (1939-1945) and the immediate reunification period (1989-mid 1990s) in Germany demarcate two intellectual battlegrounds in German history, which illustrate an ongoing connection between Germanness, ethnicity and religion. Though for different reasons, the two periods overlap in their hostility against non-Christian and non-ethnic German cultures. WWII and "Wende" map the contours of the function of ethnic bias, which German

majority culture used to deflect responsibility for its warmongering and the cost of its capitalist restructuring. Yet again, those were not entirely new or modern occurrences of racism and religious bias in German culture, nor should they be considered in geo-political isolation, as I expand on in chapter six and the conclusion. Like anti-Semitism, anti-Turkism is one of Germany's oldest institutionalised hatreds. Both discriminatory practices date back in much of Europe to the early Middle Ages. One can trace the theoretical and doctrinal context for these phobic developments while finding that, compared side by side, it took anti-Semitism and anti-Turkism at their height only decades to penetrate the general stock of political thinking and undermine liberal values in the German public. There are also similar patterns of continuity between the cultural and intellectual rooting of anti-Jewish depictions in public discourse in the lead-up to WWII and Islamophobic representations of Turkish identities in reunified Germany. It is important in this respect to stress that the killing of millions of Jewish people across Europe stands in no comparison to localised attacks at Turkish German communities. What matters here though is the aggressive propulsion of hate against alleged non-Germanness and that hate's continuation over such a long period of time. The discrimination against Jews and Turks, or those perceived as Jewish and Turkish, is marked by denigration, dehumanisation, subjugation and definition of racial lineage; most notably, this form of bigotry has usually been sanctioned by the state or national elites. It has also been characterised by readily available ethnic derision as a means of public ridicule of the supposedly wrong kind of Germanness in newspaper comics and in propaganda posters (Pratt Ewing, 2008).

Another factor in the repeat cycles of public hatred against Jewishness and Turkishness is the nation. A cataclysmic development in the narrative of hate against Jews and Turks came about when Germany turned to modern nationalism. Incidents against Jewish communities in German-speaking territories were in the main sporadic outbreaks of anti-Jewish hate up to the 18th century (Mack, 2003). The conditions enabling a systematic grouping of political ideologies around anti-Semitism had not existed before the late 1870s (see the introduction). However, with a sense of homogenous Germanness upon which to build the national German identity at the turn of the 19th century came the suggestion that Jewishness could not blend in with Germanness. Then, shortly before the height of the Nazi Holocaust, Jewish German people were denied their citizenship rights and forced to live in ghettos. "Indeed", Pulzer points out that "the word anti-Semitism itself - with its attempt to draw on the support of science - made its first appearance [only] in 1879" (Pulzer, 1988: ix). Equally contemporaneous was the idea that Jewish Germans had a transnational and diasporic subjectivity similar to Muslim ummah and that it was seen by the secular establishment as a non-homeland-related source of identity (Geller and Morris, 2016: 3-8). Due to the difference in its social and religious organisation, Jewishness was characterised increasingly in Germany by political and community leaders as the opposite of what the members of a modern nation should desire; a Self, which was primarily linked to the new political image of a self-contained nationalism and an ethno-centric Germanness. German elites projected it as a national vanguard. They regarded themselves as members of a European society, who believed that non-Christian religions would necessarily lead to flawed forms of state governance. The construction of Turkish alterity in reunified Germany thus occurred by the same means of ethno-cultural dichotomy as Jewish Othering in the early 20th century. That is, according to Schneider, as oppositional structures and binary central terms: German and Other (Schneider, 2002: 14-16). There was accepted Germanness and German sociality on one side, and there were Jews and Turks with their allegedly anti-national identity attachments beyond the German "Kulturstaat" or culture, religion and language as definition of statehood on the other. That boundary was and is to this day more efficient than any physical border to separate majority from minority communities in Germany, as the resurfacing right-wing rhetoric of AfD and PEGIDA suggests.

Expulsion from Mainstream Culture
The modern age of the German nation state and two of its most crucial events in recent history have worked fundamentally against ethnic minorities. Jewishness was presented as incompatible with Germanness for allegedly having cost Germans a loss of territory after WWI. Later, in the early 1990s, Turkishness was blamed for Germany's loss of economic dominance despite regaining the GDR as Federal Germany's national territory. Also echoing the Jewish German case during WWII, the German majority society collapsed varied Turkish groups into a Muslim Other after 1989. And they did so decidedly rapidly (Kaya, 2007: 483). The reduction of different forms of Turkish identities to a clichéd image of The Turk revolved around a functional discourse of anti-Ottoman hostility. It goes back to the allegedly despotic Sultans of the Orient, who were transforming their subjects into lazy and anti-intellectual slaves on the back of an Islamic doctrine. Such negative images of Turkish forms of governance helped to create the ethno-cultural trope of the so-called Turkish menace. Along with the trope of the lazy

dumb Turk, it had served Latin Christianity to define itself as a pan-European Christianity since the First Crusade, during which Jerusalem was conquered in 1099 (Berman, 2011). The 14th century saw an effort to strengthen Europe by proclaiming Muslims as an external threat to European countries. The process aided in the construction of European Christendom and an ethno-German, Christian Self. That kind of Christian would work hard so that the nation could thrive as a stand-in for a collective body of Germanness and Christianity and its interior be safe because it was homogenous. This ethnic and religious bias planted the seeds of an exclusionary identity practice. From the mid-15th century onwards it became the custom in German-language texts to equate Muslims with Turks. When early modern German texts mention a person having turned Turk, the meaning is that they have converted to Islam, hence making the ethnic category Turk identical with the religious category of Muslimness. Consequently, with Germany's economic downturn after German reunification, the prejudice of the anti-European, non-Christian and lazy Turk returned. Dissatisfied Germans, especially in cities and regions with high unemployment numbers and little previous contact with Muslimness and Turkish German communities, reproduced a well-rehearsed bias against Turkishness. In East German cities and areas where socio-economic trauma and the fear of instability in the country were especially high, communities developed an even more heightened sense of anti-Muslimness by projecting the German East's frustrations on The Turk.[2]

However, the exclusion discourse around Turkish Germans did not stop there. If a new national German identity was to be created, a new political order to be legitimised after the fall of the Berlin wall, it could happen only by ethnic "boundary maintenance" (White, 1997: 754-769) of some kind. Dissatisfied right-wingers sought to externalise and essentialise, and thus de-territorialise, the Turkish German community within the re-drawn borders of Germany. All the while, Germany's new federal government axed many of its infrastructure projects while the country bled manufacturing jobs. This meant that thousands of Turkish German blue-collar workers, especially those located in the reunified city of Berlin and the suburban areas around it, lost their employment in the short few months following official reunification in October 1990. "When the wall fell, it fell on us", was a common wisdom circulating among the Turkish German community at the time. The "Dolchstoßlegende", or stab-in-the-back legend, attributing insidious internal betrayal to Germany's defeat in WWI, had similarly put blame on Jewish Germans as the ethnic Others in Germany responsible for the majority society's problems. Entirely untrue, of course, and impossible because of their miniscule proportions of the general population, both groups still drew hate and fault for the consequences of German majority society's policies (Schneider, 2008). Jewish German and Turkish German Others instantly became less German, whether they had fought alongside German troops or were working on the same assembly lines.

The Janus Face of Ethnic Humour in Germany

"Oppressed groups often use humor as a form of attack on the value of a dominant society or social" (Charney, 2005: 3-4), writes Charney. I have laid out the reasons for and subjects of attack by Turkish German comedy in the new century, though an exhaustive overview of all contemporary forms of that comedy would require several books. Following on from here, this book establishes the general function of contemporary Turkish German comedy in several mass media types, which is impressive because a wider variety of comedic fictions by Turkish Germans exists. The popularity of these cultural products is also exciting, as the following chapters are going to detail. However, there is that history of "Türkenwitze" or anti-Turkish German humour which denigrates the Turkish minority for the amusement of the majority culture. To know more about it and to understand it better means an improved understanding of the pro-social agenda of contemporary Turkish German comedy entertainment and from where its makers draw inspiration.

Ethnic humour has several important qualities. One is that the story of its social functions opens a unique window into societal dynamics such as those laid out in the first part of this chapter. In Germany, the way ethnic humour worked was to separate, to hierarchise and to deride ethnic minorities, seemingly validating claims about their inferior identities. It helped German elites, the government and the wider public to turn a blind eye when ethnic minorities were mistreated, hurt or even killed. This divisive humour is a precursor to the narrative of how communities like the Turkish Germans fought back. They were the target of anti-social ethnic humour before re-appropriating its hostility, aggression and degradation. Islamophobic humour was widely consumed in German mainstream media, which illustrates the pervasiveness of certain negative stereotypes about Turkish German people. That Turkish Germans could take on centuries of demeaning jokes and racist slurs with their pro-social ethnic comedy is astonishing. Even more impressive, however, is the fact that they could use this comedy to facilitate a widening of ethnic identity discourse in Germany via the arena of popular culture entertainment.

Islamophobic humour in Germany, which one can just as well call racist propaganda, is well documented. Studies of it connect the fear of the transnational to the fear of the non-German Other, first to divisive ethnic humour and later to racialising ethnic comedy sketches and ethnic drag skits (Sieg, 2009). Those racist entertainment performances are very similar to American Vaudeville and blackfaced or brownfaced stock characters in unscripted plays in the tradition of Italian *commedia dell'arte*. Long-running jokes about Turks, appearing as visual propaganda artefacts in daily German newspapers and on television and in the cinema, go back to popular print-press comics. They were co-opted as an essential means of disseminating race-based humour by the German yellow press after the first wave of Turkish German labour migration in the 1960s and after reunification in the early 1990s. Again, none of this was entirely new and applied before to anti-Jewish German and antisemitic humour in Germany. A dearth of research studies on anti-Jewish stereotyping in racist WWII comic strips, funny stage plays and nightclub skits confirms as much for readers interested in historical ethnic comedy racism in Germany (Chapman, 2000; Dundes and Hausschild, 1988).

What was new in the case of Turkish Germans, or at least contradictory on the face of it, was that the two post-war Germanies had carefully constructed their narratives of national de-Nazification around multi-ethnic diversity. West Germany had done so by aligning itself with a pro-capitalist market economy under the leadership of the USA's so-called melting-pot multiculture. The wider public in West Germany embraced symbols of that melting-pot US culture, for example by buying American brand products and consuming American entertainment culture on German television and in German cinemas. All the while, the GDR regime was eager to construct a national story of East Germany as a utopian socialist home for and by all state workers regardless of skin colour or religious beliefs (Habermas, 1988: 3; Müller, 2000: 124). The return of seemingly racist imagery and comedy in East German and West German entertainment emphasises how short-lived the ideals of racial tolerance were within German culture. Several of the political cartoons about Turks living in Germany for the last 50 years point this out. Some of them were collected for a travelling exhibition ("50 Years, 20 Cartoons: Turkish People from the Perspective of German Cartoonists") and first put on display in 2012 at Ankara's German

Cultural Centre. Viewing them gives one an idea of how German cartoonists critiqued the pseudo-liberal perception of Turkish migrants.

"Şimdi bana Alman Anayasasının ilk 20 maddesini söyleyin bakalım!"
(Heiko Sakurai, Berliner Zeitung 2004)

Figure 2: "Döner-Centre", Heiko Sakurei, political newspaper cartoon, first published in Berliner Zeitung, 2004, part of "50 Years, 50 Cartoons: Turkish People from the Perspective of German Cartoonists" (Erdogan, 2009). The text in the speech bubble reads: "Ok, so then please recite for me the first 20 Articles of the German Basic Law charter!". Credit: Berliner Zeitung/Heiko Sakurai, reprint with permission by artist.

Anti-social and Pro-social Ethnic Comedy: "Sword" and "Shield"

Racialising comedy and ethnicity-based humour have long been a part of German culture. Their potential for varied interpretation has led to a wide range of interpretations of their effects on society, which have only recently become an area of investigation in psycho-social research into humour (Saucier and O'Dea and Strain, 2016). There are several competing opinions on the finer nuances of the subject. Existing literature on ethno-racist humour, and particularly its conceptualisation according to the "sword and shield metaphor" (Rappoport, 2005), though, suggests two primary outcomes associated with racial and ethnic humour. When ethnic comedy, that is ethnicity-based humour used in mainstream entertainment, is anti-social in intention it is used as a sword or means of attack and interpreted as such. This means that it may reinforce existing social hierarchies and divisions between certain groups along lines of ethnicity tropes and ethnic identity bias. Stereotypes about the target or targets of the humour may be reproduced, potentially giving the impression that it is socially acceptable to articulate racist prejudice and ethnic bias openly for amusement. When ethnic comedy is pro-social in intent, used as a shield and understood as such, it may serve to challenge and protect against prejudice and connect members of communities within and across group boundaries. It moves people closer together instead of separating them further.

Davies makes the point that almost all humorous approaches to ethnicity and national identities, fictional as well as in real life, inevitably involve communication about a notion of social mobility (Davies, 2002: 148-149). For example, with ethnic jokes in nation states there is always an allusion to a sense of change within and between ethnic communities and their assumed places in society: societal, occupational, cultural, educational and political. It is the very notion of the possibility of social change, upward and downward movement, Davies argues, which provides the springboard for ridicule between and even within ethnic communities. Therefore, he writes, "ethnic humor in general [and regardless of its social intent] is a relevant and important part of our modern popular culture" (Davies, 2002: 136). But it would be inaccurate to overemphasise here just two categories of ethnic humour to restrict or mobilise cultural identities in the social imaginary of a country's mainstream culture. There is a possibility that some pro-socially motivated ethnic comedy may be perceived as anti-social, presenting the possibility of unintentional reproduction of the status quo rather than subverting it. Rappoport also warns that supposedly clear-cut taxonomies and overly narrow definitions in humour theory often do not equip scholars of ethnic humour to deal with the many finer nuances of it and that which is still unclear about it: "[c]onventional analyses often just brush over the subject by referring to the humour theories summarized earlier and emphasizing the superiority theme—that by ridiculing others, people enhance themselves. Freud's psychoanalytic concepts are also frequently cited, since so much of racial, ethnic, and gender humor involves sex and aggression. This is not wrong, and much of it is useful, but the aim [should be] to show there is a great deal more to be said about humor based on stereotypes" (Rappoport, 2005: 31).

Researchers in ethnic humour studies argued until the late 1980s that ethnic humour functioned primarily to describe only the relationship between ethnic communities. Yet theorists like Giselinde Kuipers, who examine stereotype humour in the specific cultural contexts of Canada and America, argue that humour based on the identity of ethnic communities has more important functions within rather than between groups of people, as I suggest in chapter four (Kuipers, 2006: 140-142). Conspicuous examples of this can be found in most, if not all, societies around the world. Kuipers makes the point that in some societies older migrant communities or older inhabitants refuse to acknowledge and accept the values of the current mainstream culture, as indicated in chapter three (Kuipers, 2006: 144). Poking fun at themselves as perceived minorities outside the dominant community allows, for example, so-called rednecks in the United States or French Canadians in Canada confidently to mark their lifestyles as different from those of the majority, yet not as somehow lesser. The minorities can take pride through ethnic humour in forming a particularistic narrative of their cultural identity at the periphery of a multicultural society. As a reverse form of cultural assimilation, outsiders need to accept the qualities of this identity as superior to theirs in order to gain access to it (Kuipers, 2006: 145).

Is Turkish German comedy entertainment in the new century driven by similar anti-social or pro-social mechanisms? Does it present an opportunity to embed prejudice and ethnicity in self-aware discussions of contemporary Germanness? In this book I claim that it does and that Turkish German comedy productions also foreground the issue of tokenism in the representation of ethnic diversity in Germany. Neither the alt righter nor the liberal lefty, nor the comfortably neutral middle-of-the-roader, is safe from the critique of Turkish German comedy artists. They all question the identity politics of Germanness as a discrete culture complex, whose opening towards a decidedly transnational, hybrid aesthetic is at the centre of my analysis. Moreover, one can see the different mass media types of Turkish German comedy as a collective platform. It is widely accessible across multiple creative channels to interrogate normative assumptions of a white, Christian Germany. Turkish German comedy filmmakers, screenwriters, performers and authors work off it by sharing "experiences of diasporic subjects and by telling stories about the dynamics of cross-cultural encounters and postmodern multi-culturalism" (Berghahn, 2013: 6). The attentive reader will thus notice in subsequent chapters that I privilege in this book the social functions of Turkish German comedy fictions instead of reading them as representations of factual reality. It is not just about "getting" the humour which may or may not lead to a positive or negative affective response. Instead, I talk about how Turkish German comedy participates in the dissemination of ethnic communities' internal workings and how they deal with other ethnic groups.

In related aspects of modern usage, Kuipers has shown that ethnic humour functions primarily to clue in audiences on the position of ethnic identities in relation to each other. Conspicuous examples of this function appear in ethnic humour based on prevalent tropes of national, religious or regional and gendered identities. Kuipers puts forward the argument that one can read jokes about the lazy rednecks in America mentioned before as a distillation of the essence of all social interactions, namely hierarchy and ordering (Kuipers, 2006: 140-142). Proceeding on this basis, Kuipers considers this joke by US redneck comedian Jeff Foxworthy: "You might be a redneck if the stock market crashes and it won't affect you one bit." This example cites several possible ingredients of ethnic humour and its function to understand the social order through stereotyping of group identities (Kuipers: 144). In such examples identities and social mobility are inherently linked. Jackson develops the point further by arguing that humour theorists have made productive use of humour to touch on taboos or sensitive topics in society. The link between identity and mobility expresses the relationship between who we are and where we can go in life. Because of this, jokes about ethnic stereotypes show us where certain communities sit in the greater context of a society's social imaginary (Jackson, 2012: 2). Similarly, a comedic reading of popular fictions about minority characters, for instance Turkish Germans in Germany, can deliver new perspectives on the complex relationship between ethnicity, marginalisation and the novel definition of identities in German society.

Another implication of this is to place Turkish German comedy in wider research environs. Formulating a new approach to Turkish German comedy means being part of the formulation of a burgeoning field of transnational popular culture studies in the new century. Much of the scholarship in this academic project relies on established theoretical terrain. There is immigrant transnationalism (Schiller et al., 1995), which looks at the act of transfer between source and destination points and the inherent social actions and reactions migration networks generate. In the age of globalisation, diasporic and other types of trans-ethnic culture have formed new power structures (Gupta and Ferguson, 1997), cross-pollinated by anthropological sensibilities of space and the politics of representing difference (Banerjee, 2005). Between transnationally produced and consumed comedy fictions lies the centrality of mainstream entertainment, whose study has been approached from the perspectives of audience taste, commercialisation and intercultural values (Göktürk, 2004; Higbee and Song Hwee, 2010). By now, too, the recurrent crisis of German nationhood in transnational Europe has attained canonical status (Risse, 2015; Brubaker, 1996).

Studying humour, as one has seen by now, is a challenge in any domain. Interpreting the way humour emerges, which contexts it references, how its many structures and uses play out in specific settings, can be a daunting task. Comedy research is "complex and demanding—even unlimited" (Roach Anleu and Milner Davis, 2018: 6). This reality of doing humour studies may help to explain why scholars working on Turkish German culture have largely avoided a confrontation of humour styles or styles of humour with frameworks of applied social pragmatics. Even those who study the funny in Turkish German works of film, television, literature and performance have found that the things which are in and of themselves comedic or humorous are difficult to judge as inherently funny. The flavour or tone of a comedy film or a video piece can vary from being utterly sarcastic to light-heartedly warm and playful. Knock-about slapstick actions in a romantic comedy may be drawing on complex and multi-faceted, multi-dimensional notions of humour. Physical gags in online sketch reels can contain subjective, situational, multi-ethnic and plural markers for ethnic humour about multiple ethnic communities. Some think it is hilarious, some find it lowbrow garbage. It could be the reason why even Göktürk, who was the first to take on Turkish German comedy, has come to think it impractical to discuss comedy fictions just on the subjective grounds of audience perception. She has concluded as much in her numerous discussions of humorous representations of hybrid cultures in Turkish German cinema. Göktürk suggests that it is more useful to determine which aspects of identity a comedy fiction presents; and which it presents in more ways than one to propose that there are different ways of being authentically German or Turkish (Göktürk, 2000: 4-5).

But what remains absent, first and foremost still, is a systemic investigation method to merge scholarly discourse on popular entertainment culture with transnational migrant comedy. The social pragmatics of humour play a key role in responding to this gap. To question when and how humour works, where it is applied and to what end produces complex and multi-faceted examinations of subjects, situations, shared realities of living and social meanings. There are multi-dimensional strategies to the authorship of funny fictions and scripted performances. They reveal how certain cultures differ while retaining a sense of commonality, which is essential in understanding why specific jokes and puns are funny without being anti-social. In discussing Turkish German identities and Turkish German comedy, research must include a discussion of linguistic elements, verbal structures, situational elements, physical actions, a dissection of wit, and how scripted comedy in general elicits specific meanings on the textual level. This approach can be categorised as an established form of social contextualisation within the classical structure of pragmatic humour research. I would note, however, that this approach is new to analyses of Turkish German culture and Turkish German comedy. Scholars of humour, though, will recognise that I employ the classical tripartite formation of humour theory. I use it to speculate in the next chapters on how humour creates intended messages in support of Turkish German comedy's overarching agenda: pro-social, affective meanings which model positive interventions between Turkish German and other German communities in the context of everyday living and the actual reality of living in German society.

Aspects of social control as well as unbridled freedom of expression will underpin all critical thinking about Turkish German comedy as social commentary. The wealth of ethnic comedy entertainment in genres and media types is evidence enough of both a need and an opportunity to understand a hybrid form of Turkishness and Germanness as creative power, a form of new artistic labour. It questions whether the burden of uniting Islam with Western majority societies falls squarely on Muslim minority communities or groups re-Muslimised after decades of living in Germany in the wake of 9/11. I develop this point further in my analysis of inter-communal and intra-communal exchanges of Turkish Germans and other Germans in fictionalised German society through the lens of three types of humour: superiority, incongruity and relief.

Superiority, Incongruity and Relief Humour

Kuipers (2008: 388), Meyer (2000), Olin (2016) and Scheel and Gockel (2017) all agree on three broad "categories of theory or classical approaches to explaining the phenomena of humour and laughter" (Roach Anleu and Milner Davis, 2018: 6). These are the theories of *superiority*, *incongruity* and *relief*. With superiority one finds humour in the lowering of another's social station through momentary misfortune or intentional actions and speech acts. Examples of this can be found in situational comedy scripts for television sitcoms, the physical comedy of slapstick in action-driven goofball or romantic comedy films, and the quick-witted dialogue of chick-lit and dick-lit novels. Incongruity turns on the perceived difference between expected outcomes of specific situations or assumed knowledge about reality and the actual state of things or behavioural patterns of people. This mismatch is perceived by the brain as a positive stimulus of a learning experience. Incongruity generates laughter in sudden identity reversal scenes of screwball comedy and is increasingly popular with punchline pundits to elicit laughter in their stand-up routines. Finally, relief means that humour and laughter allow the sudden release of pent-up emotions or re-routing of nervous energy, thereby producing pleasure from negative sentiments and anti-social predispositions. This type of humour occurs during confrontations and stand-offs between characters, thus offering alternatives to the physical escalation of conflict and resolving contrasting viewpoints without violence. Of course, these theories overlap and intersect. They are not clear-cut paradigms. Frequently, any given instance of scripted comedy fiction and scripted comedy performance "will contain elements of incongruity, superiority and relief as well as other factors" (Roach Anleu and Milner Davis, 2018: 6).

Superiority
Superiority, *incongruity* and *relief* each have their own histories of usage and theoretical criticism in the areas of philosophy, sociology, linguistics and literary studies. Prominent supporters have repeatedly attempted to use them in different disciplines to explain laughter from the viewpoint of an intentional stimulus and a desired response to it. In the 17th century, philosopher Thomas Hobbes advocated superiority as the dominant model to explain how laugher was an individual's response to feeling superior to others. He defines laughter in *Human Nature* (1640) as a "sudden glory arising from some sudden conception of some eminency in ourselves, by comparison with the infirmity of others, or with our own formerly" (Hobbes, 1905: chapter 9, sec. 13). More recently, Arthur Asa Berger sees it as an important theory on "how humor involves some sense of superiority that people feel about those (people, animals, objects) they laugh at" (Berger, 2010: 105).

Different scholars have produced different interpretations of what the humour theories about superiority, incongruity and relief mean. Berger writes with a greater emphasis on everyday social contexts than Hobbes, "A person slips on a banana peel and we laugh because, for a moment, we who have not lost our balance feel superior to him" (Berger, 2010: 105). In contrast to incongruity theory and relief theory, laughter in the context of superiority humour is overtly directed at someone or something and looks down at the position of perceived inferiority. Berger explains this point further with a critical look at the general aspect of superiority humour defined by Hobbes. He argues that "[from] a cultural theory perspective we can extend [Thomas] Hobbes's notion of humor involving a sudden recognition of some kind of eminency in ourselves relative to others and say we may find this eminency not only in our persons but in our cultures" (Berger: 105-106).

Despite their different interpretations, Hobbes and Berger highlight several features of the same tendency of superiority humour, which is to obtain authority over certain aspects of a person's identity or a culture through ridicule. The general idea is that the emphasis of difference can position one's social status higher than that of another person. But while Hobbes remains vague about the ambivalent social mechanism of superiority humour, Berger describes it as a way of actively fighting for societal primacy. He argues that the act of reproducing perceived differences between two socio-culturally determined positions and highlighting them with humour is nothing short of an act of social aggression (Berger: 106). Berger claims further that it is undeniably also a form of aggression if the entity in the allegedly inferior social position relishes in turn the fall of a person or object from its supposedly higher place in society.

Exploring the aspect of social ordering through humour in greater detail, Sullivan makes the point that superiority humour can be perceived as a negative as well as a positive form of cultural identity politics. Superiority humour can be interpreted as a negative strategy if a majority mocks a minority, or as a struggle for social equality if the minority fights back with it. In the second case, it encourages people to fight for a better place than the one awarded to them by those in power (Sullivan, 2004: 87-88). Sullivan writes, "[A] belief in superiority produces a type of equality, albeit a particularly noxious type [because] the pervasive belief in superiority encourages violence" (Sullivan: 88).

It is the message about identities in relation to social change and society which challenges theorists not to dismiss superiority as a retaliatory practice or the one-sided form of humour defined by Davies as ethnic ridicule. But Berger argues that the ridicule in superiority humour is part of a recognition process of social contexts and subject positions, which he reads as a test of alleged differences (Berger: 107). I have described above that cultural differences are the main themes of Turkish German comedy, which suggests that superiority humour can shed new light on them as a theoretical approach. The stories I analyse start out by reproducing social differences and reifying them as potential dividers between communities. Yet, as their plots unfold, the narratives examine and comment on those dividers, they interrogate and sometimes destabilise them, and in some cases even dis-locate and re-place them to stress their artifice as makers of ethno-cultural *superiority*.

Incongruity

Put forward by Francis Hutcheson's writings about aesthetic diversity in the mid-18th century, incongruity is now the most accepted transcultural model of explaining laughter as an expression of positive surprise in the face of an unexpected situation or the experience of mismatch (Jackson, 2012: 9). Similarly, Arthur Berger defines incongruity humour as "based on some kind of a difference between what people expect and what they get. We can also look at incongruity in more specific terms as far as culture theory is concerned and say it suggests some kind of difference between what is and what is not normative" (Berger, 2012: 105). In other words, incongruity occurs where there is a mismatch, by evoking it either willingly through some semiotic stimulus or unwillingly through some other means. The stimulus activates knowledge about two diverging, incompatible frames of reference and thereby evokes an element of opposition. Laughter indicates here the realisation of an incompatibility between a concept and certain assumptions involved in a situation or thought process and the real objects thought to be related in some way to the concept or assumption (Berger: 108).

Despite its common acceptance, theorists lament the inherent lack of precision in this definition. Berger for instance finds incongruity problematic when it comes to determining in greater detail the cultural positions which are involved in the act of laughing about a perceived clash. He says: "Although incongruity theories tell us that incongruous differences in humorous texts elicit laughter, [...] usually in the form of polar opposition, forcing them into unspecified models of binary opposition is too vague as a research approach for informed inquiry" (Berger: 106). Vandaele makes a similar point. He argues that the analysis of referential conflict alone does not yield contextual results about the critical study of clashing meanings. One must rather ask how, for instance, the shock value of clashes between stereotypical knowledge and completely unexpected meanings plays out in a specific narrative (Vandaele, 2002: 223-224).

Berger and Vandaele draw explicit parallels between incongruity humour and fictions about migrant identities. Laughter emerges as the result of someone learning something new from an otherwise common situation or context in the theory of incongruity humour. The reconfiguration of the expected can happen either by people behaving suddenly differently from how they would normally or by meanings which are contradictory to their usual communicative purpose. Moreover, John Morreal points out that "expectation is a key word here" (Morreal, 2009: 60), in that what any given person may find incongruous depends largely on his or her individual knowledge about and experiences in a cultural context (Morreal: 60-61).

Ultimately, in humorous fictions about migrants and natives where the context is one in which immigration has resulted in a variety of meanings and cultural identities, the concept of incongruity becomes a question of how competently members of different groups deal with the unexpected. The comedic focus on a specific society can also indicate whether the social setting has imposed boundaries on the members of different ethnic backgrounds so that they do not share enough cultural meanings or knowledge to avoid unexpected misunderstandings. The limited knowledge and experience of their own group might not allow community members to avoid incongruent situations within the culture, much less so between cultures. If this aspect of incompetence is the humorous focus of the narrative in a film, a television show or a novel or a digital skit, the fact that both minority as well as majority members are faced with the same feeling of unexpectedness may become central to understanding difference as a shared quality in a society.

Relief

The most recent explanation of what provokes laughter is relief theory. The theory emerged in the mid-19th century and was later informed by Freud's psychoanalytical understanding of the human psyche and most recently updated by scholars in the field of neuro-medical science. The basic premise of relief is that "humor is tied to psychic economies and to aggression, often of a sexual nature" (Berger, 2012: 106-107). Berger writes that it is also "described as a rerouting or suspense theory of suppressed and suddenly released energies of the psyche" (Berger: 107-108) in the larger body of literature on humour research.

Berger's description indicates that relief theory shares several features with incongruity as well as superiority humour. Focusing on social functions of humour, Morreal notes that the homeostatic mechanism of relief humour serves much like a safety valve to release built-up pressure. It ensures that humour as a positive feeling and laughter as a non-violent reaction replace an otherwise anti-social and volatile outcome when a person is put under significant pressure (Morreal, 2009: 115). Morreal adds that the humorous outcome is "not only more enjoyable to human beings than the dissonance caused by the aggressive alternative or actual physical violence; it also presents the socio-cultural benefit of laughter" (Morreal: 115) to share in the fun as a group.

The concept of humorous relief is vital to this study because it suggests that humour is conducive to inter-communal as well as intra-communal relations by connecting people socially through their laugher. Although relief appears less frequently than superiority and incongruity in contemporary humour studies, it can be considered very useful, in that an individual constantly experiences identity pressures within a group. The role of affinities and affiliations which ethnic communities develop to foster a notion of cohesion are crucial in multicultural societies. This is particularly relevant for people who are required to indicate their social belonging through language or a certain behaviour despite a dislike of either or both.

The notion of a sudden discharge of accumulated tensions of the psyche also plays a central role as far as repressed groups in society develop an acute sense of belonging, which humour helps them to advocate. According to Russian literary critic Mikhail Bakhtin, who published most of his work under a repressive authoritarian regime, the social ritual of carnival demonstrates this vividly. Bakhtin writes in his study of the medieval European novel, "during no other time more than at carnival, and even though only for a short while, the carnevalesque parody and self-parody of one's outwardly-projected and/or internalized identity display to the world that folk laughter is knowing resistance to oppression from above" (Bakhtin, 1965: 2). He explains that the oppression is exercised by elites, who impose their dominant views and values on the oppressed under their rule (Bakhtin: 3-5).

What can be inferred from Bakhtin's connection between fictional carnival and a form of relief in actual reality is that cultural insiders need to adhere to the normative ways of their groups to benefit from the community's social status or to signal loyalty. Any departure from the norms means a rejection of the authority over a cultural identity and is usually penalised. Yet, if a rejection of authority is not feared but instead intended because it elicits laughter temporally in the fictional realm as the expression of a constantly changed actual reality, then relief is the sign not of social suppression but of social progress. The different instances of Turkish German comedy I analyse in this book demonstrate this.

CHAPTER II
Clash Films

"Hast du schon mal einen Türken einen Kinderwagen schieben sehen?"
"Have you ever seen a Turk push around a pram?" [1]
—Marion Martienzen to her daughter Patritzia "Titzi" (in *Kebab Connection*, 2005)

Summary

Culture clash cinema originates from fish-out-of-water comedies, which go straight to the heart of perceptions of Turkish German Muslims as Other. Clash comedy films usually depict a disenfranchised or disaffected individual whose rebellious stance against the rich and the powerful goes back to the American screwball comedies of the 1930s. Rebel and counter-culture protagonists of 1960s and mid-1970s comedy films in Western societies continued the refusal to assimilate into the majority society. They would not easily let go of their original identity. Only with the onset of the 1980s did a continuous line of films about the clash itself establish the genre of culture clash as a mass-cultural audience favourite. Workers and middle-class people in British cinema clashed over socio-economic differences while young women refused to conform to gender norms in the United States. Race issues featured prominently in the 1990s as non-white Americans and newcomer migrants to the US sought to normalise their marginalised identities.[2] It would take ten more years for Turkish German cinema to present its version of culture clash comedy in the new century with Anno Saul's *Kebab Connection* (2005), which based the clash between first-generation immigrant Ibo and his girlfriend Titzi on Turkish and German gender models. This chapter suggests that Turkish German culture clash comedies have followed the structure of Anglophone precursors of the genre. Yet, filmmakers have added with great success political issues such as same-sex marriage (*Evet, ich will!-Evet, I do*, 2008) and aspects like urbanisation in Berlin (*Meine verrückte türkische Hochzeit-Kiss me Kismet*) to the clash genre and experimented with non-linear narratives and even elements of augmented realism (*Almanya: Willkommen in *Deutschland-Almanya-Welcome to Germany*, 2011). Turkish German culture clash comedies have evolved, and in only a short period they have become synonymous around the world with a new brand of transnational German cinema.

Ethnic Clash Films as Social Commentary

Culture clash comedies are most potent if they dramatise the theme of cultural tension pleasingly yet offer enough scope for the plot to work through the social context of why people and their values clash. The clash comedies in this chapter do this, too, to question and challenge essentialist notions of a migrant community's perceived difference in its Germanness. Based on the generic structures of clash comedy film to turn that which makes us different into the joke itself, they giddily subsume Germans' obsession with the boundaries of cultures and a preoccupation with difference in culture, sexuality, language or religion. This means that I will concern myself here mostly with examples of incongruity and superiority humour. Culture clash comedy appeals to a large audience, both majority and minority communities, by appropriating elements of foreignness and Otherness and developing new ones, such as hybrid, in-between, familiar, relatable or fusion. Those audiences who watch them and the filmmakers who produce clash comedy films find pleasure in the avoidance of being contained within a stereotype attached to a certain place in society or social status, as Halle (Halle, 2010) and Naiboglu (Naiboglu, 2018) have found. This makes Turkish German culture clash cinema doubly relevant, as the culture clash punchline is a delicate line to walk on for both the viewers and the producers. The makers of these films must consider that some audiences may consume the material at face value while other viewers may misunderstand what is supposed to be funny and at whose expense (Benbow, 2015). To portray colliding cultures through superiority, incongruity and relief humour generates plots and characters. They appear in the pairing of lovers, families and ethnic communities during romances, family celebrations or community rituals. The clash comedy which ensues offers an opportunity for social commentary and satire of societal issues. Though emphasising the "odd" identity versus the identity of the allegedly "normal community" has a precarious place in German ethnic humour. Culture clash comedy can play for cheap laughs while perpetuating racist attitudes and religious bias. Jewish Germans and Turkish

Germans have paid dearly for this flipside of anti-social ethnic humour, as I explained in the last chapter.

The characteristics of the four films discussed in this chapter suggest that Muslimness is not a punchline pun. Neither is it a barrier. Just like non-Muslim Germanness, it is a platform to think about the feeling of being misunderstood. It is an opportunity to imagine multi-ethnic coexistence in the same country without the need for total assimilation. Within the arena of the popular culture industry, ethnic identity is not a joke unto itself if played for nuance. It is an opportunity to explore when and why culture clash occurs. *Kebab Connection, Kiss me, Kismet, Evet, I do,* and *Almanya-Welcome to Germany* use humour to critical comedic effect. Their range of topics shows how helpful popular culture cinema can be in fostering and sustaining a debate around a nation's cultural identity. The communities contributing to it reflect through their representation on screen that there is joy in Otherness; that the positioning as Other and a clear-cut identity per nationality is reductive; and that difference and diversity always rest in the eye of the beholder.

Anglophone Precursors to Culture Clash in Turkish German Film

Culture clash comedies are not mimetic representations of social realities. Hake argues that verisimilitude is also not the point of the genre. That the figure of the cultural outsider and insider follows a trajectory of confrontation and disillusionment is more important (Hake, 2013: 167). The collision between two communities creates a tension which invariably tests and confirms the limits of social change and progress. Clash comedies in Germany like Wolfgang Becker's *Goodbye Lenin-Good Bye, Lenin!* (2003) have a history of framing the clashing characters' self-images through German-specific events like labour migration and reunification (Hake, 2013: 168). Thus, it is important to situate the genre in a broader historical and functional context to address the specific form in which contemporary clash fictions make sense of specifically German affinities. German film directors such as Wim Wenders have already explored the Germanness of German national cinema in numerous feature productions since 1989 in "the search for authenticity, immediacy, and belonging and the desire for freedom and movement [which have led] to the feared disappearance of the real" (Hake: 168).

The Turkish German culture clash comedy films in this chapter act in service of the same agenda.

The most important precursor to the clash motif in contemporary Turkish German comedy is a spate of 1970s and 1980s American films. Those works thematically involve "conflicting and clashing cultures or subcultural attitudes, perceptions and lifestyles" (Fuller and Loukides, 1991: 171). The majority of cinematic clash comedies in Germany's cultural mainstream which have emerged since the 1990s have been following the popular American model of adopting and occupying existing stereotypes about certain groups or identities and exaggerating them to the point of absurdity (King, 2002: 152). Multicultural comedy in German cinema of the 1990s, as described in the introduction, is largely congruent with the mass-market norms of Hollywood-produced fictions. But Turkish German comedy has perhaps more than any other genre embraced America's comedy antics of excessive and stylised caricatures of racial and ethnic essentialisation, as Halle's study maintains in the context of German film after 1989 (Halle, 2009: 40).

Some film scholars claim that the "line between exaggeration, parody, and a simple re-enactment of stereotypes is often hard to draw" (King, 2002: 153), which makes it difficult to determine the influence of earlier clash comedy formats on later ones. Here, however, the motivation of Turkish German culture clash comedy to subvert reductive perceptions of an identity as a woman, as a non-Westerner or as a Muslim does go back to America's multiculture and clash comedy cinema. There is a fine line between pro-social and anti-social comedy, and its function as sword and shield, as I described in chapter one. In the heyday of culture clash cinema in the United States, this became apparent in the underlying self-consciousness of the Other as someone who lives outside the dominant community. In most instances the Other's awareness of cultural difference is explicitly marked as a self-parodic routine, as illustrated by the black American comedian and actor Eddy Murphy. Murphy adopts a clumsy "dumb black" behaviour to outsmart racist white criminals as Axel Foley in the *Beverly Hills Cops* film series (1984-1994). Then there is Chicano celebrity Richard "Cheech" Marin, who undermines any realism in the Mexican-American image of the "lazy Latino" in his *Cheech and Chong* stoner comedies (1978-1984). Or we have Jewish-American comedy star Mel Brooks, who reaffirms his permanent displacement from America's cultural "WASP" (White Anglo-Saxon Protestant) mainstream as a Jewish-Indian chief in *Blazing Saddles* (1974) (King: 152). All this reverberates in the comedy aesthetics of Turkish German culture clash comedies.

The hostility between characters with different cultural identities living in the same country is the main focus of culture clash comedies, though there are some variations.³ Comedy provides the genre with a safety net to explore, for example, antagonisms based on religious bias and ethnic difference without controversy or violation of public norms when material or language is used which might otherwise be impossible, or at least highly controversial, to include. The scandal surrounding Sarrazin's books vividly illustrates the difference between fictional discourse and reality. The audience of culture clash, however, expects a prejudiced viewpoint and permits it under the premise that the trading of insults, fights and controversies will help to improve the initially hostile relationship between the clashing identities with the possibility of a redemptive experience (Kopp, 2014: 61). Despite the unwillingness of culture clash "to develop and dwell on the dark side of comedy" (Fuller and Loukides: 171), the clash treatment makes it possible to read even the most insulting rant or ethnic slur as an entertaining commentary on societal tensions between groups. Culture clash, with some exceptions, also usually emphasises family-friendly comedy and focuses less on graphic images and explicitly sexual or violent themes due to censorship concerns (Fuller and Loukides: 176). As I show in chapter five, this is radically different with social media and streaming platforms like YouTube.

Culture clash comedy films are a representation of social consciousness. The format has become centred on forms of cultural self-defence and on resistance to being placed in a social position rather than placing oneself in it. It turns on the unwillingness to being reduced to a cliché and the awareness of identity typing. Gurinder Chadha's British culture clash blockbuster, *Bend It Like Beckham* (2002), proved at the beginning of the new century that the tried and tested clash comedy formula has remained popular with audiences. While Benbow rightly suggests that not all culture clash films are able to convey a critical message to the audience if viewers consume the material at face value (Benbow, 2007: 519), the development of culture clash has always included the undermining of social inequality and a support of social change (Fuller and Loukides: 170). The interaction of disenfranchised and disaffected figures, who butt heads with antagonistic characters of higher social rank, is an exemplary feature central to a strain of regional-themed satire and black humour films in the Hollywood cinema of the 1980s. These films in turn refer to the US screwball and romance comedies of the 1930s and the social rebel and counter-culture films of the 1960s and early 1970s (Fuller and Loukides: 170). There is an element of social progress in every one of them.

Not all comedy clash films are the same, but all share the genre's most fundamental plot element. There is the chance encounter and conversation between allegedly polar opposites such as conservative males and eccentric women, blacks and whites, criminals and cops, Jews and Christians, the fringe of society and the core, rigid conservatives and cultural progressives, the poor and the affluent, and the domestically encultured and the societal newcomers. Germany is now experiencing a heyday trend similar to the American one with the culture clash comedies of Turkish German cinema, which "[far] from merely 'aiming' to please,' [...] challenge even smug progressives, consumers of ethnic difference who fail to recognize their own perpetuation of racist traditions" (Benbow: 519).

Kebab Connection as Cultural Re-Mixing

Cultural conventions are a central element in culture clash comedy. They are highly revealing of power relations and of dominant values in society (Fuller and Loukides, 1991). Anno Saul's *Kebab Connection* (2005) explores their subversion by mixing a diverse set of characters across cultural boundaries in German society. This exploration of undoing cultural homogeny and the film's multicultural imagery make *Kebab Connection* an important opportunity to "examine the place of the Turkish diaspora [...] within a transnational rather than a national context" (Cooke and Homewood, 2011: 4). The film's young hero is an aspiring filmmaker and screenwriter named Ibrahim "Ibo" Secmez. He was born in Germany as the second child to Turkish guest worker parents. He is in love with a native German woman called Patritzia "Titzi" Martienzen. Titzi is an aspiring young actor who studies for her entry exam to a prestigious acting school in Hamburg where both characters live. It is Ibo's quest to make the first German Kung-Fu film. Meanwhile, Titzi is obsessed with acting and religiously memorises the German translation of Shakespeare's *Romeo and Juliet* as her audition monologue. They are already in a romantic relationship at the beginning of the film. Their different cultural backgrounds could not hinder their bonding and developing affection for each other over a shared passion for the arts. They frequently meet in one of Hamburg's outer districts, the so-called Schanzenviertel, to discuss their dreams.[4] Tizi wants to have a career as an actress, whereas Ibo sees his future in directing transnational fusion films.

Kebab Connection opens with one of the cinema commercials Ibo produces for his Turkish German uncle. The uncle owns a small Turkish takeaway called "King of Kebab" in the heart of the "Schanze". Despite the popularity of Ibo's commercials with local audiences and although he can cast his lover Titzi as the female lead in most of the short productions, he aspires to more than making money with advertisements. The 21-year-old cinephile wants to fuse the aesthetics of East Asian film classics, more precisely the Kung-Fu feature films starring his idol Bruce Lee, with the realities of migrant life in Hamburg. Ibo thinks he can establish himself internationally as a global filmmaker that way. His dream of film auteurism rests largely on his ability to mix elements from different cultures in a funny and cool way without turning the East-West fusion into a farce for cheap laughs. This premise captures the basic attitude of Turkish German comedy clash films. It suggests that a mixing of identities should be open to reinterpretations and creative experiments grounded in pop culture.[5] *Kebab Connection*'s opening scene illustrates this with a fierce Kung-Fu fight between an AfroGerman man and a Turkish German man over the last delicious Döner at "King of Kebab".[6]

The Kung-Fu scene immediately references the notion of multiculturalism as a form of unexpected incongruity. Two non-white characters inhabiting roles common to popular Asian cinema have the humour in the introductory scene tread a fine line between tradition and innovation. However, the lack of what is presumed to be ethnically correct casting for this commercial styled as Asian Kung-Fu is no coincidence. Identities in *Kebab Connection* constantly bring up questions about politically correct or appropriate behaviour while they clash in contexts of cultural re-remixing. Ibo's fusion identity as a Turkish German man is scrutinised the most. Other characters who represent culturally diverse Germanness are also critical of the norms around ethnic identities, much more so than any Germans who think of themselves as historically "native". Some of those German characters who think of themselves as native German are happy to stick to racist clichés as established knowledge about German society. Titzi's German mother, Marion, is eager to reduce Ibo to the stereotype of the Turkish male chauvinist referred to in the quotation at the beginning of this chapter. Yet, some Turkish Germans are also equally reluctant to accept Ibo's lifestyle choices. His parents repeatedly push him to take up an allegedly traditional Turkish German blue-collar trade, like being a mechanic in a garage or working as a butcher in a halal meat processing plant. When it comes to gender, some Turkish German men find it hard to deal with Ibo as an artist. Some refuse to accept that he is dating a non-Turkish woman. His "King of Kebab" advertisements however fly in the face of all these restrictions on Turkish German hybridity outside the alleged norm. A wide range of cinemagoers enjoy Ibo's innovative take on cultural fusion as it reverberates with their truth of living as Other yet not lesser German in multicultural Germany's "Schanze" neighbourhoods. The wild mix of cultures in the Kebab ads encapsulates a critical comment on the creative labour of migrant filmmakers for which scholars have lauded the film's scriptwriters, Fatih Akin and Anno Saul.

More elements of social critique have been recognised by now in *Kebab Connection*. Some researchers emphasise the clash comedy hit's connections to other German films about hybridity with allegedly more highbrow substance. Hake sees striking similarities between Saul's film and Dani Levy's Jewish German comedy *Alles auf Zucker!-Go for Zucker* (2004). She points out that both films pursue a complex investigation of contemporary hybridities in German society (Hake, 2008: 218). Because it makes a powerful statement about the difficulty of translating other cultures and languages into German contexts, Cooke and Homewood find conceptual parallels (Cooke and Homewood: 4) between *Kebab Connection* and Hans-Christian Schmid's Polish German drama *Lichter-Distant Lights* (2003). And, as in *Distant Lights* and *Go for Zucker*, both hybridity and border crossing between cultural communities feature prominently as the main themes in Saul's film. Sometimes, though, the effect of the incongruity and superiority humour in *Kebab Connection* exaggerates the cultural clash framing in a way that only a light-hearted film comedy can. *Kebab Connection*'s younger target audience may be a reason for this. For example, the Kung-Fu fighters in the opening scene are evidently Afro-German and Asian German and speak perfect German. One fighter, though, even keeps on speaking after his head has been severed from his neck. He cannot stop praising the snack foods at "King of Kebab" for their glorious taste.

Ibo's filmmaking is an eclectic mix of different cinematic styles. This makes it harder for the older generation of Turkish Germans in Germany to understand his vision of a transnational cinema where ethnic difference borders on ethnic travesty. Ibo's uncle and father still think of German and Turkish culture in discrete national and not hybrid transnational categories. Hence, they prefer tradition and expect Ibo to reproduce a Turkish cinematic culture which is plausible to them. Ibo's uncle expresses this after watching a preview version of the Kung-Fu-styled "King of Kebab: Two-for-One Döner" commercial with Ibo and Titzi. He dismisses the ad's artistic value for its unusual aesthetics and is enraged by its production cost. As soon as the lights come back on in the shoddy surroundings of a run-down cinema hall, he screams at the top of his voice at Ibo: "All my money went up on the screen?! All my money went up on the screen! This...! This is some of the worst stuff I have ever seen! And believe me, I've seen plenty of shit in my time!!! The 74/75 [football] season of Galatasaray, for instance!" The viewer sees Ibo cluelessly shrug off the reference to Turkish premier-league football, not least because the film fanatic has only the outward signs of a stock type, Turkish identity. While his name and his physical appearance reference Turkishness, Ibo lacks the knowledge about Turkey's favourite national sport, command of the Turkish language and Turkish cinema. He would need all that to be accepted as a real Turk, a real man, and arguably as an artist, by Turkish Germans like his older uncle. It is telling for the clash between Ibo's and his uncle's Turkishness and knowledge about Turkish culture that Ibo was not even born in 1974.

There are more demands for an impossible allegiance to authentic Turkishness and loyalty to one's cultural traditions throughout the film. Ibo's reactions to them stress the importance of the transnational mindset with which the makers of Turkish German culture clash approach the mixing of ethnic identities and national cultures. For instance, Ibo calms Titzi down after she angrily labels the outburst of Ibo's uncle as "total crap, because [Ibo] worked on this commercial for three months like a madman and it is genius". "And the thing is, I don't even like Döner", he responds with a smirk and thanks Titzi later with a kiss for coming to his defence. As Ibo's uncle storms off, the lovers assure each other of their creative and artistic talents as director and actor, respectively. Their transnational artistry bridges the alleged culture gap between Germans and Turkish Germans and forms the basis for the titular "Kebab Connection". This represents the core of my work here, showing that all cultures residing in the country are equally representative of Germany's diversity in the 21st century.

Of course, this is only the first ten minutes of the film. Saul waits to bring on the real clash test for the romantic link between the couple. As the plot moves on, Titzi finds out that she is pregnant. The responsibilities of parenthood force her and Ibo to reflect on their identities in more complex and less romanticised terms. This places *Kebab Connection* in the broader tradition of the so-called New German Comedies, because the film provides an amusing but at the same time very informative window onto "the changing norms for gender and mixed families in Germany [which] we could first see in Doris Dörrie's groundbreaking comedy *[Männer-]Men* (1985)" (Ferree, 2012: 13).

Ibo's and Titzi's romantic relationship is based on a love for cinema. This premise suggests that migrant identities in Germany are flexible and that it should be easy for everybody to live together if they have a shared goal. However, the reality of an unplanned pregnancy means that the couple must suddenly agree on life-altering decisions, testing the idea of easy multicultural differences while arriving at that shared goal. The plot twist reminds the viewer that much work and many clashes still lie ahead for German society.[7] That message plays out in various ways. One is the presentation of non-German culture commodities the "Schanze" offers to its residents like a multicultural buffet. There is food (Turkish kebab), fashion (Albanian headgear), dance and music (Sirtaki at the Greek Tavern) and, of course, language (Italian, Turkish and Greek). In line with Sieg's analysis of ethnic Others as "the fetishized objects of profitable multicultural industries" (Sieg, 2002: 254), one could say that Germans were premature in claiming a multicultural success story. The constant rivalry between the Turkish eatery of Ibo's uncle and the Greek restaurant across the street can be read as a projection of how the Germans' naïve vision of "multi-culti" clashes with the sober reality of ethnic coexistence. The diversity in German society is not necessarily integrated on a deeper level in the country's public spaces or in the private sphere.

It is a problem for multicultural societies to sustain social cohesion. The relationship of Ibo and Tizi demonstrates this vividly. The two lovebirds regard their intercultural romance as perfect. That is until the prospect of having a baby requires them to negotiate their cultural belonging through profound introspection. *Kebab Connection* constructs the need for its characters to confront their own identities. They achieve this by immersing themselves in cultural references, the building blocks of who they are at their core. The process suggests to viewers that long-term reconciliation between clashing cultures depends more on the critical thinking of individuals than on multicultural platitudes, as observed by Ebert and Beck (Ebert and Beck, 2007: 92). Ibo's drug-induced nightmare after breaking up with Titzi, triggered also by a fight with his father over Turkish tradition, bears this out. It warns the audience against consuming interculturality only at a superficial level, which is the stereotypical knowledge one receives without critically interrogating it.

Ibo's vision has him running away from his role as a Turkish father and Turkish manhood. A previous flashback scene reveals that his father had instilled both concepts into him since early childhood. A generous amount of pot immobilises Ibo, so he cannot move and is forced to confront the different expectations and cultural roles pulling at him. Finally, he ends up crashing from the marijuana high and sees Titzi on the street with a baby's pram. Another scene has already shown men pushing prams as the symbol of Ibo's idea of emasculation. He calls after Titzi and begs her to her stay as she walks away. The pram is important. The viewer will see it again at the end of the film after Ibo has refashioned it in his cinema prop shop. Ibo's version of a baby's pram is uniquely his, neither conventional nor afraid to draw attention to the person pushing it. It features a bronzed dragonhead, welded-on metal wings and a dragon tail made of steel. "A sick ride! It's cool and comes with an extra diaper bag", he explains excitedly as he presents it to Titzi. As Ibo describes his creation, the joy he finds in the redesign of the pram eventually invokes relief humour like the other clash films I discuss. Ibo finds amusement in the redefinition of his identity as a father instead of being frustrated and acting out aggressively like the clichéd character of a Turkish German man.

Saul suggests to the viewer that the process of self-reflection is crucial and needs to be profound to achieve a happy end. After the image of Titzi leaves Ibo's drug hallucination, he thinks he has come to but is still hallucinating. The figure of Bruce Lee suddenly appears to teach the Turkish German a life lesson and to bring him enlightenment—though one might be surprised that Lee fits into Ibo's bar fridge. After the transition to a dark environment, there is only a spotlight to shine brightly in the centre. It looks like the theatre stage Titzi performs a Juliet monologue on in preparation for drama school. Lee, the Kung-Fu icon, explains to Ibo, "Every step on a steep path reduces the journey. Stepping onto the top of the mountain makes the mountain disappear". Ibo does not understand how this Kung-Fu wisdom applies to his situation, prompting the Asian sage to simplify the proverb for his Turkish German disciple: "Show her that you are a man. Go to a Lamaze class!".

That Bruce Lee and not the Prophet Mohammed guides Ibo refers again to an incongruous transnational imaginary in the context of modern Turkishness in Germany. The advice of the Asian icon, whose role as a messenger and wise man one could liken to that of the friar in *Romeo and Juliet*, motivates Ibo to overcome the cliché of the Turkish macho. Ibo follows Lee's instruction and enrols in a pre-natal parenting course. The Lamaze classes signal to the viewer a turn of events and that the happy end is near. For now, though, as another instance of incongruity humour, Ibo's best male friend takes Titzi's place. He is another male, second-generation migrant born to parents from Albania. The unusual Turkish-Albanian couple, two young men who pretend to be expecting a baby, raises eyebrows in the antenatal class. It also aligns Ibo's initial view on stereotypical Turkishness with the German audience's preconceived ideas about two Schanzenviertel migrants. But Ibo's drug vision, along with the ironic nod to Bruce Lee as a "racial noble Other like Karl May's *Winnetou*" (Sieg, 2009: 223), wipes the slate clean. The young Turkish German man can finally accept that identity formation is a complex process and that he needs to find his own way. Similarly, German viewers without the lived experience of migration can understand that they also should consume ethnicity more critically.

One could argue that the word connection in the title encapsulates the film's central message about the acceptance of different identities as well as their complex fusion. As I have described, the re-connection of characters despite incongruities is a central feature of culture clash. Saul uses it effectively. While older Turkish and German characters have difficulty accepting a mixing of Turkish and German identities, younger characters are more likely to think of their identity as a diverse construction. Social innovation is something *Kebab Connection*'s clash plot foregrounds and on which its comedy trades. The downside of being stuck in one's ways when it comes to an imagined authenticity of being Turkish or German or another nationality is made explicitly clear as the target of ridicule in Saul's film. Characters like Ibo's uncle and his father are suspicious of his liminal identity as a Turkish German Kung-Fu filmmaker. They try to instil in him a sense of Turkish belonging as the husband of a "nice Turkish girl" and refuse to accept that he will have "a child with a German, an infidel".

Kebab Connection suggests that people can change and that taking on board other cultures is okay. How Ibo's uncle and father change their minds illustrates the integrationist idea of culture clash comedy. They end up wanting him to be a hybrid filmmaker and father to a child whose mother has no Turkish identity. Though, while the uncle changes his mind only because Ibo's commercials earn him money, the father changes his attitude because he is genuinely impressed with Titzi. She educates the first-generation migrant passionately about the equality principle of multicultures and thereby proves her Turkish qualities: "[a] love that knows no borders and no differences"—and she asks him, "How could this be wrong?" "Turkish fire like girls from Anatolia", Ibo's father mumbles to himself long after the young woman is gone. Here, Titzi quotes lines similar to Juliet's plea for borderless love in the fifth scene of the first act of *Romeo and Julie*. The irony of this is not lost on viewers familiar with the Shakespeare classic.

Saul's film makes a statement about the transnational development of art. One can see that the fading of boundaries leads to productive mixing of highbrow and lowbrow in the cultural context in which the transformation of other characters around the protagonists appears. There is a proliferation of ethnic diversity. There is also an acknowledgement that one can be authentically Turkish or German, a valid artist or a good parent in many ways. This addresses all the characters' affinity for stereotyping themselves and others. The clash narrative emphasises that people can do away with clichés just as easily as they accept them. For instance, in a scene after Ibo's drug high before the finale, Ibo is sceptical of his father, who wants him to reconcile with Titzi after first rejecting her: "I get in a fight with Titzi because she is a German and she is pregnant with my child, and you kicked me out because of that. And now you tell me I did the wrong thing and that I let her down?" "Yes"—the father responds smugly with a grin on his face. Ibo replies, utterly perplexed yet with visible relief, "Those Turks are barking mad!"

Kebab Connection's cultural remixing does not fully resolve all culture-clash problems. Some of the social tensions between Turkish Germans and Germans remain. Cultural hybridity and Turkish German liminality happen only within the boundaries of the multi-ethnic "Schanze" despite the happy end. Titzi's and Ibo's union emerges from the union of the fictional couple in Ibo's last Kung-Fu commercial, and it blurs the boundaries between film and reality. That act of crossing borders is celebrated only in the context of the hybrid space of "King of Kebab" and Hamburg's migrant district. This suggests to the viewer that the acceptance of alternative identities is still only tenuous. The alternative identities represented in the form of interethnic relationships and their fictional representations, as indicated by Ibo's transnational film aesthetics, are innovative connections in German multiculture. However, not everybody is ready to embrace them.

Reversed Roles in *Meine verrückte türkische Hochzeit-Kiss me Kismet*

The theme of modelling cultural diversity continues in Stefan Holtz' *Kiss me Kismet* (2006). The story of the culture clash comedy centres on Götz Schinkel, who is the last of two native Germans in Berlin Kreuzberg. At least, that is what his best friend, who also narrates the story through voiceover, tells the viewer at the beginning of the film: "Berlin Kreuzberg-Little Istanbul. You're a minority here as a German. We two are the last ones, and we'll keep the flag flying", he gravels in his deep baritone as if he were narrating the introduction to one of Sergio Leone's cliché-laden Spaghetti Westerns. Götz is the owner of a small speciality store for vinyl records. He is obsessed with music and lives for his nights as a club DJ. The backdrop to the story of Götz, the hip young man with a trendy haircut and skinny jeans, is a culturally diverse neighbourhood. Turkish and Arabic are the dominant languages here. Streets are populated with exotic fruit stalls, spice vendors and all kinds of culinary takeaways. The jury who awarded the film the 43rd Adolf Grimme Award for outstanding German film and television in 2007 wrote this about that feature of the film:

> German film can also be different. "Kiss me Kismet" does away with a couple of dozen prejudices which Germans and Turks in Berlin-Kreuzberg and in other places have. [...] It is so funny, fast-paced, full of comedy and gags, it can easily keep up with your big American cinema blockbusters, from "My Big Fat Greek Wedding" to 'High Fidelity' to "Notting Hill". Others may try to avoid cultural clichés: "Kiss me Kismet" emphasises them instead in order to find pleasure in poking fun at them with nuanced irony or hard-handed gags.[8]

The first scene of Holtz' film includes wide-angled shots of Berlin's skyline. The director uses a split-frame technique to suggest that German high-rises, glass and steel constructions, can blend in seamlessly with Muslim mosques and the towers of small minarets. The panning movement of the camera then focuses on the gritty urban grounds of Kreuzberg's concrete towers in Berlin's migrant housing estate. The multicultural neighbourhood is covered in a sea of satellite dishes, connecting a million television sets in Germany via satellite to a wide range of free Turkish-, Arab- and Asian-language channels every night (Göktürk, Gramling and Kaes, 2007: 332). Ibo's parents in *Kebab Connection* live in a similar neighbourhood.[9]

The initial shots present the cultural cartography of *Kiss me Kismet* and they give details of Götz' environment. Spray-painting youths are covering walls with colourful graffiti. Young children play football in alleyways. There are many adult and older men and women, marked as Muslim and dressed in Western plainclothes, business casual, veils and headscarves. Their ethnic difference is not emphasised by stereotypical Oriental sounds or garments meant to indicate an association with Muslim fashion. British cult clash comedies like *East Is East* (1999) start out that way to mark British spaces as occupied by Muslim Others. While Götz strides through the diverse crowd of his multi-ethnic neighbourhood, face beaming with the joys of having all kinds of Turkish and Arab deli foods at his fingertips, the Berlin hipster runs into two youths who bully a small boy. It is the first time that the viewer sees the tensions of culture clash at play in the film.

Holtz uses the scene to introduce Götz as a foreigner. The German encounters two young men and a boy who speak Turkish. It is a language Götz cannot speak or understand. The linguistic aspect stresses his Otherness together with his expensive leather jacket, blond hair, blue eyes, pale skin, lanky body and towering height. Speaking German and referenced by his appearance and language as a non-Turkish figure in the film, Götz would like to intervene in the fight in order to show that he cares about his neighbourhood. The bullies dislike his involvement. One pulls out an impossibly large Crocodile Dundee knife and threatens Götz before the two thugs take off at speed. Instead of thanking the German man for his help, the young boy who was bullied purposely pushes Götz aside as he runs away, too. What relieves the tension humorously in this scenario is the voice of the narrator who shrugs off the incident as Götz' inability to face the reality of his environment: "Oh well, from the looks of it, Götz has still not learned how things work here. He's just too nice for this world". Götz dusts himself off in the meantime and gets on with his day.

The scene considers how German majority society can react to changing definitions of its spaces and cultural boundaries. Both Götz' reaction and the narrator's comment promote alternative solutions to negative emotions such as fear and anger in response to a society in transition. The actions of the Turkish-speaking thugs and the Turkish-speaking boy also draw attention to Götz' inability to interfere as a native German in cultural affairs he cannot fully understand. He must accept his position as an outsider and trade on Turkish expectations of his Otherness to participate in the cultural milieu of Kreuzberg. This means that somebody needs to mediate the clash context of Berlin's Little Istanbul for him and translate what the disputes among Turks involve. That part goes to the other main character in *Kiss me Kismet*, a young woman named Aylin. She explains to Götz, after ending a brawl between Turkish German men and him in another scene, what he misunderstood about the three Turkish German boys: "[w]ith Turks it's all about honour and keeping face. It's not real, it's all just for show". Aylin is a beautiful young woman with Mediterranean features, long dark hair and dark eyes. It is a purposeful aesthetic construction. I expound on in greater detail in chapter four with the example of Hatice Akyün's chick-lit novels. Weber calls such sexualised fantasies of the Oriental woman's body functional count-discursive tropes of Turkish German female bodies and identities. They relate to earlier German films which showed Turkish German women as the exotic

Other, a desirable non-white object for male Germanness (Weber, 2013: 144). German men like Götz had to protect it against the violent abuse of Muslim men, which fed right back into the cliché depiction of Muslimness and Turkish German gender roles as described in the reductive Turkish German drama films mentioned in the introduction.

Kiss me Kismet shows Aylin to be more than just a token character. She is no damsel in distress and needs no saving. In fact, the eloquent lawyer intervenes in both Turkish and German and ends the violence quickly when Götz gets involved in a clash between his German co-worker and the Turkish shop-owners right outside his record store. He goes down with a head-butt to his face while Aylin does not even break sweat in perfect makeup and high-heeled stilettos. The humour in this scene relies on the viewer's knowledge that Götz is a hopeless romantic. The audience may laugh at the aggression of ethnic Others because it serves to ridicule Götz' act of German chivalry. Viewers can simultaneously admire Aylin's ability to control the violent group of male Muslims because of her Turkish identity. As Aylin shoos the men away like children while Götz is ridiculed by them in the previous scene, the clash comedy plot harks back to conflict resolution through its trademark reversal of roles. This convention of the culture clash comedy genre emerges early in the film as a critique of gender roles and ethnic as well as male superiority.

The reversal of roles also frames the clash between familiar and unfamiliar cultural spheres. One can read the brawl scene as a criticism of German cinema's Eurocentric attitudes. Stepping into what the film construes as Muslim Berlin draws attention to Götz' German exoticism by conspicuously contextualising it during his everyday routine. His daily walk to his workplace is part of that. The viewer sees numerous shots of men with Mediterranean features talking in rapid Turkish and Arab while the camera walks with Götz at eye level. During the brawl in front of his shop, the camera catches glimpses of older onlookers wearing kaftans and full beards. All this stresses the juxtaposition of Götz and his ethnically diverse neighbours. In contrast, the German's clothes are indeed very similar to the Western designer labels worn by most male leads in contemporary culture clash. Holtz adds to this jab at German male ego and being a white knight in shining armour with interspersed soundtrack hits from *High Fidelity* (2000) and *Notting Hill* (1999). As I detail in chapter four on Turkish German dicklit, both of these films are hallmarks of anti-macho messages during a period obsessed with constructing new masculinities as less toxic and less self-obsessed than the "Rambo 80s" (Jeffers McDonald, 2007: 3).

Götz and Aylin develop romantic feelings for each other after their first encounter. The German, a DJ and music lover, is attracted to Aylin. His is a creative spirit and finds her outlook on life invigorating, especially her ability to maintain a work-life balance. Aylin enjoys life and hard work without losing out to late Western capitalism and turning into a corporate suit. In turn, she falls for Götz because he values artistic passion more than money in an embrace of the late 1990s rom-com's concept of tender millennial masculinity (Palmer, 2013: 122). Titzi loves Ibo in *Kebab Connection* for the same reason. This is, however, not to say that love conquers all in a naïve resolve of multicultural tensions. Despite their affection for each other, Götz and Aylin seem to put the interests of their families and friends before their own as the story unfolds. When they struggle to find common cultural ground, they give in to their cultural communities' constant in-group pressures to stick with "people who are just a bit more like you and me". Götz' conservative German mother cites the line of "apples-to-apples" frequently to discourage her son from pursuing Aylin. Though Götz and Aylin fall for each other regardless.

Just as do Ibo and Titzi over their passion for filmmaking, *Kiss me Kismet*'s protagonists bond over a permeating creative force, which is music.[10] This matters because music, just like the creative art of filmmaking and acting in *Kebab Connection*, decentralises certain stereotypes attached to gender, ethnicity and religion. The stereotype in *Kiss me Kismet* is that of the arranged marriage imposed on the Turkish German woman by her father and a male-dominated community. Aylin's Turkish German wedding ceremony with her Turkish fiancé Tarkan who speaks only Turkish is constructed as reductive space for her ability to love freely.[11] A music track exclusively created by Götz for Aylin highlights this further. It turns into the couple's love theme during the film. Towards the end of the film, the theme plays on a small boom box at Aylin's arranged wedding with Tarkan. Hearing the song compels Aylin to reunite with Götz after an interim break-up, hence foreshadowing a harmonious conclusion to the clash comedy.

It is common for lovers in interethnic clash comedies to keep oscillating between culture and romance and alleged tradition and supposedly modern thinking. These films emphasise an initial incongruity or discord between characters and modulate it later into love or another form of productive togetherness. Happy ends happen if different ethnic life models combine without replicating their shortcomings and failures. Berghahn's take on recent German film comedies with hybrid characters suggests that this impulse has come to dominate the genre. There is a rift between family loyalties or attachments to one's ethno-cultural community and romantic love. The schism hints at culture as an implicit hierarchy of values German-speaking film audiences are now questioning through the motif of romance (Berghahn, 2013: 4). The cultural identities of clash comedy protagonists are deeply engrained in them, which makes it hard to be compatible with members outside one's own community. This works as the main trope for ethnic culture clash. That one character complements the other is simply not enough to assimilate into another culture or community. Götz for instance grew up with a loveless German mother who put her career first, while Aylin rarely encounters loveable goofballs like this German DJ in Berlin Kreuzberg. Theirs is a love based on the romantic comedy clash logic of opposites attract. This appears to be Berghahn's idea of "crossover appeal" (Berghahn, 2013: 4) in family comedies with ethnic Otherness. It all turns on a greater sense of partnership if multicultural love between a Muslim and a non-Muslim, and not just a man and a woman, is to succeed.

As its clash story unfolds, *Kiss me Kismet* becomes less interested in merely reproducing comedy tropes of Germanness or Turkishness. The more Götz and Aylin try to accommodate their future in-laws, their cultural customs, their religious beliefs and their cultural values, the more the couple fails to negotiate a genuine hybridity. According to Burns, *Kiss me Kismet* mocks the German "multi-culti" fantasy of performing Germanness or Turkishness until one is "desperately locked into that fantasy" (Burns, 2013: 57). Götz and Aylin arrive at this conclusion when they face exclusion from their families for a commodification of ethnic differences. They decide to circumcise Götz and have him convert to Islam while Aylin tries to teach her parents the ways of a proper German dinner conversation. The final scenes of the film reveal and ridicule these actions as the undue imposition of Otherness. They are superficial gestures at best. When Götz suffers from the removal of his foreskin in his skinny jeans in the office of the Imam who performed the procedure, Aylin's father still refuses fully to acknowledge the German's Muslimness: "Bin Laden will be Santa Clause before this ever happens!", he says half-jokingly. Aylin fails just as much in trying to win over Götz' mother with a non-halal German pork roast.

Holtz complicates the notion of respect for ethnic diversity with lovers who must be loyal to multiple identities. Quick-witted banter scenes between Götz and Aylin after their failure to be more German or Turkish draw attention to the simultaneous reproduction and exclusion of ethnic Otherness in German society. Instead of empowering intercultural relationships, the xenophobic attitudes towards cultural outsiders feature a problem of not only the German majority but also the Turkish minority community. Aylin demonstrates this when she shouts at her parents for their rejection of Götz as a Muslim spouse, "Because all you care about is your fucking honour!". As Ezli notes of the scene, "This scene, as all other scenes in the film, is resolved through comedy. However, closely attached to the immense visibility of Islam here is its immovable position, which is the real condition for Götz' integration into the Turkish family" (Ezli, 2013: 203).

The from-two-different-worlds theme makes clear how important the introductory scene in *Kiss me Kismet* really is. "The culture war over taking on the Other as part of the Self" (Ezli: 204) first happens here as a central element. Holtz repeats it in variations throughout the narrative. Goetz is mixed up in a stand-off among Turkish German youth. Then he becomes involved in a brawl among Turkish German men because of his inadequate knowledge of the Turkish concept of honour. Later he visits the home of Aylin's parents where he commits one cultural faux pas after another because of his lack of Turkish language skills, knowledge of Muslim rituals and of Turkish cuisine. In the end, even the marriage between the German and the Turkish German characters happens amidst another street side brawl after Aylin tells Tarkan and her whole family in clear terms what she thinks about sacrificing love for Turkish tradition whilst dressed in a white wedding gown: "No!"—to which her father appreciatively remarks to his displeased wife in accented German, "*No*. Her favourite word".

Aylin's rejection of what the film alleges to be Turkish tradition and certain family expectations foregrounds the subversive quality of culture clash. She rejects a Turkish spouse by speaking in German. At the same time, she asserts herself as an independent Turkish German woman. Despite its lack of nuance regarding cultural diversity within Turkish German culture and tradition, the general thrust of this comedic clash scene bears out a disruption or rejection of the audience's general knowledge about ethnic diversity in Germany. Aylin's actions turn Germans' essentialising ideas about Islamic forced marriage and female Muslim victimisation on its head. Also, Götz, and even more so Aylin, find relief from ethno-cultural normativity because they behave in ways in which no authentic Turkish woman or real German man should act; that is at least according to Götz' racist friend, Horst, and Aylin's extremist uncle, Melek. Götz and Aylin may experience cultural bias because of their innovative behaviour. Still, the couple is willing to stick it out through brawls, insults and a fight with Tarkan's angered family members until there is a happy end. That dedication implies that Germans and Turkish Germans must consume ethnicity with a multicultural appreciation for diversity and problems along the way if they expect any form of positive co-existence.

There is religious bias in *Kebab Connection*, just as there are the racist friend of Götz and the prejudiced uncle of Aylin in *Kiss me Kismet*. Both suggest that Mandel's idea of cosmopolitan anxieties is the flipside of openness towards social change (Mandel, 2008). Götz' and Aylin's impromptu wedding in the back of a VW beetle demonstrates this. It is the final scene of the film. Götz and Aylin appreciate each other's presence because both have proven that they are more open-minded than the fist-fighting crowd outside the car. Aylin's father drags the Turkish Imam who officiated at her and Tarkan's ceremony into the car. Even the Imam recognises the borderless love between the intercultural couple and blesses it in the eyes of Allah. This marks the interior space of the VW Beetle, a quintessential German car, as emphatically transnational. Individuals in this space are free from stereotypical expectations about cultural norms and their life partners.

However, the ending remains ambiguous. The couple may or may not get to live out its cultural hybridity and its clash romance as part of the wider community in Berlin Kreuzberg (Ezli, 2006). *Kebab Connection* also leaves viewers unsure about the likelihood of greater change in Germany's society outside the multi-ethnic neighbourhood of the Schanze. As it is with Ibo and Titzi, all ends well for the clash comedy protagonists in *Kiss me Kismet*, too: that is they can live as a couple. Yet, the cultural transformation around Götz and Aylin is significantly limited to the interior of the car in which they get married. The people outside are still fighting and fail to recognise that their aggressive energies could be rerouted to serve a much better, socially productive purpose than to clash violently.

Cultural Redefinitions of *Evet, ich will!-Evet, I do*

A third culture clash comedy to complicate the integration of ethnic Otherness in Germany is Sinan Akkuş' *Evet, I do* (2008). The wedding-themed comedy centres on three couples. They form a diverse ensemble of characters with varied ethnic identities and sexual orientations. As with the protagonists in *Kebab Connection* and *Kiss me Kismet*, this links the film's representation of alterity to a self-conscious engagement with societal acceptance of difference. In *Evet, I do*, the Sunnite Kurd Coşkun and the Turkish Alevi Günay, the German Dirk and the Turkish German Özlem and the Turkish German Emrah and his German boyfriend Tim, act as "brokers of cultural difference" (Berghahn: 8) when they respond "Evet", or "Yes, I do" to their partners' marriage proposals.[12] Viewers hear these words during the first few minutes of the film. The phrase signals the beginning of a clash between the future spouses' families, their cultural differences, and all their multiple attachments to a certain religion, a specific neighbourhood, a language, a tradition or a minority and majority community, respectively.

Evet, I do revolves around the exposure of its characters' identities to each other and to their communities. The stereotypical inscription of the characters with imagined identities clashes with their actual selves. None of the weddings can go ahead until this is resolved. Akkuş uses the characters' intercultural clash dilemmas to comment on a defensive attitude towards inter-ethnic fraternisation in German society. It plays out as instances of superiority humour, which delegitimises some identities and validates others for the same reason. For instance, Coşkun and Günay indirectly clash over their ethnic backgrounds. Günay's Kemalist father suspects Coşkun of Islamist extremism due to his Kurdish heritage. This is false. The liberal radio host Coşkun only stands in for his community's conservative reputation. In yet another family context, Özlem's parents insist that her daughter must marry a Muslim. This disqualifies Dirk and requires his conversion to Islam like Götz in *Kiss me Kismet*. And in the Turkish German neighbourhood of young Emrah, coming out as gay to his family is not an option for the closeted car mechanic. He presents boyfriend Tim to his father and mother as his best friend instead. As the wider context for the wedding motif, culture clash challenges and eventually disavows here the ethnic purity and compatibility test, which stands in the way of multicultural relationships.

The couples falsely assume that they need to hide their true identities to be accepted by and not to stir up controversy among other ethnic communities or in theirs. For characters such as Coşkun that assumption means downplaying his Turkishness and his identity as a Kurd, whereas Dirk needs to downplay his Germanness. The challenge for Emrah doubles in that regard. He needs to hide his homosexuality and his relationship with a German man from his Turkish German family and his Turkish German father, who is unsupportive of men being proudly gay. However, the pretence only works on a superficial level. The gay closet trope of "butching up", and that of "Turking up" or "Turking down", respectively, indicate that hiding alleged difference turns out to be less satisfying than probing its interstices. Berghahn and Sternberg correctly outline this realisation under the rubric of "the redemption of the marginal" (Berghahn and Sternberg, 2010: 41). Other and more social issues connected to identity and belonging are raised as well in recent German comedy cinema with films like Maren Ade's *Toni Erdman* (2016) and David Wnendt's *Er ist wieder da-Look Who's Back* (2015). There are claims that issues of race, colour, nationality, religion, ethnicity, regionality, language, generation, class, gender and sexuality still divide society. The clash plot of *Evet, I do* refers to them all.

Akkuş makes it very clear that his point of view is about a critique of normativity. He also leaves no doubt with his bilingual film title that there is a difference between communities, which one cannot deny. Rather than catering to the notion of superior and inferior identities, the filmmaker teaches the audience how to find joy in not fitting into established categories and coming out as something Other. His characters play a host of stereotypical roles for all they are worth to make this point. They deliver over-the-top performances of ethnic, linguistic, religious and sexual identities they assume others to expect of them. To put on an identity performance is a popular feature of culture clash as described above. It is a big part of the meet-the-parents scenes of *Evet, I do*. They prelude the actual weddings of Coşkun and Günay, Dirk and Özlem, and Dirk and Emrah, though only Dirk's and Özlem's wedding is included in the film. The Turkish wedding and the gay wedding never make it on to the screen.

Initially, Günay's father foils Coşkun's wedding plans. The widower and devout secularist refuses to entrust his only daughter "to a religious fanatic, who locks up his wife at home and forces her to wear a headscarf! Your mother and I didn't come to Germany for this", he explains to his daughter in an angry and bitter tone. Coşkun refuses to give up. The father's disapproval requires Akkuş' most romantically minded groom to prove his cultural compatibility. Of course, that plan spirals out of control and turns into the actual danger for true romance to succeed. Coşkun follows his elderly Turkish uncle's advice. Viewers may remember that red flag from *Kebab Connection* with Ibo's uncle. Coşkun kidnaps his fiancé as a hyperbolic gesture of love. According to rural traditions in Turkey, so his uncle tells him, such gestures demonstrate the groom's sincerity and should help to bring the future in-laws round. The allegedly authentic Turkish tradition does not work here. Instead it turns into a farcical performance somewhere between Hollywood gangster film and cheesy romance. In fact, it backfires. Coşkun appears less like a romantic and more like the cliché of the aggressive honour-killing Muslim when he stands with a toy gun in the apartment of Günay's father. It takes only five minutes for German police to have him surrounded by a special weapons and tactics team. The police arrest Coşkun for public endangerment and "for suspected attempt to take a hostage and resisting police authority".

A similar, albeit less dramatic, mishap unfolds when Dirk's parents accompany him on a visit to Özlem's parents. For Dirk, and indeed for the viewer, *Evet, I do* confirms that purposeful catering to someone else's ethno-cultural expectations is a disservice to one's own identity. What Sieg calls "commodified ethnic mimicry" (Sieg, 2009: 231) leads to disappointment. Dirk shares Coşkun's eagerness to act like an authentic Other and he recreates every step of a Turkish wedding ritual as conveyed to him by Özlem. Traditionally, as Özlem explains to Dirk in an earlier scene, the groom's father must ask the bride's parents to consent to the marriage.[13] The performance fails and is already revealed as a charade while the couple make their way to Özlem's parents. It starts with Dirk's mother. She insists on wearing a headscarf without knowing how to wrap it properly. Dirk finds that the way she puts on the head covering makes it look as if she has run away from a peasant theatre troupe. Indeed, she ties the scarf into a thick simple knot under her chin rather than wrapping it artistically round her head. Dirk's father shares his wife's gift for stepping right into cross-cultural blunders. Where possible, he embarrasses his son with several of them. Berghahn argues convincingly that the father's refusal to say the phrase, "We ask you for the hand of your daughter in the name of our Prophet", is evidence of a native German society plagued by xenophobic sentiments (Berghahn, 212). The German father's compromise of saying "in the name of A Prophet" illustrates this.

Akkuş delivers further criticism of a naïve form of easy multiculture with Tim's and Emrah's storyline. He draws attention to the inability of individuals to accept that there are ethno-cultural alternatives to established identities and lifestyles. Benbow describes the latter as "recognizable ethnic stereotypes" (Benbow, 529) which work in culture clash to contrast innovation in society, mostly in countries with diverse ethnic paradigms and migration histories. Akkuş uses well-known stock imagery from wedding comedy films to focus his poignant ridicule on the centrality of the heteronormative family. The light-hearted ending of a typical romantic comedy generally demands a festive celebration if a young man asks a young woman to marry him. However, Akkuş' film takes a more sobering perspective on the idea of a transgressive couple, both gay and transnational. They need sympathy more than they would need conformity when saying I do and coming out to the family (Berghahn: 212-219).

The meet-the-parents scene with Emrah makes fun of normative thinking from the outset, his and that of his family. There is the idea of heterosexual masculinity, which Emrah's conservative Turkish German father ostensibly supports and sees as superior to that of homosexual men. The father's attitude towards his son's arranged marriage with a middle-class Muslim girl can also be described as outdated kinship thinking to safeguard the status quo, as I show in my discussion of *Kiss me Kismet*. The prospect of being married to a woman pushes Emrah into the climax of his clash narrative, which is a coming out scene. The fear of losing Tim and being caught in a sham marriage motivates Emrah to out himself in the living room of his bride-to-be's parents. The arranged marriage would have suited her well. She had planned to trick the closeted homosexual into marriage and being a father to her unborn lovechild with her black American ex-boyfriend. Shouting and yelling ensues. The situation makes Emrah's Turkish grandfather wonder how to fix his grandson's faulty "sex organ in the head". The grandfather, who came along to the proposal ritual, still ponders this question while Emrah's father inspects a pin-up photo of his half-naked son. Emrah had planned to give the picture to Tim as a gift for the anniversary of their relationship. He drops the nude photo by accident as he storms out, only for his father to pick it up from the floor while general chaos ensues. The next scene then tops things off, as a nosy German neighbour uses the intercom system to call up to the apartment of the sneaky bride to be. As she leaves the living room and runs into the hallway, the intercom system rings and she answers. While all hell breaks loose around her, the neighbour tells her something which sets up yet another clash scenario: "At the door, there's a negr ... urrhm ... eerrhmm ... there's a bla ... oh well, blimey, so what do you call that now? HE IS FROM AFRICA". It is the American father of her unborn child, who is black.

Akkuş refuses to supply the viewer with easy solutions to complex social issues. The couples must deal with their families and figure out how to express and negotiate their cultural, religious, sexual and racial identities despite assumed superiorities or allegedly correct behaviours. Some norms remain firmly in place. The reaction of Emrah's father to his son's coming out and relationship with Tim illustrates this best. The German-born Turk asks Tim never to kiss his son in front of him. He forbids them to hold hands. Tim and Emrah also need to keep their relationship a secret from the wider Turkish German community. "They ain't all as modern as I am. And besides, gays and cars don't mix well", the car mechanic says sternly. This does not correspond to Wartenberg's definition of ethnic romance comedies as "unlikely couple films" where eventually love between individuals has love win out over tradition, too (Wartenberg, 1999: 7). In the same vein, Akkuş puts Coşkun under the constant surveillance of Günay's distrusting father, who believes Turkish Kurds are religious extremists and oppressive husbands. Also, through the failed engagement ritual with Dirk, *Evet, I do*'s director cures Özlem's hopelessly romantic sister of her romantic delusions of a German prince to sweep her off her feet. Danielle Steel fantasies are one thing. Negotiating the realities of interethnic romance is quite another.

Akkuş criticises the commodification of cultural traditions and Turkish diaspora through the three couples' problems with established norms or assumed knowledge about certain identities. It goes to the heart of this culture clash comedy, which is that life in Germany has fossilised certain Turkish rituals and significant acts, reducing them to a short-lived performance and a couple of rehearsed lines. Coşkun performs a popular practice in regional Turkey like a Hollywood cliché. If anything, it turns out to be an obstacle to his father-in-law's appreciation of him as an open-minded Muslim in Germany. Coşkun complains regularly about outdated traditions and Turkish machismo, but he still adheres to alleged authentic Turkish-Kurdish norms despite thinking of them as inferior and out of place. He simply reproduces them because he considers them a means to an end. Similarly, Dirk's lack of critical self-consciousness motivates his performance of an equally superficial reproduction of Turkish masculinity and Turkish customs related to weddings. He pushes his parents to do the same, thereby ignoring their reluctance to act Turkish. Emrah seems to be the only character able to muster enough courage to stand up for his hybridity because he rejects playing the straight Turk. Cultural norms need critical redefinitions, and their performance must allow for diversity. That message plays out in Emrah's unintended outing. He sobs like a child in the arms of his totally perplexed mother.

Evet, I do offers a less cohesive vision of a society in transition than other Turkish German culture clash comedies. This may explain why the film ends on an even more ambivalent note than *Kebab Connection* and *Kiss me Kismet*. Akkuş's film encourages the mixing of different cultures and identities and portrays romance as an entertaining learning experience. Yet, it also suggests that nobody should surrender their individual identity or assume that assimilation is an easy path to authentic multiculturalism. Some differences remain and new forms of Turkish German identity are still forming. At the end of the film, the character of the old Turkish man Songül delivers a zinger on this issue. He watches as Dirk's mother performs a belly dance at her son's wedding reception. Songül is a Turkish migrant who has lived in Germany for more than 50 years. He is part of the so-called first generation. His one-liner smacks of superiority humour: "Everything moves, but the belly". "Well", responds a Turkish woman next to him, "it can't be helped". It is his Turkish wife, Nazime. Turkish German writer Emine Sevgi Özdamar plays that part in a rare on-screen appearance. In Turkish and with a giggle, her character adds before the film ends on a black fade-out, "That's what a German belly dancer looks like".

Identities across Time and Space in *Almanya-Willkommen in Deutschland-Almanya-Welcome to Germany*

Another popular comedy critique of exoticising Muslim migrants in German film is Yasemin Şamdereli's *Almanya-Welcome to Germany* (2011). *Almanya* uses culture clash to comment on ethnic identity role-play like the other three productions I have discussed. The film also highlights what Berghahn points to as "aesthetic strategies [in German film which] conform to mainstream Western generic templates instead of embracing a 'diasporic optic'" (Berghahn: 168). *Almanya*'s storyline follows the Turkish German Yilmaz family. The clan's three generations encompass a host of different identities. The first generation consists of Hüseyin and Fatma Yilmaz. They were born in rural Anatolia, growing up there in a small village. Hüseyin and Fatma are the parents of three boys and one daughter. Muhamed and Veli were born in Turkey. They came to Germany as children in the 1960s with their parents and their younger sister, Leyla. Ali, the youngest son, was born in West Germany in the 1980s. He is the only member of the second generation who cannot speak proper Turkish. His father never tires of reminding him of that. The second generation has produced four grandchildren, of whom the young Cenk, son to Ali and his German wife Gabi, and his cousin Canan are featured with central prominence as the clash film's commentator and voice-over narrator, respectively.

The film tells the story of how Hüseyin and Fatma met in Turkey. Then they had three babies and came to Germany when the children were old enough for the journey. *Almanya* describes how Hüseyin arrived as a guest worker in Germany. He came on his own by train before later bringing over the family in a second-hand Mercedes. The children and their mother settled into their new home in another society. The new residence included a German "water closet" or toilet. Fatma wonders what kind of furniture item this is. Other scenes depict language barriers and cultural customs, and some revolve around the iconography of Christianity. These are myriad clash moments for the viewers to laugh at as the plot unfolds. They also set up the context for the film's use of flashbacks and foreshadowing when the whole family comes together for a nice Sunday brunch in what the story action marks as the present. Here, an elderly Hüseyin declares to the rest of the family that he has bought a house in Turkey and that they are all going on a road trip back to the old "Heimat": "Family, I have surprise! I have bought house. In Turkey. In Sommer, we all go together there", he lets them know with a big smile on his face.

The patriarch's idea of a return home to Turkey is a one-sided love affair. As he shows old sepia-coloured photographs of Anatolia to his grandson Cenk at the dining-room table in the first scene of the film, his wife and children only frown and scowl Cenk seems to be the only character thrilled to explore his family's Turkish roots. The boy's enthusiasm for the trip, the viewer finds out in another early scene in the film, is due to an incident at Cenk's elementary school. Other children reject him for being a Turkish German hybrid. During a football game, neither the German nor the Turkish German children want to have him on their team. The children tell Cenk in a mocking sneer, "You're not a real German!". Others chime in: "And you're also not a real Turk either!". Cenk starts a physical fight with one of the children because he feels frustrated. The result is a black eye, which he shows his grandfather Hüseyin at the family brunch. Angered by the inconclusiveness of his in-between identity, he demands to know from the assembled Yilmaz members, "Well, so what are we now?! Turks or Germans?!".

To negotiate one's ethno-cultural belonging is crucial in Turkish German culture clash comedies. Cenk's "all-important question" (Berghahn: 1) is the same as the one Ibo asked himself a decade before the release of *Almanya* in Saul's *Kebab Connection*. To define the nature of Turkish German hybridity is a challenge. Nobody in Cenk's family knows the correct answer. Immediately, this draws attention to the same staples of "commodified ethnic otherness" (Sieg, 2009: 241) as in all the culture clash comedies preceding Şamdereli's film. *Almanya*'s crucial clash scene confirms that Turkish food has a history of being used to express cultural identity. That food, which is too spicy for Ali, becomes a marker for Cenk to prove his Turkishness. Ali's son devours a Börek with hot chili flakes to show he is a real Turk and to have the naïve performance validated by Hüseyin. The grandfather looks on with pride as his grandson eats. Then there is the outward appearance Ali's older brother Veli presents through his Turko-stache or Turkish moustache. Ali teasingly calls it a Turkish greengrocer moustache. There is also Fatma's headscarf. Finally, there are the Turkish and the German languages. Only Veli, Muhadem and Leyla can converse competently and without accent in both languages. According to Ali, "Hüseyin should finally take a German language class", while Cenk complains that his Turkish is as non-existent as that of his father.

A heated debate around Cenk's question about identity ensues among the family but produces no satisfying results. And so the boy must make do with a frustrating response: "You can be both, can't you?". That statement draws attention to ethnic Otherness and underlines a conspicuous element of multicultural universalism. The complex phrase confuses Cenk even more. To help the nine-year-old with his dilemma, Canan tells him the story of the grandparents' and his parents' migration from Turkey to Germany. By retelling the story of Turkish German migration, *Almanya* combines incongruity, superiority and relief humour more intricately than any of the other films discussed here in order to construct a "multilayered diasporic consciousness" (Hake and Mennel: 1). The film simultaneously disavows naïve integration fantasies and ironises German culture as a commodity one could consume like food or even this integration film itself (Reimer and Zachau, 2017: 247).

Almanya frames the question about Turkishness or Germanness with nostalgic memories. They tell of the first and the second generations' experiences. For instance, the first flashback scene shows Hüseyin courting Fatma in Anatolia. Their wish to secure economic status in the West starts the larger story of labour migration from Turkey to Germany. Another scene a little later in the film shows the family's first trip back home to Turkey with a boot-load of German chocolates, bottles of Coca-Cola and other souvenirs from the capitalist West. Şamdereli's version of Turkish German hybridity paints culture clash with fondness. It is a sentimental fondness, which accompanies many moments of insecurity and failed assimilations. Those, in turn, are resolved with light-hearted humour to reveal that conformity does not have to be desirable and that ethnic identity typing in comedy is not a domain of Western films. In one scene, shortly after the family's arrival in their first apartment in Germany, Fatma wonders why Germans put fancy porcelain chairs in their bathrooms. "And this? What kind of funny chair is this?", she asks puzzled. In another scene, Muhamed has a nightmare after drinking too much Coca Cola, the quintessential Western beverage. In his dream, the Muslim boy sees Jesus Christ stepping down from a large wooden cross in his family's German living room. The figure bleeds from his stigmata wounds and moans. With the slow growls of a zombie, which seems to be Muhamed's explanation for the miracle of Christian resurrection, nightmare Jesus draws nearer until the child wakes up screaming his head off. The German Dachshunds in the neighbourhood are totally alien to the children, too. Veli experiences a tremendous fright when he first sees a Wiener Dog: "Oh NO! There are monster rats!! There are monster rats!!".

The Yilamz family's journey to Germany looks like Alice's travels to Wonderland. The purpose of this is to stress clash incongruity for humour, not realism. Normativity in *Almanya* is suspended as the comedic mode prepares the viewer to buy into Germany as an unfamiliar, outlandish landscape. To make this logic credible we see reality through the eyes of the Turkish protagonists. According to Emeis and Boog, "*Almanya*'s family portrait and the image it draws of society moves back and forth in episodes between [imagined] 'orient' and 'occident'. It profits that way from the spirit of *Culture Clash* and the friction between different values systems and forms of belonging" (Emeis and Boog, 2011: 166). A montage scene with impressions of the family's first Christmas in Germany stresses that discrepancy. In one shot, Muhamed, Veli and Leyla demand of their parents a proper Christmas celebration "just like all the other kids at school get". In the next take, they accuse the mother of not wrapping the presents properly and of decorating a measly pot plant with only two baubles and the sparsest amount of tinsel. Hüseyin watches his favourite Turkish soccer team, Galatasaray, on television, whereas the children want to have Santa bring their presents. The exoticisation of German culture is complete as, finally, the lyrics of the German equivalent of "Jingle Bells", namely "Kling Glöckchen Klingelingeling", become a rather slurred "Plüm Düng Dong Plümmeldingellüng".

Almanya is a hilarious apprenticeship in cultural mimesis, the darling trope of assimilationists. Most attempts of the Turkish migrants to duplicate Germanness fail, yet the Yilmaz family is not broken up about it. Its perception of the German language oscillates between Charlie Chaplin's nonsensical Hitler-bark in *The Great Dictator* (1940) and an onomatopoeic "mooooh", which a German retailer uses as a phonetic crutch to communicate to Fatma the concept of cow's milk on her first grocery shop in Germany. Şamdereli reserves the actual German language for the memoir sequences of the Turkish characters. Switching languages easily from Turkish to German so that Cenk can understand, young Hüsein's and young Fatma's native Turkish tongue becomes the language of the native German audience. In this sense, the director indicates that alternative languages and an embrace of the unfamiliar are long overdue in German cinema. This is supported by Whittier, who sees the end of linguistic hegemony in German film as a productive substitute for the strained discourse of "Eurocentric paternalism" in Turkish German cinema (Whittier 2011, 1).

Almanya also suggests that there is danger in glorifying the settler society. A good example emerges in an earlier scene. Canan tells Cenk why his grandfather moved to Germany as a guest worker. She tries to explain to Cenk that Hüseyin followed Germany's call for an international "workforce" in the 1960s. The young boy pictures the German state as a loud and disembodied voice. The voice booms out of a loudspeaker to a crowd of young men in the Turkish city of Istanbul, men gathered around a hole in the frozen sea ice at the North Pole, a man sitting at an Italian family dinner table in Naples and a couple of males on the Greek island of Rhodes. Germany's booming voice invites them in the motivational tone of a gym instructor to be part of the Federal Republic's new labour force: "[d]ear citizens of the world, this is the Federal Republic of Germany! We are looking for workers. If you are young, strong, and possess a good work morale, then immediately contact the next official authority". That all these guest workers were the victims of economic exploitation, lured by the capitalist promise of Germany's economic miracle, becomes clear in the last scene of the film. The screen fades to black and Max Frisch's 1965 comment on West Germany's labour arrangements appears: "[w]e called for labour, but what we got were humans".

The incongruity in the final statement of the film is not an accusation, although the gap between fantasy and historicity of German labour migration emerges constantly throughout the film. Rather, it works as *Almanya*'s explanation for Hüseyin's diasporic desire to return to his birthplace as a human, not a guest labourer. Hüseyin's return to his Turkish birthplace mirrors Cenk's question at the beginning of the film. However, Hüseyin never makes it back all the way to his old village in Anatolia. He dies of a heart attack after making it at least to Turkey. The family decides to have him buried at a local Turkish cemetery before going back home to Germany. There, Cenk delivers an official speech in front of German Chancellor Angela Merkel at a special anniversary event: "50 years of labour migration in Germany". Hüseyin was supposed to deliver his thoughts on coming to Germany as the country's 1,000,001st guest worker. Talking about mutual understanding, he jokes with Cenk in an earlier scene at a Turkish barber's shop about addressing Angela Merkel rather informally on this festive occasion: "Angela. You are from the EAST. I come from the EAST AS WELL. We both—EASTIES". In his stead, Cenk delivers his grandfather's prepared speech to German politicians, the media and his family: "I have been living here for 45 years. Sometimes it was good and sometimes it was bad. But now I am happy".

The film concludes with a supernatural scene following the speech. Hake and Mennel describe this complicated ending as the nuanced aesthetic of a bittersweet "tragicomedy", with death as the flipside of life (Hake and Mennel: 4). The ambivalent resolution of the narrative acknowledges the complexity of Turkish German identities in the last scene of *Almanya*. The transformed family, changed by the trip to Turkey and the flashback narrative, is distanced from the rest of the world. The viewer sees the Yilmaz family's younger selves and older selves grouped next to each other as the camera moves slowly across a final shot of all the family members. The concept of change and sustaining German multiculture becomes considerably more complex here than in the conclusions of *Kebab Connection*, *Kiss me Kismet* and *Evet, I do*. Time is undermined while self-reflexivity and the simultaneous co-existence of multiple identities are foregrounded. One might refer to the surrealistic reconfiguration as an augmented realism reflective of a Turkish German consciousness of multiple identities. This ending very much leaves it up to the viewer to decide what kind of comment and insights into the question of Turkish German belonging the culture clash comedy delivers.

CHAPTER III

Television Narratives of Ottoman Invasion and Cohabitation

"*In Ihren Filmen und Serien geht es um den Zusammenprall der Kulturen. Was gefällt Ihnen daran?*"
"*Außer in 'Türkisch für Anfänger' spielte dieses Thema nie eine große Rolle. Ich achte darauf, dass nicht alle blond und blauäugig sind, die in meinen Projekten mitspielen, weil das nicht zeitgemäß wäre und nicht der Realität entspricht, wie ich sie—vielleicht auch durch meinen Migrationshintergrund—wahrnehme.*"
"Your films and TV series revolve around the clash between cultures. What do you like about that?"
"This was never really something that was that important, only in 'Turkish for Beginners'. I make sure that not everyone in the projects I put together is blond and has blue eyes. That wouldn't be the time we live in and it wouldn't correspond to reality and how I—maybe because of my migrant background—see it."
—Bora Dağtekin (*KINO.de* magazine interview, 2014)[1]

Summary

Sitcoms about blended families have helped to create discussion among American audiences about societal change and non-traditional structures of social organisation. In the 1990s German public broadcasters noticed the sitcom's mass-cultural appeal after private networks had already imported numerous US sitcoms during the 1980s. Public as well as private television network providers aired a host of original German sitcoms shortly after the first attempts at German adaptations won over audiences and critics alike. The audience's initial disinterest in Bora Dağtekin's blended Turkish German family sitcom in 2006 however showed that alleged lowbrow humour and ethnic diversity in Germany were still a hard sell. The Turkish German screenwriter's *Türkisch für Anfänger-Turkish for Beginners* was the first mainstream comedy series on public primetime television (ARD, 2006-2010) to feature Turkish German individuals and native German individuals as members of the same household. Turkish German Metin and native German Doris pursue their romantic relationship. Their children Lena, Nils, Cem and Yağmur, and extended family members, Grandfather Schneider and Grandmother Öztürk, reject the multi-ethnic living situation. In time though the characters come around and the viewers, too, warm up to the idea of ethnic sitcom families as the new normal in German society. This chapter dissects *Turkish for Beginners* as a televised comedy in Germany about different kinds of Germanness and related identities. The process of cultural integration, which arises from situational humour among family members in everyday life situations at home, in school or at work, is the series' most prominent element. The ethnic sitcom helped German and international audiences to extend the meaning of the wider German family and disprove the myth of cultural normativity.

A Sitcom to Capture the Turkish German Zeitgeist

In the quotation at the beginning of this chapter, Turkish German television and film screenwriter Bora Dağtekin points out that his work in the German entertainment industry captures a current aspect of German society, and that it links the issue of social diversity with the cultural phenomenon of migration. "Zeitgemäß", or being contemporary, as Dağtekin says while reflecting on the screenplays and scripts which he has been writing successfully for more than a decade now, is as much a concern of his as is presenting diversity. Not all of Dagtekin's writing and comedy projects focus on Muslimness in Germany, but his sitcom *Turkish for Beginners* (2006-2009), the long-running series about a blended Turkish/German family, is a reflection of the transformation of German society and directly related to non-native and Muslim Germans' increasing visibility in popular culture and being more equal to the majority population.

As I mentioned in the introduction and in chapter one, the need to reposition the national within popular culture has become increasingly important in German politics, international affairs, as well as in transnational criticisms of social relations. *Turkish for Beginners* can be considered a Zeitgeist commentary, in that Dağtekin focuses on issues of Turkish/German living, migration and integration in contemporary German society in the new century in all of his episode scripts. The series is set in an era of unmatched global travel, trade and migratory movements. I have described these circumstances before in the context of pro-social ethnic comedy and Turkish German culture clash film as examples of Arjun Appadurai's claim that mobility is vital for transnational societies in terms of changing cultural spaces and cultural worlds. Distance and proximity have become synonymous with difference and sameness, respectively, as he argues (Appadurai, 1996: 21).

Dağtekin's comedy series partakes in the German discourse on social change in the 21st century. It asks what defines cultural mainstream and what constitutes authentic Germanness or Turkishness, or a hybrid form of the two, while it traces the co-existence of four generations of a blended family. *Turkish for Beginners* starts with its German and Turkish German protagonists moving in together. Once set in motion, the story about a "soft undoing of the so-called parallel living in society" (Boss, 2015), as one media commentator referred to the plot of the series before it first aired in 2006, presents the struggle of the Schneiders and the Öztürks to live as one family under one roof. The narrative moves forward until the family members reach a point after three seasons at which all can define their identity in more complex terms than before because of their cohabitation. However, despite its title, *Turkish for Beginners* does not cater to the majority audience in Germany. The sitcom depicts the Turkish German minority experience in German society and balances it with different facets of alleged native Germanness, for example gender issues and pseudo-liberal politics. Dağtekin uses incongruity, superiority and relief humour explicitly to create more than one viewpoint in the narrative. The mix of different social pragmatics of humour complicates the viewer's interpretation of Dağtekin's fiction as an immigrant comedy.

My analysis here complements Benbow's study of gender in *Turkish for Beginners* and Peterson's discussion of a cosmopolitan didactic in the show to teach multiculturalism to German viewers (Peterson, 2012: 96). Benbow outlines an important model of how a sitcom with a focus on ethnicity can instruct viewers how to see, and more importantly how to be, a female in Germany in different yet "equally valid or authentic ways" (Benbow, 2014: 234). She focuses in her analysis less on the spatial aspect of the narrative though, which is part of Peterson's work on the narrative arc of "home-making" with the show's characters and their "positioning" in a shared household (Peterson, 2012: 97). The concern of cultural studies with representations of diverse ethnic space(s) in popular culture contexts, as indicated by Stehle's work on cultural spatiality in contemporary films and fictions about ethnic minorities in German society (Stehle, 2012: 122-123), is however a crucial issue I examine here.

I have outlined in the previous chapters that there is a push to reposition identities as hybridities in more recent German film to avoid the idea of clear-cut national, cultural and socio-economic community lines. This promotion of diversity and social cohesiveness between ethnic communities in German society has become a matter of urgency after 9/11. *Turkish for Beginners* uses three generations of Turkish German/German identities to achieve it. The sitcom does this also in an attempt by the show's screenwriter to include a historical dimension. It is similar to the function of the multiple temporal layers the story switches back and forth to in Yasemin Şamdereli's *Almanya*.² The narrative of the series involves individuals who lived through WWII, like the German grandfather, the old Schneider. Some lived for most of their lives in rural Turkey, like grandmother Öztürk. Some of the characters were born in the 1970s, like the Turkish German father and the German mother, although the former, Metin, came to Germany with his first wife as a migrant, while the latter, Doris, was brought up and socialised with her sister in Germany. The teenage children featuring in the series were born in the 1990s and they were all raised and socialised in Germany. The generational identity aspects place the terms of the Turkish German debate about Muslim integration into a broader timeframe and ethno-social context. The different ethnic identity types also acknowledge that German culture relies on a long tradition of consuming ethnicity in mass media fictions, as argued by Benbow and Sieg.³

Television and media critics in Germany, such as Alexander Kluge and Hans Magnus Enzensberger, have placed television at the centre of debates about the representation of social change and cultural diversity.⁴ The prioritisation of a mainstream medium is crucial to my work for, as the iconoclast of sitcom research, Mills, observes, "all entertainment, including the sitcom, plays an important role in society. Its effects may be deemed incompatible with critical thinking and rigorous analysis; but a sitcom is good entertainment precisely *because* it doesn't require us to think critically. Yet [...] the pleasures of sitcom are not simple, and certainly require an understanding of complex social conventions and generic rules in order for them to be enjoyed" (Mills, 2009: 5). My focus is therefore specifically on the plot structure of an entertainment format, which viewers in Germany and internationally have consumed as a representation of modern German multiculture (Yeşilada, 2008: 6).⁵ References to other popular sitcoms and comedy genres devoted specifically to questions of ethnicity complement my analysis of the multicultural and multigenerational family in *Turkish for Beginners*, which illustrates the potential of German mass-media as a pioneering forum for ethnic minorities to participate in German culture with a "distinctly diverse voice" (Yeşilada: 7).

Co-Existence Modelling: The Ethnic Sitcom and Its Close Cousins on Television

Situation comedy on television enjoyed unprecedented levels of popularity in 1990s Germany. It did so because audiences had already been trained to recognise the pattern of a hate-them-love-them family comedy in popular sitcoms imported from America, such as *The Cosby Show* (1984-192), *Family Matters* (1989-1998) and *Roseanne* (1988-2018). German viewers thought the sitcom was a television format in service of the search for the Golden Age of the German Family. Their family appeal and rather simple, relatable plotlines had sitcoms reaching across traditional entertainment and cultural boundaries. Both public and private television channels with no extra costs to German viewers offered many versions of the sitcom at the turn of the century, though most were imported. Some featured apartments (*Seinfeld*, 1989-1998; *Friends*, 1994-2004; *Caroline in the City*, 1995-1999) and workplace settings (*NewsRadio*, 1995-1999; *Scrubs*, 2001-2010) as their organising principle. Yet public television channels in Germany preferred sitcoms produced in Germany, revolving around domestic issues and featuring German family life in houses or house-like settings. Germany's leading taxpayer-funded public television channel, ARD (Public German Broadcasting), produced situation comedies like *Berlin, Berlin* (2002-2005) in accordance with that premise. To add to this point, German-specific content is the trade mark of Germany's state-run broadcasters, who offer public broadcast television. Channels like SWR (Southwest-German Broadcasting), NDR (Northern-German Broadcasting) and BR (Bavarian Broadcasting) are by definition German region-specific or culture-specific networks. They must adhere to an educational mandate for Germany's national broadcasting guidelines. The Federal German Council for Public Broadcasting and Media Oversight sets and revises those guidelines every year (Kosnick, 2007: 53).

Germany's public television channels have a history of following highbrow standards for their programming. They see themselves as successors of earlier government radio and tax-funded newscasters in Germany. Cooke thus claims that the German public broadcasting channels' issue with American comedy as lowbrow art has to do with concerns about the upkeep and safeguarding of Germany's national culture and the traditional canon (Cooke, 2005: 156). Such concerns intensified after reunification. Original German television entertainment in the 1990s was considered central to revitalising a sense of modern Germanness, particularly in light of a surge in xenophobic attitudes and a stark economic division between East and West Germans (Cooke: 157).

A counter-trend to this was lowbrow, mass-culture comedy formats about multicultural Germany. They went on air in the late 1990s and played on the many references to ethnicity and easy German multiculture in the country's public discussions on social change. One of the hottest topics was the clash between supposedly native German and Turkish German migrant culture. Some references, for example the headscarf, Islam, the Turkish masculinities, the class struggle and lack of education of migrant communities were frequently cited in intellectual debate, in literary circles and in the wider public. They were overused to the point of being cliché, soon appropriated as stock comedy props by popular shows like *Erkan & Stefan* (Dunphy and Emig, 2010: 4-5). That sketch show aired on ProSieben, a German commercial television channel. On the show, two German comedians play a rather dim-witted German-Turkish low-life duo, who find themselves in everyday-life situations: "[d]öner and dance club, totally cool dude, ey!" (Dunphy and Emig: 8). *Erkan & Stefan* did not last long in the pantheon of German television comedy. The duo failed to open up Turkish stereotypes and minority issues like religious discrimination and social bias for more critical readings and multilateral foci. Other comedy shows like Kaya Yanar's long-running sketch series *Whatcha Looking At?!* (2001-2005) had more to offer to the audience. It aired on ProSieben's private competitor channel, Sat1, and outlasted the competition (Bower, 2011, 378). Yana's show was better, albeit still not good enough for the programming directors of German public television, at thematising the problematic environment of ethnic discrimination and religious bias in German society.

Yanar usually gets the credit for being the first non-native German to combine ethnicity and mainstream comedy on German television. He does this by augmenting ethnic stereotypes until they become visible as cultural myths. The performances are as overdrawn as Groucho Marx's stage makeup and as easy to recognise as Yanar's costume-like repertoire. One may think of them like the beaglepuss, the novelty pair of horn-rimmed glasses with attached eyebrows, plastic nose and bushy moustache caricaturing Groucho Marx (Struppert and Keding, 2006: 22).[6] In his popular show, *Whatcha Looking At?!*, Yanar took the audience through short clips of caricatured ethnicities and bits of Seinfeld-like stand-up He performed them in fast-firing gag reels. He was dressed like a Turkish bouncer, a German welfare recipient, an Indian IT specialist or a gypsy woman telling fortunes to customers. The principle of Yanar's comedy was interchangeable ethnicities. He offered through his comedy sketch reel a variety of ethnic performances and exaggerated costumes to motivate viewers to inspect ethnicity and ethnic roles "as discursive constructions of a wider social dialogue" (Struppert and Keding, 2006: 23). The German media lauded Yanar for this innovative use of mainstream comedy. At the time, talk show hosts and opinion journalists assured their viewers that this kind of ethnic humour rerouted tensions in Turkish German migration discussions into comedic relief. *Whatcha Looking At?!* was a way of exposing sentiments of superiority about ethnic prejudice in both host and migrant populations. It was meant as a lesson in self-ironic deprecation. Struppert and Keding make a case for the innovative quality of Yanar's television comedy similar to my argument. The show took ethnicity and ethnic essentialism to mainstream audiences without keeping their enjoyment off limits. I revisit this duality in chapter five with a discussion of contemporary Turkish German stand-up comedy on YouTube.

Yanar injected his status as a German person of colour into clichéd representations of Turkishness. He was the principal cast member in a family TV show. He was perceived as brown, or at least as ethnically non-white. Spielhaus describes with great insight into the Turkish German integration discussion that this opportunity for Yanar to present something new was astonishing for mainstream ethnic comedy on German television screens. 11 September had caused a new wave of "Muslim othering in Germany" (Spielhaus, 2013: 182) and a distrust of the Germanness of those self-identifying or being perceived as Muslim. The subsequent increase in discussions about non-native populations in German society, and the promotion of their visibility could just as easily have pushed ethnic comedy to the fringes of German television. The viewer numbers for *Whatcha Looking At?!* however held steady and host channel Sat1 became the weekend winner in primetime ratings. The loyalty of Yanar's audience prompted other German networks to follow suit and produce formats with Turkish German themes to get in on the ethnic comedy business. There was *Kebab Pretzels – Integration in Bayern* (2011, BR) and *The Özdags* (WDR, 2007-2008). RTL, another private broadcaster, entered the ethnic comedy ratings race with *Everyone Loves Jimmy* (2005-2007), which was a sitcom about a Turkish German family in German suburbia. The working title of that show was *Crescent Moon over Little Istanbul* (Spielhaus: 183). The ratings success of RTL's as well as Sat1's comedy programming eventually carried over to non-commercial broadcasters. In 2005 ARD executives ordered the first ethnic situation comedy ever to air on public German television. In 2006, the genre of ethnic sitcom in Germany came of age when *Turkish for Beginners* began its award-winning three-season run.⁷

My So-called Hybrid Life: The Setup

Lena Schneider's narration is the focal point for the story of a Turkish German Brady Bunch. She talks directly into a hand-held camera at either the beginning or end of each episode to sum up the previous episode's plot or to lead into next week's episode. Through voice-overs and close-up face shots, Lena shares her experiences with best friend Kathi, who went to the United States for a study year abroad. Kathi's eventual return causes a shift of video addressee. Lena then talks to her father Markus in her videos. The German father lived with the family in the Amazon jungle before his divorce from Doris when their children were still young. This kind of the classic "Dear Diary" form, a self-reflective narration style (Allrath et al., 2005: 3-6) and the trading-places scenarios are the sitcom's dominant aesthetics.

The series opens with teenage drama in the blended family. Lena tells viewers how *Turkish for Beginners* is about a patchwork family after they all move into a shared house in Berlin's migrant district of Neukölln. She calls the neighbourhood "difficult to say the least, problematic at best". The Schneider-Öztürks/Öztürk-Schneiders move from two separate houses into a new home, an "old shed with a garden fit only for middle-class squares who like to live around a boring ass ghetto in the middle of nowhere", as the 15-year-old Lena describes it. "None of my friends will even dare to set foot in this slum! How for God's sake am I meant to explain THIS to my friends at school on Monday?", Lena asks her German friend who went to America on a student exchange programme. During the first episode, Lena is recording her family's moving day on camera to document the horror of it all. The family's relocation is Lena's own personal nightmare. She refers to the unwanted situation of living with two Turkish Germans as "bogan internment". The viewer knows already from this episode that Lena is referring here to her new stepsiblings, Cem and Yağmur. The three of them get into a massive fight over storage space on the removal van. Lena immediately resents 16-year-old Cem for being "a total dick-driven pseudo macho". Things are equally bad with her de facto stepsister. The 15-year-old Yağmur, a devout Muslim who wears a headscarf, has already clashed with Lena, an "infidel", over religious beliefs and moral values during their first family dinner.

Fighting with other family members during dinner, breakfast or lunch over different opinions or values is a go-to comedy scenario in *Turkish for Beginners*. That a conflict plays out over a family meal is the classic trope of basically any sitcom's Thanksgiving episode. Viewers see during the pilot how the fighting over a large family meal gathering first happens in *Turkish for Beginners*. A flashback cuts from moving day to a dinner scene in a Chinese restaurant. Here, haram Peking duck and unblessed soy sauce cause serious trouble. "That's just barbaric and improper", finds Yağmur, disgusted by Lena's favourite dish. She gets even more enraged about the "faithless German airhead girlie" when Lena disrespects Metin, Cem's and Yağmur's father. He is a police detective with Berlin's criminal investigation unit and a widower. Lena shouts Metin down when he breaks the news of the family reshuffle to his and Doris' children. Lena's 14-year-old brother, Nils, "Nille", likes Metin. This drives Lena's anger up to the next level. Lena, who had expected to hear news of a break-up instead of a lifelong union, unleashes her frustration at mild-mannered Metin Öztürk. Metin tries to reason with her, "this usually works out well with kidnappers", which makes Lena's liberal mother who is a psychotherapist by trade object vehemently to her partner's idea of the parent foot coming down: "Let's not be that militant, honeybunny!", Doris tells Metin in a soothing voice. The 39-year-old has been a single parent for most of Lena's and Nils' life. Her parenting style is distinctly New Age. Doris' "Gefühlskreis", or "circle of feelings" is indicative of this. It describes the German mother, making her children sit with her on the floor and hold hands. While articulating their emotions, eyes closed, they sway back and forth with Doris beating rhythmically on a drum draped in faux fur.

The dinner scene is so memorable because of its utter failure to reconcile cultural differences. There is reductive knowledge each side presumes to have of the Other. If not to a full-blown food fight, the scene leads to the teenagers flinging ethnic clichés back and forth, and then turns into a stand-off between reductive ideas about Germanness and Turkishness. Dağtekin's script splits the two families right down the middle of the screen to reinforce that point visually. The German Schneiders are on one side of a large dinner table. The Turkish German Öztürks are on the other. The placement mirrors the so-called parallel society in Germany. No character refers to it specifically, but it conjures up the two-world paradigm mentioned in chapter one, which Zafer Şenocak and Emine Sevgi Özdamar write about in their prose novels on social change and cultural spatiality in Germany. The majority society lives in one cultural sphere and the minority society inhabits another. To live in both worlds requires a dual perspective. The quotation placed at the beginning of this chapter explains that Dağtekin's intention is to recreate but also challenge that viewpoint in *Turkish for Beginners*. Dağtekin uses comedy to cut across cultural spheres by entertaining the people in each world with life on the other side. His let's-live-together, blended-family sitcom works through long-held stereotypes to get there. The scriptwriter refuses to reproduce earlier integration discourses, which had The Turks and The Germans live in separate places and/or houses and interact only in public spaces. Benbow observes that integration in that sense is presented in the show's initial episode as a *fait accompli*. The characters load all their things on to the removal van despite the fights they have had and those still to come. Like it or not, the diverse members of German society are ready to take the next step and move in together (Benbow: 248).

A Space for Difference

The incongruity humour of *Turkish for Beginners* quickly moves past the idea of ethnic stereotypes and stand-off clashes for cheap laughs. Episode two shows how. The plot in this episode is all about the new family home and mundane actions such as getting up in the morning and standing in line for the bathroom. The show's iconic yet also quotidian aspects of how people live their lives in German society are purposeful. Family members live together but may differ from each other in how they are typical Germans, Turks, women, men, mothers, fathers and Muslims. In fact, the whole of the rest of season one of *Turkish for Beginners* lets characters explore how well they fit into certain identity moulds and whether they actually want to fit into them. These explorations play out in countless family quarrels, walk-by banter, hefty burns and stinging one-line zingers. It all happens inside the shared home of the blended Turkish/German family in corridors, bathrooms, on staircases, in the garage, living and dining room, or the kitchen. The funny comes from everyday forms of difference in all ordinary spaces. One can assume that viewers have experienced such moments in their own families. Turning ordinary life into funny situational comedy, in this context, is also to suggest that there is humour in travesties of hyperbolic ethnic biases. Most episodes of *Turkish for Beginners* focus on that message instead of pointing to fundamental disagreements over politics or religious beliefs. Initially unwanted, the ethnically Other side of the blended family ends up enabling personal growth rather than stunting each other's identity development.

Congruent with this goal, *Turkish for Beginners*' focus is on living areas as spaces with cultural significance and an awareness of identity-specific chores. Gendered chores feature more than others in the plot. They connect closely to daily routines like doing the dishes or preparing a meal, as there are minor dissimilarities in each of these performances in each family home. Benbow describes the deliberate emplotment of spatiality and ethno-sexed identity as an invitation of the viewer "into the intimate domestic sphere of a Turkish-German family and its roles" (Benbow: 235). And in this sphere, the basis of the ridiculous and the ludicrous is the departure from the norm, the incongruous. The deviation from standard ways of doing things or being something outside the expected becomes the relatable butt of the joke without tearing the difference down. This definition proposes comedy as intimately concerned with normative behaviours of all kind, which *Turkish for Beginners* exploits in the most common setting of sitcom families and a staple sitcom locus: the kitchen. Dağtekin's characters do the cooking as they do gender, as they do culture. They are funny when they get it wrong and even funnier when they try to fix what was never broken. Doris is leading the charge in that regard. For instance, there are the family dinners. It is here that something as trivial as preparing supper triggers an ethnic clash storyline when Doris insists on being a happy housewife, although she loathes cooking. She takes over the kitchen only accidently to feed pork meatballs to the Öztürks. Yağmur sprints to the toilet to throw up the non-halal meat in a panic when she finds out. A staunch vegetarian, Doris wonders why meat eaters would care anyway about the different types of meat they eat: "[p]igs, cows, sheep, they all had a face before they got minced up. What does it matter?".

Wary of another "international incident", as Lena calls the pork episode in one of her video messages to Kathi, Doris turns into a very conscientious cook. The German mother resumes kitchen duty the morning after "Piggate". A reluctant chef, she boils eggs for almost an hour just to be sure that she has killed off any hint of salmonella. "You could use those as ammunition in warzones", Lena remarks in a snarky tone while pounding an egg with a metal spoon. Metin prefers "one egg, soft yoke and firmly cooked whites, please and thank you, honeybunny". He then receives an egg so overcooked it could be a piece of rock, but rather than hurt his partner's feelings Meting silently forces it down. Assured by Metin that she was successful, Doris beams with pride after having mastered the art of boiling eggs: "It ain't all that hard after all!", she says with confidence in her culinary abilities. Metin shudders, his face hidden behind his broadsheet newspaper as she goes on, "And tomorrow, it's omelette for breakfast, my darlings!". Another household chore Doris has failed to master is the laundry. Her understanding of how to wash whites and colours lacks some nuance: "[s]eparating whites, colours ... and whatever goes into boil wash - total waste of time!". Metin volunteers to do his own laundry when he hears this. He loves to separate whites from colours as well as fold, press and starch his shirts for work at the police station, but Doris bans him from the laundry room. "Oh, come on now, Metin. That's so easy and simple anyone could do it", Doris explains to him. "Why, do you think I'm too stupid for this?", she asks him with an angry undertone in her voice. The scene cuts to night-time and the linen cupboard in Doris' and Metin's bedroom. The viewer sees Metin getting ready for bed. For most of season one, he sleeps in pink-stained singlets.

The series' humour is often rooted in the subversion of normative identities, including enjoyable missteps around certain gender roles. The way in which it dives into the domestic space and works in sexist subtext makes *Turkish for Beginners* more complex than the average German sitcom. Dağtekin complicates the ethnic identities of his characters through their interactions with and perceptions of each other primarily on the premise of gender-based stereotypes. For instance, Turkish German Metin serves as the "poster child for a Turkish migrant father's integration into German society" (Wellgraf, 2008: 36). Notably, however, the show makes the point that this is only a fantasy. Mainly, though, it is a fantasy of Metin's. His attempt at a neat and nice family dinner during the flashback scene in the Chinese restaurant elicits annoyed frowns and mumbled asides from Cem, Yağmur and Lena. These reactions address several incongruities between the way other characters think a supposedly real Turkish man should act and the way Metin behaves on his own terms as a Turkish German. Every person at the table reacts differently to Metin's behaviour. This raises questions about restrictive imaginations of Turkish masculinity reminiscent of the male protagonists in Turkish German culture clash comedy. At the first family dinner, Metin performs the identity of a father, a Muslim, a migrant, a man and a romantic partner. And the other characters let him know that he fails at all of them.

Cem finds it embarrassing that Metin is not willing to act in the way his son thinks a real Turkish man should act: "Oh dude, what kind of impotent Turk are you?! You can't even get that little Missy (looks at Lena) to shut up". Yağmur's reaction to her father's behaviour suggests that she thinks Metin should act less German: "[t]he Quran says that a woman should be obedient to a man, and the daughter should please the parents, not like this ... (she looks at Lena with an angry expression)". A self-declared hippie, Doris rejects what she sees as Metin's old-fashioned Germanness, which complicates a simple alignment of normative Turkish-German with normative male-female stereotypes. She says in the tone of a patronising primary school teacher who is trying to explain something to an angry child, "Now, now, Metin, let's not be an authoritarian. You're much worse than any German stiff! And besides, this is all so totally forced. One has to allow one's feelings to come out and to articulate them. Otherwise this all just builds up on the inside and we all need to feel that we are in a safe and loving space, don't we? After all, we are now O-N-E family". The middle-aged, blonde German woman ends her reprimand with a wide, toothy smile. "Oh boy, how great! Circle of feelings", Nils adds happily. A close-up shot of Metin's face reveals that all those different reactions are utterly confusing for him.

A Family and Its Generations to Mirror Social Change

Dağtekin emphasises the incongruity of certain characteristics and clichéd behaviours. Because each of his characters acts in accordance with the imagined ethno-sexed behaviour of a certain type of Turkish or German stock-type personality, they remain individually distinct but retain a generational quality. There are the children and the parents, while the grandparents come in later in the series. One may argue that they all represent the first, second and third generations of Turkish German migrants and the corresponding German counterparts. This set-up accounts for the plot's ongoing concern with identity formation. Each episode turns on how a character finds a more authentic version of the Self in negotiation with other characters. The characters of all generations in the Schneider-Öztürk family serve that purpose in their identity performance, funny and flawed as it may be.

In a similar reciprocal relationship, *Turkish for Beginners* invokes the culture-clash premise and the hybridity theme in the pilot to satirise what viewers may think Turkishness or Germanness should look like. The family dinner at the Chinese restaurant cites Turkish machismo and German pseudo-liberalism. The scene is laden with generational conflict, opposing ideas, culture clashes and different lifestyles. Even the issue of language and mutual understanding emerges briefly when Metin tells Cem in Turkish to "behave and shut up" or, as the subtitles read, "there'll be some bitchslaps coming right your way". While those tropes of gender and ethnicity appear, they do not make for big and overly dramatised events in the lives of Turkish German people. Benbow finds that the sitcom already moves on in the second episode from any damaging stereotypes about aggressive male Turkish Germans. There is no domestic abuse at the hand of Turkish German men or any honour killings. Dağtekin instead addresses issues like the depiction of modern womanhood in German society in more complex and nuanced terms with Doris', Lena's and Yağmur's character development (Benbow: 248).

The whole premise of the series' pilot episode can be understood as a *Zeitgeist* platform for the ensuing narrative of Turkish Germans living with Germans, and vice versa. The show's producers manage to negotiate the line between overdoing the representation of identity and reducing its importance to inconsequential comedy. *Turkish for Beginners* redefines Germanness and Turkishness through a complex in-between identity and cultural hybridity, which is enacted by each family member. The last line of the show's theme song goes "Nothing bad can happen to us/All of us together do our best /(We all) against the rest". The song suggests a close-knit relationship between Turkish Germans and Germans when the opening credits are rolling. It plays on while close-up shots of the family members' faces are montaged together at the end of the introduction sequence to form a family portrait. The viewer can see in the montage that Doris and Metin are in love while Lena, Cem and Yağmur appear upset. The dysfunctional family image also serves as the show's promotional picture and can be found on the DVD compilation covers of season one and season two. It morphs into the snapshot of an idyllic family portrait before the scene fades to black and the show ends in the final episode of season three.

This is a valuable clue. The purpose of the show is not to delve into the psychological damage of decade-long assimilation angst or the dangers of living with Others. It is to try to reduce that damage and diminish the anxieties of inter-ethnic coexistence by styling cross-cultural living as a funny family experience. Next to the catchy pop song of the introductory sequence, the last image of the happy Schneider-Öztürk family at the end of season three suggests that the blended family can laugh off the tensions inherent in the ongoing debates about ethno-cultural problems in Germany; in particular, as alleged by Sarrazin or the AFD, those problems which come from mixing Muslimness and German culture in marriage. The opening credits depict children who are reluctant to become a new family. The parents are clearly smitten with each other. They kiss while they are holding hands. Benbow writes about the trope this image seeks to undo, "Years of portrayals of forced marriages and honour killings—culminating in the middle of the decade [2004] with a notorious issue of *Spiegel* magazine on 'Allah's outcast daughters'—have created the expectation in the German mediascape that Turkish [German] marriages are at best unequal and at worst abusive" (Benbow, 2014: 2).

The perceptions Muslimness and Turkish Otherness in *Turkish for Beginners*, which readily surface during the first episode and in many other moments of the series, underscore the prevalence of negative views on cultural hybridity. The show does not shy away from the precarious us-versus-them tenet of anti-Muslim-migrant arguments like that of Sarrazin. I described in chapter one how his bigoted rhetoric participates in a long history of anti-Muslim bias in German-speaking cultures. According to Peterson, who accurately recaps some of Sarrazin's controversial concepts, Sarrazin's claim is that German society would be better off without migrants who refuse to assimilate. This means "that, conversely, Germans are fine just the way they are" (Peterson: 97). Viewers of *Turkish for Beginners* also frequently encounter this neo-segregationism during the show. For one, there is Doris' father, Grandfather Schneider. With a seemingly perpetual gusto, he focuses in his xenophobic rants on Turkish Others as "goat herders" and "terrorists". Peterson's referencing of what Sarrazin states in his demagogic books is almost verbatim a copy of the Old Schneider's usual performance of anti-migrant hate speech. "They [the Turks in Germany] have not learned our language; have not succeeded in our school system; have not taken on our norms, values, customs and habits; and, most visibly, have neither emancipated their women nor left the neighbourhoods where they congregate" (Peterson: 97).

Apart from contemporary dealings with immigration, *Turkish for Beginners* invokes Germany's past dealings with ethnic difference and minority identity politics. At the end of season one, Old Schneider moves into the Turkish German household. Doris' father is an old Nazi remnant and a self-proclaimed former "business tycoon". Grandmother Öztürk mirrors his prototypical German identity. Metin's very conservative mother from Turkey moves in with the blended family at the end of season two. The German granddad and the Turkish granny stress through their dislike of ethnic diversity a perspective on German society which Corkhill and Lewis point out "can benefit from the acknowledgement that the 'German' in German culture, whether we are talking about nineteenth-century or contemporary German culture, is always already shot through with influences and elements from other cultures" (Corkhill and Lewis, 2014: xv).

"Gy-Gy-Gy... - Gyros Vendor?—No. Gynaecologist"

It is vital to analyse the diversity of identities as one of the features in Dağtekin's pro-social ethnic comedy. It is also important to consider the de-centralisation of the Western gaze through a focus on what the series seeks to teach the German audience.[8] Peterson contends that "there are, of course, other frameworks that might prove useful for thinking about the issues that *TfB* [Turkish for Beginners] raises. The model of intercultural communication helped to legitimate the study of literature and film produced by minority authors in Germany, and the instruction paradigm that frames [Peterson's] analysis is certainly communicative" (Peterson: 98). However, these approaches reveal little about humour as a complication strategy to suggest that ethnicity cannot explain every difference between certain identities; and, as Göktürk asked in her reading of earlier comedies about social change in Germany, how the mode of comedy can highlight a newer generation of Turkish German narratives and character developments in a pro-cosmopolitan portrayal of Turkish German life (Göktürk, 2008: 2). While Benbow warns about "a certain fetishization of Turkish German otherness" (Benbow: 249) in the context of light entertainment like ethnic sitcoms, *Turkish for Beginners* extends national cultures and established identities. That the sitcom was liked and lauded because it explored more complex notions of Germanness may suggest more optimism in the wider public about the diversification of Germany's mainstream culture.

Turkish for Beginners depicts expectations regarding gender, religion, class and nationality as a dense network of stereotypical knowledge about people's identities. The pilot episode makes clear that the first impression of the Other relates to many generalised assumptions and premature judgement of character. Dağtekin then disentangles that network to reveal its inaccuracy. He suggests that there is a host of naïve assumptions about what constitutes authentic Turkishness or Germanness and how allegedly real Turks or Germans should behave; what they should look like; how they should talk, dress and think. I have described how the dinner scene in the pilot lists certain incongruous characteristics and behaviours. Dağtekin assembles them around a dinner table and highlights their clash through the different characters who participate in the blended family's first dinner fight. Fostering social tension is a way to put a sitcom in the service of the discovery of new social realities in a society. The way in which some community members perceive other community members may show up in conflict situations, when one side hurls easily available tropes at the other. Wellgraf notes that Dağtekin uses that context for a comedy of conflicts, but also a comedy of democratic resolutions: "both sides make fun of each other in equal terms and on equal footing" (Wellgraf: 39).

There is situational humour in this family fight and the many other fights which happen afterwards. It encourages discussion about what each side thinks of the other and when and why it is socially permissible to laugh at the heated issues around migration. That means superiority humour complements incongruity humour. In the series, this combination reminds the audience that a critical self-perception is as important as being critical with the perception of the Other. Later episodes of *Turkish for Beginners* provide the viewer with numerous scenes about characters who make fun of Others because they consider themselves superior to them. Though, when failing to justify the logic of their own flawed identity performance, they suddenly recognise that they are mistaken in demanding normativity from Others. Characters may fall from their imagined superior height, feeling more educated, emancipated, sophisticated, modern, wealthy, attractive, masculine, feminine or German or Turkish than another individual or group. Introspection leaves them as the laughed-at dupe of an episode. But it is not necessarily a one-dimensional or extreme-minded character who bears out the ridicule for feeling superior. In the context of ethnic sitcoms in Germany in the new century, the dupes are also younger and relatable figures in whose heads some clichés about other communities are still firmly anchored (Benbow: 239).

In the fifth episode of season two Dağtekin presents the most poignant display of superiority humour combined with incongruity humour. In a short exchange, Metin has a father-to-suitor conversation with Yağmur's future love-interest, the Greek German teenage boy Costa. Costa has been Cem's best friend since Kindergarten, "when we two were still in the 'German For Foreigners' class that they put all migrant kids in". Costa is a close family friend. The viewer has no reason to doubt Metin's respect for the non-ethnic German with a Greek migration background. That is until the police officer informs Doris of his views on migration in a scene before talking to Costa: "Oh well, honeybunny, I don't mind foreigners of course as long as they make themselves useful in Germany as proper members of society". Metin says the same thing to his own mother in season three when Granny Öztürk tries to make money with textile brand forgery. "Anyone who doesn't like it here can just leave", he says sternly while Doris seems rather shocked. Even just the semblance of improper behaviour puts Metin on high alert after Cem and Costa perform a "street gangsta minority rap" in the living room of the Schneider-Öztürk's house so that they can become famous on

YouTube. Metin pulls Cem's sidekick aside and asks Costa about his parents' jobs. He believes that they are blue collar workers and hence may have a bad influence on his family's middle-class status: "Hey Costa, tell me, what's it that your parents do for work?" Costa, who suffers from a bad stutter, responds: "My mmm-mm—mother is a ttt-tt—tteacher." — "And your father?" — "Gy-Gy-Gy…" — "Gyros vendour?" — "No. Gynaecologist!".

Metin's assumed superiority evaporates instantly. The Turkish German middle-class man is shocked, as his reaction suggests: "WHAT?! So, then, you come from a family of academics?!" Metin applies to Costa the same reductive thinking which the openly racist Granddad Schneider applies to Doris's life partner in the second episode of season two: "Oh come on! Turks are all goat-herding Kanacks! The lot of them!", Old Schneider yells during one of his temper tantrums. The racist remark follows on the heels of a television newscast about the German federal government's integration policy and German Chancellor Merkel's diplomatic engagements with Turkish German politicians. The realisation that he behaves like Old Schneider is enough to leave Metin flustered. The Turkish German father continues to grapple with his fragile illusion of being the "modern man" and a "good German citizen". A later episode bears this out. In their nightly conversation before the couple turns in, Metin recapitulates the events of the day and turns to Doris. He asks her, "Mrs honeybunny, tell me, am I really that insensitive? I try so hard to understand everyone. Like I try to understand women and do everything to be an enlightened male". Doris rolls her eyes while directly facing the camera, her head turned away from Metin. She turns her face to him, putting on a doting look, albeit with a hint of attitude: "Well, Mr honeybunny, I think we'd better talk about this another time. Good night". Doris turns off the bedroom lights. All Metin can do is look utterly perplexed as the lights fade and he is left to ponder this question on his own.

The awkward pillow talk shows that the series thematises gender roles and political attitudes just as much as ethno-cultural identity issues. *Turkish for Beginners* puts them in a relatable social dimension. It all goes back to everyday life and the comedy arising from common family matters. One instance of this plays out in a dance club scene in season one's third episode. Lena wants to go out for drinks and tricks Yağmur into accompanying her: "You can very well sit here at home in front of the telly and grow old and bitter under your headscarf, but that's no fun at all. There'll be some dingbat dude even for you if you come along to the club. They let in minors tonight, even ones dressed as prudish as you", she teases the conservative Muslim. At first, Yağmur refuses. She finds that

Lena should stay at home and watch television rather than jump around half-naked in a discotheque with drunken boys drooling over her. But with her ego challenged, Yağmur agrees to "underage hours at the club". Doris is happy to play along with her daughter's proposal, namely that Lena and Yağmur should go out unsupervised and without a curfew. "Of course, my little gherkin! Young women must be able to master life and draw their own boundaries. Don't come home early, not before 11pm!" This positively horrifies Metin. "Should you need me, call me! Call my mobile or, better yet, call me on my on-duty phone. This means I get to turn on the siren and I'll be there in a jiff!". Of course, the pseudo-emancipatory attitudes of Lena and Doris backfire. At the end of the episode, Doris is worried sick with fear. She believes that something has happened because the girls stay out until midnight. She needs Metin to calm her down. Lena, who wanted nothing but strict rules from her laissez-faire mother, ends up hopelessly drunk and potentially vulnerable to sexual assault. Yet, she arrives back home safe and sound thanks to Yağmur.

Notably, the series lets Turkish German as well as German characters take comfort in learning that they can still evolve beyond the stock identities they had imposed on themselves. Again, introspection is key. Benbow points to season two's plotline here. It is consumed with the storyline of Metin's proposal of marriage to Doris and her repeated refusals of the "yoke of marriage" (Benbow: 246-247). In episode three, Doris yells at the top of her voice at a puppy-eyed Metin: "I! DON'T! WANT! MARRIAGE!". Dağtekin channels in episode six of season two a feminist critique of Western notions of "romance fluff" in a reversed mother-daughter talk between Doris and Lena in the family kitchen: "You're such a feminist, you can't even take it that the man is the one to propose", says Lena. Doris responds while cutting onions for dinner, "Yes, but I'm going to make an effort. That's why I do the laundry more often now and I don't always have to be on top when Metin and I have sex. I'll just have to grin and bear it when he proposes". - "Is that supposed to be some kind of practice for you in how to be a woman?" — "Oh my, it's going to be horrible. Just what kind of gender role has history burdened us with?" [...] — "Gee, you're so unromantic, Doris. You don't even cry when you're cutting onions".

Predictably, however, the preliminary superiority of Doris' feminist protest at marriage turns out to be susceptible to the alleged inferiority of traditional romance and female stereotypes. The German woman finally allows herself to be whisked away by her "middle-class Romeo" after a botched Botox injection to keep her looking young and after buying a reasonable wedding gown, a beige trouser suit. "There are just so many occasions I can wear it to", explains Doris while she models the purchase to Lena in what is the anti-climax of every rom-com's get-the-gown scene. Metin accepts this all as part of Doris' complex personality, which reassures her that it is the right choice for her own life. "I have a kitchen and kids, and I cried when someone asked me to marry him. I am a real woman". Doris says these lines in an over-the-should shot while dancing her first dance as a married couple with Metin. She says the words to herself rather than to Metin, who leads her across the dance floor. The camera zooms out while the couple keeps dancing on a barge on the River Spree in Berlin after their wedding ceremony. Peterson writes that, here, the didactic message of the comedy series hinges on the fact that *Turkish for Beginners* "humanizes and complicates issues that are both intensely personal and highly charged politically" (Peterson: 101), while the humour turns on the acceptance of Otherness in Others and the Self.

When Grandad had a Girlfriend

The narrative of *Turkish for Beginners* repeatedly suggests that predetermined ideas about migrants or other narrowly drawn identities are undesirable. There is also a rejection of aggressive behaviours towards Others because they seem different. The end of the series demonstrates how liberating the reflection on incongruities and a more critical self-image can be. One could call this a form of relief humour. It encourages individuals to refocus their energies on maintaining and developing relationships rather than pushing away Otherness. Several of the show's couples come to that happy-end conclusion. Lena and Cem can find common ground and their relationship ends on a happy note in the final episode. Lena gives birth to their mixed-ethnicity child after dumping her German boyfriend Axel in season one. That relationship was too easy and unsatisfying for Lena. In contrast, the effort it takes to work out her problems with Cem turns into a desire to understand the Turkish German character better. Ultimately, the process of getting to know Cem's true identity turns into romantic love. Cem vows in turn to clean up his act because he wants to be there for his family—"not like those loser-dads in the papers, those who simply run off. That ain't me", he assures Lena.

The substitution of anger with enjoyment culminates in the final episode of the series. Lena and Cem repeat the insults for each other from the first episode's dinner scene. However, the context has changed completely. "Stupid German bitch princess", says Cem to Lena with a big smile on his face. "Turkish macho dick", responds Lena in a kind tone. They look at each other and cannot suppress their giggles. Amusement has replaced aggression. The moment both characters laugh off their initial hatred for each other while holding their new-born child illustrates this. The scene reminds the viewer of the promotional image of the series. It featured the bickering children and the smitten parents. At the end of the series, Yağmur has learned to accept more diversity in her life and to embrace the Turkish German duality of her identity. She marries Greek German Costa before starting a career as an interpreter for Turkish and German at the Federal German Parliament in Berlin. In episode two of season one she had still yelled at Doris for buying Greek olives and being totally mindless of the long-standing conflict between Greece and Turkey: "Are you out of your mind, Doris?! GREE-EEE-EK olives?!". In the finale, Costa and Yağmur hold hands and smile at the camera.

Second- and third-generation characters enjoy the liberation from resentment and aggressive energies. Their plotlines end in love stories. The first generation may find love, too, despite being firmly set in its ways. Dağtekin's series suggests that members of the grandparent or first generation can still learn to embrace ethnic diversity and social change. Something positive will happen to them if they do. Hermann Schneider lives and dies to prove this point. Economic failure forces Doris' father to live with his daughter in a multicultural household. Nothing could displease the alt-right nationalist more. He is forced to enter hostile territory where his blonde German daughter is fraternising with "a Muslimist". Hermann's racist rants and "kick out the foreigners!" ramblings are hyperbolic. He shouts in a militaristic style at people and plays military parade music in the family's living room to romanticise the "good old times" of his youth. His character is caught up in a stereotypical Germanness. All the other members of the Schneider-Öztürk household agree that he is a "Nazi artefact". Yet, a feeling of relief also comes to this character as well as those who initially hated him. The joy over his ability to change ensures that Hermann's reductive portrayal as a racist does not overshadow his rendering into an identificatory figure with positive attitudes towards a modern Germany.

Old Schneider harbours a great amount of hatred for everyone who is different from his generation. He objects to everything who and which is not historically Bio-Deutsch. This negativity must be gradually replaced by positive emotions before his character can find joy in how German society has changed. Doris finds her father's presence revolting until he shows signs of moral betterment. The sitcom puts the figure of Hermann through its paces, a fact which is mirrored in his journey through the living areas of the Schneider-Öztürk house. The series highlights Old Schneider's initial disappointment with what he calls his Turkish prison camp. There a numerous instances of quick-witted dialogue between father and daughter ending in humorous dismissal of his anachronical mindset: "In the olden days they wouldn't have served that dog chow to any decent German", he rambles during the family's weekly "Kebab and Köfte" dinner. "In the olden days you also still fit into your Hitler army uniform", counters Doris. "Now shut it. Eat your salad and then it's off to the attic again!".

Hermann is an obnoxious character who reluctantly inhabits the blended home. His daughter stores him away in the attic of the Turkish German house because of his continual hate speeches. Hermann Schneider is the spectre of Nazi Germany. It occasionally makes an appearance in the spaces connoted as the present, the living areas of the second and third generation on the first and second floors. There, Hermann regularly encounters the introvert Yağmur. He finds joy in poking fun at the oversexed German women appearing on German television programmes with her. It is not until his death that the macho-chauvinist ceases to dwell both in a racist past and the attic, where he denies the demographic reality of present-day Germany: "We'll have those foreigners kicked out eventually. All it would take are decent politicians like the ones we had before", he regularly shouts to nobody while pounding with a fist on his old "Volksempfänger", a kind of radio receiver developed by engineer Otto Griessing at the request of Propaganda Minister Joseph Goebbels.

Granddad Schneider's identity is conflicted. The conflict is similar to that of older German sitcom characters such as "Nasty" Alfred in *A Perfect Match*.[9] The grandfather's racist mindset has endured despite his increasingly frail body and his economic losses. Both have damaged his sense of pride and his ego as "a German of yonder, who never needed the help of others—and in particular not the help of no foreigners!" He repeats this Sarrazin-like rhetoric in various forms to Doris and the other members of the multicultural home. It is only gradually that Hermann gradually warms to the idea of becoming reacquainted with his hippie daughter, his granddaughter and "the in-house Turkos" after he suffers a stroke and is moved down from the attic to the second floor. Doris and the rest of the family decide to nurse him there and include him in their lives. The family cares for Hermann despite his disrespect for them. Their acceptance for him motivates Old Schneider to rethink his behaviour. His redemption arc therefore closes with a love story, too. He finally changes his ways when he falls in love with a Jewish German woman. Her name is Esther. When Doris asks if Esther is offended by Hermann's Nazi past, the octogenarian proclaims with a wink and a wave, "Oh no, not at all. I mean, I've always had a thing for bad boys".

Love and romance are a staple of most mainstream sitcoms (Benbow: 247). Where it gets mixed up with ethnicity, the sitcom genre simply adds that aspect to its situation humour plotlines and revises a character's story as an arch of redemption. These are quite popular with audiences for offering images of harmony and resolve, as is the case with Old Schneider. His love for others compels Hermann to come to terms with modern-day Germany and his place in it. A positive outlook on life in the New German Family offers Old Schneider an insight into non-aggressive ways of being German, a father to his daughter and a member of a Turkish German family. The grandfather transforms. He ends his existence with a changed perspective on different communities and their existence in Germany alongside Germans like him. His final deed is representative of the transformation from hateful to loving being. He convinces granddaughter Lena not to abort her Turkish German child. What Old Schneider believes to be the "only good thing" in his life finally allows him to die in peace. The death even moves Doris to let go of her negative feelings for Hermann. Two episodes later, she laughs tears of joy at the memory of Granddad Schneider while looking at the first ultrasound pictures of Lena's baby. As Benbow interprets such metaphors, of which there are many in Dağtekin's series, "The family—like Germany's multicultural society—might have its share of conflict, but there is plenty of love there" (Benbow: 247).

Granny Business

Another example of how Dağtekin's situation comedy moves beyond the standards of Turkish German stereotypes is Granny Öztürk. She enthusiastically takes up the idea of textile brand piracy in old age. Metin's mother is initially portrayed as an old-fashioned Muslim. The widow moves from Turkey to Germany to be with her son and to make sure that Yağmur grows up a proper Turkish woman. Metin's daughter likes her conservative grandmother, whereas Doris receives nothing but negative comments from the old woman: "Her [Doris] no can cook, no good Turkish woman, no good wife". Lena's wardrobe elicits similar criticism from the old woman, who insists that female emancipation in Western countries is ludicrous. "If you not be good housewife, you not have good husband". This is a nugget of gendered wisdom the old Öztürk matriarch tries to instil into Lena. Another is: "Who dress like tramp, is tramp".

The granny settles quickly into the multicultural household and tries to set in motion a process of re-traditionalising the family, both Turks and Germans. The turn to rural Turkish tradition refers to the stereotypical norm of Turkish-German femininity in relation to motherhood and matriarchy: "that Turkish terror Granny and her old-fashioned bs", Cem complains when the old woman kicks him out of his bedroom. It would be unthinkable for her to share a room. Then the grandmother demands that Cem do something worthwhile with his time like finding a job or marrying a decent Turkish girl. At the very least, "not hang around and waste time, like that Coos—taaa".

The arrival of the Turkish Granny bears a resemblance to the earlier arrival of the German Granddad. Both figures are first generation and they cater to the clichés of their respective cultures. The Turkish woman appears moral, pious and family-oriented; she wears a headscarf and speaks only very little and broken German. The German grandfather, as described, is the poster child of an aged Nazi in a Hollywood film. Initially both characters seem to be defined by little other than their love for their national heritage and the long-gone past. Their negative reactions to mixed cultures hint at this. The old Schneider and the old Öztürk dislike the in-between identities of Metin, Doris, Lena, Cem and Yağmur. They reject the way these hybrids dress, think or re-define their nationality as their characters change. However, Dağtekin avoids in the storyline of "When Granny Makes Big Business" the relief humour perspective viewers had with Herrmann Schneider. He focuses instead on the incongruity humour arising from her role as the old-fashioned Turk and the not-so-innocent and, one might say, borderline criminal entrepreneur. She does business "like a Baller Boss"—this is Cem's definition of a self-made man who runs his own company and makes money by doing virtually nothing, mostly Turkish Gangsta rappers he watches on television.

Turkish for Beginners parodies here the cliché of an old-fashioned granny who is more Turkish than most Turks. The viewer finds out after a couple of episodes in season three that Granny Öztürk regularly sneaks out of the family home at night for a joyride in Doris' car. One night, Doris and her sister Diana catch Granny red-handed. Both Schneider sisters are blonde and blue-eyed. They vehemently advocate female empowerment, gender equality and the study of sexual self-help books to find one's G-spot without a male. Their shock at finding Granny Öztürk behind the steering wheel starts off a conversation about female identities in Turkey. The old woman reluctantly tells the two German women that she quite enjoys driving because Turkish women were extremely limited in their life choices when she was young: "[b]ack then in Turkey, women may not drive, may not get driver's licence". Yet, the stern Turkish matriarch admits that she and her late husband always dreamed of the time when Turkish women would be allowed to drive a car. In fact, they conspired to break the law in Turkey to do so: "[e]very Sunday, when us drive together out of the city to countryside, I do the driving".

The revelation is greeted with curiosity by the whole family when they eventually find out about grandmother Öztürk. Cem is happier than all the other Schneider-Öztürks to hear of his grandmother's night-time excursions. Acknowledging that his grandmother "has quite a cool attitude for such an old bag", he tries to put her to work accordingly. She is a skilled seamstress, so Cem ropes her into working in a rag-tag sweatshop where she is supposed to sew designer brand labels on Aldi polo shirts. However, the joke is on Cem and Costa, whom Cem has recruited as an accomplice in the scheme. The Granny they think is a naïve old lady blackmails them into doing most of the sewing themselves when she realises what Cem is up to. "If you not play along, I go to police and tell all. Then prison! And this one here, with pretty face"—she points to Costa—"will have much fun there".

The plan fails in the next episode when Metin closes down the backdoor business: "[w]hat in the world are the people going to say when they find out that my mother is a brand forger? This is a misdemeanour!" Cool as a cucumber, the grandmother cannot see the harm. "Should only big brand companies in West get all the money? Why should I not get my share from rich tourists who would buy totally overpriced things in Turkey?", she asks reproachfully in Turkish before moving out of her son's home.

Here, as it is with all characters I have described, the ethnic sitcom makes short work of reductive identity typing to convey its most poignant conclusion with a sense of humour: it is never too late to understand how different contexts add new layers to the production of one's identity.

CHAPTER IV

Bridget Jones's Halal Diary

"Lass mal gut sein, es hätte schlimmer kommen können. Immerhin kann sie ordentlich Deutsch. Und sie trägt kein Kopftuch."
"Never mind. It could have been much worse. At least her German is good. And she doesn't wear a headscarf."

—Mariechen, an old German woman who comments on Lale Akgün's ability to fit into German society as a second-generation Turkish German (in Lale Akgün's *Tante Semra im Leberkäseland-Auntie Semra in the Land of Pork Meatloaves*)

Summary

Millions of readers around the world know chick-lit because of Helen Fielding's *Bridget Jones* novels (*Bridget Jones's Diary*, 1996; *Bridget Jones: The Edge of Reason*, 1999; *Bridget Jones: Mad About the Boy*, 2013; and *Bridget Jones's Baby: The Diaries*, 2016). A large readership also knows dick-lit because of Nick Hornby's successful novels (*High Fidelity*, 2005; *About a Boy*, 1998). Both genres are popular fiction and usually depict the lives of single women and men who work in white-collar jobs in urban environments through first-person narrations. Chick-lit novels gravitate towards overbearing parents and outdated life models, while much of dick-lit revolves around neurotic obsessions with popular culture to escape adulthood and responsible behaviour. Romantic relationships and sex are the most poignant aspects of chick-lit and dick-lit characters in their twenties. Characters in their thirties are usually married and contemplate family life or consider the validity of alternative lifestyles as singletons. Turkish German versions of chick-lit and dick-lit add to the traditional structures the perspective of non-Western men and women who grew up in Germany as sons and daughter of Turkish migrants. They write as narrators of their own life stories, using a first-person viewpoint. The added layer of Muslimness complicates the negotiation of previous and contemporary identity models despite the authors' ability to work the issue of their ethnic identity seamlessly into Western life stories. This chapter claims that Turkish German chick-lit and dick-lit authors write in their fictions astute observations on changes in German society, specifically the debate about the ability of Muslim migrants to become German and their children to value German culture. Selected works of Hatice Akyün, Lale Akgün, Hülya Özkan, Kerim Pamuk, Ihsan Acar and Murat Topal show that Muslim Germans are just as neurotic, obsessed with shoes, cars and the allure of home ownership as are their fellow Germans. A change in economic status of first-generation migrants and their social upward mobility through bilingual language proficiency and access to education and jobs in media and entertainment have cast their personal stories in the light of funny life writings. The majority population in Germany increasingly seeks access to them.

Turkish German Comedy Literature as Part of the Global Funny

The commercial success of Turkish German chick-lit and dick-lit in Germany arises in part from the genre's position in the larger comedy entertainment culture of the West. The novels I discuss here remained on the bestseller lists of *Spiegel* magazine for months and more. As I pointed out in the introduction, some even claimed a top ten, if not top rank, spot for several weeks. Some topped *amazon.de*'s download charts for e-books for months on end. Akyün's two novels are already in their seventh reprint due to an increasing demand for their protagonists' funny attitudes to relationships, love and society. It is doubtful whether *Einmal Hans mit scharfer Soße-A Spicy Kraut* and *Ali zum Dessert-Ali for Dessert* will ever outsell the *Bridget Jones* series (*Bridget Jones's Diary*, published in 1996, *Bridget Jones: The Edge of Reason*, published in 1999 and *Bridget Jones: Mad about the Boy*, published in 2014, all by the large British publishing house Vintage Press). But the success of the German-language variant of chick-lit and dick-lit rivals the Anglo-American original's popularity in the context of Germany's crowded book market. *A Spicy Kraut* has already been adapted for cinema as a film version called *Spiced Up Jack* (2013), which the film adaptions of three of the Bridget Jones novels show is good business. A cinematic release based on Lale Akgün's *Auntie Semra in the Land of (Pork) Meatloaves* premiered in 2015.

One explanation for the local competitiveness of contemporary Turkish German chick-lit and dick-lit in Germany is the way the literary genre has adapted the comedy elements of earlier English-language versions. Smyczyńska stresses in *The World According to Bridget Jones* the (self-)ironic attitude of chick-lit and dick-lit protagonists in which they take on "normativity" and their perceived "failure" as "conventional" men and women (Smyczyńska, 2007: 3).

Women like Bridget make fun of their consumerist desires through their own commodification (Smyczyńska: 4). The cliché that they are obsessed with their body image plays out in Bridget Jones's tally of weight, and alcohol units and cigarettes consumed per day. Hatice Akyün, inversely, keeps a log of l her stiletto shoes. Faulk meanwhile argues that dick-lit men write about (gendered) norms through "trends" in consumer culture (Faulk, 2007: 25). In Nick Hornby's *High Fidelity*, the protagonist Rob Fleming sorts people and, in particular, his ex-lovers into top ten lists and labels them as "hip" or "lame". Kerim Pamuk describes German culture in a similar way by listing the country's regional identities from "normal" to "intriguingly quirky" (Pamuk, 2009: 24).

The aspect of self-irony in chick-lit and dick-lit novels also relates to several facets of incongruity, superiority and relief humour as I have outlined them in chapter two. Deeply ironic humour in Anglo-American chick-lit and dick-lit frequently involves incongruity and discordance with norms. German chick-lit and dick-lit authors rely on it as well. Turkish German characters who target themselves and their foibles for comedic effect entertain the reader with exaggerated characterisations of allegedly typical Turkishness and Germanness. Hatice Akyün and Murat Topal utilise outsized self-portrayals with which they ridicule what the German media refer to as "Klischeetürken" or basic Turks. The basis of both Akyün's and Topal's humour is that they play with expected clichés and what happens in the actual everyday lives of Turkish German individuals. Their unexpected normality runs counter to certain expectations that Turkish German women are forcefully married off or that all Turkish German men are aggressive machos and misogynist brutes. I have already touched on these discourses in chapters two and three in my discussion of a nexus between gender roles and both ethnic and religious clichés.

Superiority humour in contemporary chick-lit and dick-lit of Western mainstream cultures is closely interwoven with incongruity humour because both rely on hierarchical structures and evaluative judgement. From the contrast between two identities one may emerge as the supposedly more civilised or, in myriad other ways, the superior one. Bridget Jones's refusal to be the dumb office blonde demonstrates this when she pushes back against her male and female colleagues' prejudice. Why not just be the best dumb blonde then is also a question which Amanda Brown's popular chick-lit heroine, Elle Woods, asks herself in *Legally Blonde* (2011). There are also several instances of humour in Lale Akgün's novels where the author reveals implicit social pressure in German society simply because others consider her inferior as a woman, as a Muslim and as a non-native German. One can relate to her opposition to being reduced to something less than German men, which the humour in her writing bears out in reversals of assumed hierarchies in German society. Specifically, Akgün targets the sexual self-esteem of German male politicians, which Ihsan Acar and Hülya Özkan echo in their description of Turkish and German attitudes towards overused assumptions about other cultures.

Incongruity and superiority humour serve as components of an overriding structure in chick-lit and dick-lit. Both Fielding and Hornby in their chick-lit and dick-lit novels use incongruity and superiority humour as reference schemes for cultural bias and to show just how available discriminatory sentiments are. Relief humour, in contrast, highlights a person's reaction to these schemes and how to deal with discrimination, which Benbow describes as the didactic agenda of modern chick-lit (Benbow: 90). The mock-aggressive play of chick-lit and dick-lit authors with prejudices against certain groups of women or men bypasses a distressing affect. When chick-lit and dick-lit characters laugh at potentially offensive stereotypes, they exploit the harmful energy in them (Ferris and Young, 2006: 43; Pearce, 2007: 216). Readers can then understand that certain tired expressions and assumed roles stand for hostility and repressed anger, which chick-lit and dick-lit authors re-route into laughter. The allusion-transgression mechanism is the trademark relief humour of "Bridgets who deal constantly with male fuckwittage" (Smyczyńska: 3). It is also a prominent humour mechanism in Kerim Pamuk's dick-lit novel each time the Turkish German author ironises the social habitus of Germans to group-related feelings of ethno-cultural superiority vis-à-vis ethnic minorities who identify as Muslim.

Ethnic Chick-Lit and Dick-Lit as Constructions of Gender(ed) and Turk(ed) Identities

Contemporary Turkish German chick-lit and dick-lit are indebted to a global comedy phenomenon. The defining features of Fielding's and Hornby's novels, like so much chick-lit and dick-lit following after them, appear in Akyün's, Akgün's and Özkan's novels with female authors who work in or with the media "and have either autobiographical elements (Bushnell) or use an autobiographical format (Fielding's diary format). Texts that started life as a newspaper column (such as Bushnell's) are also common in chick-lit" (Benbow: 92). The resemblance to Anglo-American precursors reveals that light-hearted Turkish German chick-lit and dick-lit is not as new as German publishing houses like Rowohlt may want their audience to believe (Yeşilada, 2009: 118). However, two features of the genre are certainly innovative in the context of Turkish German literature. They concern the issue of transnationalism and the focus on stories about Turkish German suffering and marginality preceding them. The themes are hybridity, liminal identities and the negotiation of a new identity across the borders of established ones. This defines the Turkish German chick-lit and dick-lit novels I discuss here as cosmopolitan comedy narratives. They reject national cultural borders like those outlined in the introduction and chapter one, keeping Jewish Germans and Turkish Germans out of mainstream German culture at arm's length. Because of that, the writers reclaim "socio-spatial constructions like borders, fences, houses, kitchens, and backyards" (Cisneros, 2014: 4) and invite readers to join their transnational lives in all these spaces (Seyhan, 1996: 16; Fenner, 2011: 13).

I examined the exploration of cultural spaces and the crossing of ethnic and gendered identity borders in chapter two in my analysis of Turkish German culture clash film comedies. The idea that Turkish Germans are incompatible with the majority society as described in chapter three's ethno-spatial and multi-generational analysis of *Turkish for Beginners* is also central to Turkish German chick-lit and dick-lit. All this connects the novels here to culture-clash comedy films and ethnic television sitcoms about non-native women and men who are more concerned with how their hair looks than with proving that they are not part of "a violent and threatening global Islam" (Benbow: 89). And while some novels like those of Hatice Akyün and Murat Topal are informed by discourses on forced marriage and honour killing debates and Islamic extremists, they are instead more interested in debunking the myth of the between-two-worlds paradigm Adelson writes about in *The Turkish Turn* (Adelson, 2005: 4-5).

The notion of Turkish Germans as exotic, non-European Others still interests German-speaking audiences. Contemporary Turkish German dramas in film and on television, such as Fatih Akin's *Aus dem Nichts-In the Fade* (2017), resemble earlier films and television productions. The common scenario in the 1960s and 1970s was that of violent husbands abusing their wives and Muslim fathers brutally attacking their daughters. The success of Feo Aladag's *Die Fremde-When We Leave* in 2010 therefore blindsided critics who believed that audiences were no longer interested in Turkish German female suffering at the hands of Turkish German males. Some researchers were not surprised though. Benbow details how there was a renewed curiosity after 9/11 about life in Germany's parallel societies, which she calls *"autoethnographies*, a genre that [set] the agenda for subsequent literary portrayals of Turkish German women, [combining] elements of sociology, ethnography, and autobiography to various degrees" (Benbow: 15). Cheesman insists that these texts were instrumental in heightening existing anxieties about a sense of disintegrating Germanness (Cheesman, 2007: 2-4). Stories "ghost-authored by German journalists" (Benbow: 15) appealed the most to audiences. Weber adds that Turkish and German gender roles became intricately bound up with ethnic identities in this context. That connection still dominates contemporary Turkish German entertainment fictions in the new century (Weber, 2013: 2-3).

Not all chick-lit and dick-lit authors from ethnic minorities focus on the undoing of an association between ethnic identity and gender identity. Scholars like Yeşilada have argued that only female migrant authors with certain privilege in society, through liberal upbringing, high levels of education, monetary wealth, family support can reject ethno-gendered victimhood as an issue of the past (Yeşilada: 118). There is a "new confidence of nice Turkish women living next door" (Yeşilada: 117). "These new German-Turkish women" have optimism about their own lives and they publish books about it with large German publishers like Rowohlt, but it is not a reality for all migrant women (Yeşilada: 117). One could however argue that the direction at least seems promising. Second-generation chick-lit authors and, as I propose in this chapter, also dick-lit authors want to highlight positive alternatives to overly sensationalising representations of Turkish German identity tropes. It is a pertinent aspect in promoting independence and the privilege of not having to reproduce these tropes for commercial benefit as a result of the first generation's struggles.

Turkish German Chick-lit and Dick-lit

Turkish German comedy novels by male, first-generation authors like Şinasi Dikmen and Osman Engin have already presented a view of hybridity which starkly contrasts with "the agonies described by Turkish-German autoethnographers" (Benbow: 90) about suffering and exploitation as documentary fiction in the 1960s. Dikmen and Engin wrote in the 1990s about skinheads too dumb to tell Indians from Turks and about German bureaucrats as senseless and dictatorial as *Alice in Wonderland*'s Red Queen. The authors I discuss here take it a step further by writing about shoes, good sex, top-ten lists and their in-laws from rural Swabia. Audiences still perceive Turkish German authors of the first generation as excessively Other, yet things have changed in the new century for Turkish German chick-lit and dick-lit novels of second-generation authors (Burns, 2007). German-speaking readers consider their books as sufficiently Western and German, so the focus in those stories could shift from accent to accessory in the first place.

A shared feature of the chick-lit and dick-lit novels in this chapter is the rejection of Turkish German women as victims and Turkish German men as victimisers. Instead, maternal advice about late-age pregnancies replaces female suffering, and well-meant meddling of blood-relatives and in-laws in one's career choices and personal affairs substitutes for a brutal Muslimised machismo. The beneficiary of this shifting viewpoint is the audience, which can catch a glimpse inside the daily life of novelists with parents as overbearing or spouses as infuriatingly passive-aggressive as their own. Hülya Özkan's novel, for instance, revolves around the idea that mother knows best, while Murat Topal agrees to his father's notion of happy wife, happy life. This is not to say that Turkish German Otherness has disappeared in the second generation's negotiation of Turkishness and Germanness, but the focus is more on dual identity and German transnationalism than it is on dealing with a new culture and a new home country.

Hatice Akyün: Intercultural Romance

Hatice Akyün's first autobiographical novel *Einmal Hans mit scharfer Soße-A Spicy Kraut* (2007) and the follow-up novel *Ali zum Dessert-Ali for Dessert* (2010) remain to-date the most prominent examples of contemporary Turkish German chick-lit. Akyün introduces her family and her family's migration background in the first novel. In the second she goes on to tell readers about her life as a single 30-something woman in modern Germany. She describes in "jaunty, accessible prose" (Benbow: 89) her day-to-day "living in two worlds", as the subtitle of her books reads. This includes a doting father and a nosy mother, a conservatively minded sister and a self-declared ladies' man of a brother. It matters for the novel that Akyün identifies as Muslim and was born in rural Turkey in the Anatolia region. Yet, the chick-lit theme of finding a husband and marriage while pursuing a career is more central to the narrative than the negative stereotypes about Turkish German femininities. The focus on family and relationships is also important in Akyün's second novel, in which the choice of male partner continues to eschew a stereotyped discourse on violent husbands and forced marriage. The perspective is decidedly positive when the story ends happily and with Akyün's partner by her side (Benbow: 97).

A Spicy Kraut borrows heavily from Bushnell's *Sex and the City* and Carrie Bradshaw's obsession with having Mr Right and having great orgasms, too. Akyün's most urgent concern is to find a suitable lover and the perfect pair of high heels. Each is a necessary component for a life which she models on the consumerist ethos of Western chick-lit heroines like Bridget Jones. Female second-generation authors with a migration background like Akyün's have a history of defining their modernity through independent consumption (Butler and Desai, 2008: 10). Their works' didactic message is that women are now in charge of choosing both footwear and life partner, which Benbow writes "characterizes chick-lit above all" (Benbow: 96). This confirms Butler's and Desai's statement that "neoliberal feminist subject-making [is] based on the notion of 'choice'" (Butler and Desai: 8). Akyün's choice falls on a German Hans with Turkish spice for a husband, despite this being unheard of in her Turkish family circles.

While her parents would prefer a Turk for their daughter, Akyün wants a German. Only one dipped in hot sauce though will strike the perfectly palatable balance between the cultural stereotypes of German reliability and the sensual passion of a Mediterranean man: "the sex appeal of a Ferrari, but the reliability of a Volkswagen" (Akyün, 2007: 106). This image of cultural hybridity reveals a conflicting desire in Akyün's first novel. Ommundson refers to it as reflective of "the challenges facing young women as they navigate between careers and relationships, independence and commitment, and commodity culture and traditional values" (Ommundsen, 2011: 108). The point chick-lit makes about middle-class women is that they must negotiate feminist gains and consumerist motivation through gainful employment. It is by that logic that Akyün uses the established structures of Turkish German ethnic humour, which I have described previously as pro-social, to insert her life story into a popular chick-lit universe. The in-between identity of "a spicy Hans—just dare to imagine that!" (Akyün: 87) trades on the interethnic romance motif viewers can see in Saul's *Kebab Connection* with Titzi and Ibo, and in *Turkish for Beginners* with Lena and Cem.

There is a tension in Akyün's longing for cross-cultural romance. It provides the impetus for her reflection on the complexity of second-generation migrant identities as integrated. These reflections emerge from the circumspect nod to a first-generation discourse on violence, Islam, and Muslim women. Weber observes that there has not for a long time been an alternative to the portrayals of Turkish German women and their romantic relationships in German society (Weber: 152). Harsh Islamic laws which punish adultery are of no consequence for Akyün's life. She is not interested in sensationalised honour killings or overly dramatic tragedies in the life stories of Turkish German women. However, she acknowledges both jokingly when she talks about her own family as an example of the contrary: "[m]ost German [...] men don't believe me when I tell them that the men in my family are totally harmless. German men were so afraid for no good reason that my father would have his sons beat them up, only to save the honour of the family" (Akyün: 64).

Akyün makes clear to the reader that she and no one else controls her life, her bed and her shoe cupboard. She recognises what Montoro calls the basic premise of post-feminist chick-lit, namely that life on one's own terms and credit card should be the norm for women (Montoro. 88). Such normality does not mean that Akyün is less aware of the normal realities and everyday lives of many Muslim women in Turkey who are forced into marriage by their fathers or brothers. She uses incongruity humour to establish a tie between her German lifeworld and the Turkish flipside to her modern lifestyle. When the question of a forced marriage in rural Turkey is put to her, Akyün simply responds with a flippant answer which has a serious undercurrent. There was once an Anatolian groom, she tells the reader, but his relatives found the marriage dowry being offered by the groom's family, the al-Mahr, unaffordable: "[y]es, his family didn't want to pay four camels and their farm truck for me. It turns out that they wanted to save it [the al-Mahr] for their older son's future wife, which meant that I just barely got off the hook" (Akyün: 105).

The key to Akyün's light-hearted portrayal of second-generation Turkish German women as allegedly just as modern as other German women is romance between interculturally competent men and women. She is comfortable with living in the liminal space between two worlds, as the blurb inside the dustjacket of *A Spicy Kraut* reveals. The only problem is that Akyün's multi-ethnic competence restricts her dating pool to men who equally live between two worlds. One could call it a test of second-generation transnationalism, or looking for Mr Cosmopolite-Right on the pages of Turkish German chick-lit. Akyün's novel shows how potential suitors fail this test because they act too German or Turkish and, thus, are incompatible with transnational Germanness. Akyün's German "Hans", for example, almost dies of eating a Turkish dish with extremely hot peppers. Hans' real name is Stefan. He eats the peppers only to impress Akyün's father, which Nick Hornby would refer to as a balls-to-the-walls moment. Stefan fails both the food test and the couch test. He cannot find the mustard-coloured couch in the living room of Akyün's family and gets lost in a sea of shaggy Turkish carpets and colourful wall tapestries. Akyün describes the clash of Germanness and German body with Turkishness and Turkish space in this scene with observational relief humour. She comments on every shade of red and green in Stefan's face and the amount of sweat the six-foot-two man can produce. Scared that Stefan's cultural competence may be as limited as his palate and sense of direction, she declares the relationship a failure.

Akyün's romantic preference for a *Spicy Kraut* was an illusion of her own making. Because of this, she questions her personal cultural prejudice against Turkish German men in her second novel, *Ali for Dessert*. After a period of intense reflection, she ends the dating embargo on Turks and starts seeing a Turkish German man: "[b]ut, what was I to do with a Turk who can't even speak proper German? One who goes around breaking women's hearts? Now it turns out it was I who have fallen for this stereotype" (Akyün: 58). But there is a happy ending after all, as Akyün decides to date and later have a child with a so-called Turkish "Ali". He is a second-generation Turkish German man with dark eyes, brown skin and raven hair. Akyün reveals that he teaches literature at a German high school and that he holds a university degree in German Studies, just like herself. It is a classic turn of events in chick-lit and most mainstream romantic comedy. There is the obligation of chick-lit authors to "kiss many frogs until Mr Right appears" (Ferris and Young: 17). And kissed many frogs Akyün has, because she stereotyped instead of acknowledging diversity among Turkish German men. The second novel ends in a long-term, monogamous relationship and a baby daughter for Akyün. This serves as confirmation that Akyün is right to pin her hopes of continuing her Turkish German identity development on her life partner's education and emotional intelligence rather than his ethnic background. In *Ali for Dessert*, Akyün admits that she has freed herself from a desire to choose a partner who is bio-Deutsch. She admits that this obsession was mainly to mark her status as a professional Turkish German woman in modern Germany, which was all about being seen with the right brand of husband on one's arm like an expensive bracelet. However, this kind of transnational femininity in German society is anchored in Western domesticity and essentialist identity thinking. It is a criticism of scholars of Turkish German chick-lit I engage with in the next section on Akyün's fellow chick-lit author, Lale Akgün.

Lale Akgün: Hybrid Women

Lale Akgün devotes her two novels, Tante Semra im Leberkäseland-*Auntie Semra in the Land of Meatloaves* (2009) and *Der getürkte Reichstag-The Turk(ed) Parliament* (2010), to the experiences of second-generation Turkish German women. Akgün migrated as a very young child to Germany with her father, mother and her younger sister. Her first novel, which centres on the time between the family's arrival in Germany and Akgün's marriage to Turkish German husband, Achmed, puts a positive spin on the supposedly woeful tales of Turkish newcomers in 1960s Germany. Her second novel picks up Akgün's later years in life. Its plot starts after she has completed a German university degree in clinical psychology and has been running a private practice for several years in the German city of Cologne. *The Turk(ed) Parliament* details her career change from therapist to politician as the first elected official in the German Parliament who is of Turkish descent and a practising Muslim. Both novels have been in high demand in the media since their publication, and Akgün herself has appeared many times on television like Hatice Akyün.

Akgün's public persona is primarily that of a female intellectual. The image of Akyün and similar Turkish German chick-lit authors features more as that of *Sex and the City* alpha chick fashionistas and girly girls despite their invitations to expert roundtables on Turkish German integration. Akgün also fits less into the mould of a "media-savvy, articulate, photogenic [example] of a new cultural phenomenon" (Benbow: 100), by which Benbow refers to Hatice Akyün's description as an "'integrated', non-threatening, refreshingly uncomplicated face of Turkish German femininity" (Benbow: 100). While Akyün talks publicly of cold waxing her upper lip and intercultural dates in keeping with her chick-lit author's image as a modern woman, Akgün defines her own modernity through socio-political activism for marginalised Turkish German youth in urban areas and lower-class city spaces.

Akgün's chick-lit comedy and her idea of femininity are more reflective and contemplative than Akyün's. *Auntie Semra in the Land of Meatloaves*, which was made into a film in 2015, also focuses overall more on female character diversity than Akgün's novels. Akgün draws for humour on the clashes among women like her mother and her aunt, whereas *A Spicy Kraut*'s and *Ali for Dessert*'s humour hinges mostly on funny dating scenarios between women and men. This is not to say that Akgün rejects the German reader's multicultural curiosity in what Yeşilada has termed "profitable *Chick-Lit alla turca*" (Yeşilada: 135).

Akgün's books feature her as the Turkish native informant. She narrates as the ethnographic insider, who presents Turkishness to the German majority society with a self-ironic take on integration, abused Muslimas and orientalist clichés. Directly addressing the readership and a look inside the daily life of her Turkish German family thus put Akgün in the same genre category as Akyün.

Akgün in her focus on how hybrid identities of Turkish German women clash with each other deviates somewhat from the romance plot of the chick-lit mother genre. Central to *Auntie Semra in the Land of Meatloaves* is the explicit contrast between Turkish German femininities, specifically first- and second-generation. The relationship of Akgün with her mother Latife, for example, represents an acknowledgment of women in reference to modern Turkishness. The title character of Akgün's aunt Semra adds yet another layer to that context. Latife is a Kemalist mathematician. Her identity confronts the domestic stereotype of the first generation's veiled Turkish German housewives, who supposedly all took care of household and children while the husbands did manual labour in German factories. There are several instances in the novel where Latife reads her husband the riot act or where her academic training enables her to put racist German officials in their place. That Akgün's mother also clashes frequently with senior citizen and Turkish national Semra, who bends the rules of Islam according to her own needs, ironises the notion of anti-modern Turkishness and a generalising perspective on womanhood even further.

There are today still pressures in German society for Muslim females to perform their identity in clichéd ways. Landfester in her analysis of contemporary Turkish German literature finds that Akgün's women figures can violate these expectations. Yet they can do so only because genres such as chick-lit put the feel-good aspect for the female, integrated and modern reader before religious or ideological problems (Landfester: 2013). What Montoro describes as the female individualism of Bridget Joneses who rebel against others wanting to speak for them plays out in Semra's unapologetic love for finely ground pork loaf, a Southern German dish known as "Leberkäse" or liver cheese. Latife insists that Aunt Semra is a religious hypocrite and that she cherry picks from the rules of Islam for women despite Semra's hajj to Mecca and the holy places. Semra shoots down the criticism with a simple pun before she bites into her pork sandwich, decorated by a wide grin on her face: "I don't know whatever it is you are talking about [...] but my German is just as good as yours. This stuff here is made of liver and cheese. I mean, that's what it's called, right? Where in the world would any pork in there come from?" (Akgün: 115). The battle between Latife and Semra over who is more modern and more emancipated ends when the old woman makes another un-Muslim choice. The 65-year-old does as she pleases and washes her meal down with a big glass of cold German beer.

Similar incongruous humour moments resurface in *The Turk(ed) Parliament*. Akgün is confronted with German women who fear the alterity of Turkish German femininities and German men who want to exploit it: "Oh dear, oh dear, we cannot vote for you if you wear a headscarf" (Akgün, 2010: 1), say two old German women to Akgün in the pre-election phase of her campaign. "Why for heaven's sake aren't you veiled? That would get us the Turkish vote" (Akgün: 46), old, white German MPs say to Akgün on her first day as an elected member of Germany's Federal Parliament. The struggle with reductive images of Muslim women is clear. Akgün laughs these off with the same laid-back attitude Semra's character displays in the first novel when confronted by Latife.

In fact, Akgün decides to enjoy clichéd perceptions to teach the reader about a persistent bias against Muslim women in Germany. Her Turkish German husband chuckles as she tells him of her male colleagues' issues with sexual "endurance" (Akgün, 2010: 34) in a chapter entitled "Soft German Wood". Akgün reduces Germany's most influential individuals to their limp penises. This mirrors the reduction of Turkish German women to mute bodies under veils and exotic beauties with no brains.[1] In her thoroughly modern way, though, the board-certified psychiatrist prescribes a generic brand of Viagra, which her husband traffics across borders from Turkey to Germany. Akgün finds delight in her ability to show smug German men how much they depend on Turkish migrants, and the allegedly less modern Muslim women, to please both their German wives and mistresses (Akgün: 34). "Putting a couple of the members of this old boys' club in their place" (Akgün: 34) reflects how the chick-lit agenda of Turkish German women defies assumptions about male dominance in society (Ferris and Young: 43). All that is needed is a little resistance to hegemonic identities. Hülya Özkan approaches her identity as a modern, Turkish German woman in ways similar to those of Akgün and Akyün. She self-styles the world to which she invites the German reader. I discuss her book next, before turning to the perspectives of Turkish German dick-lit authors on the nexus between gender and Muslimness in German society.

Hülya Özkan: Border Crossing

Hülya Özkan participates with her novel "in the [Turkish German chick-lit] project of inducting the German reader into the normalcy of Turkish German lives" (Benbow: 96). Özkan's *Güle Güle Süperland-Bye Bye Süperland* (2011) is the narrative of what her novel's subtitle describes as "A Trip to My Scary Nice Family". The text starts and ends with Özkan's Turkish German mother, who declares excitedly to her daughter in a long-distance call from Turkey as the story begins, "We have sacrificed a small goat for you!" (Özkan: 1; 187). It is an annual tradition for the mother to have her daughter visit her during Eid al-Fitr. At the time of the Muslim High Holidays the mother's immediate family gathers to celebrate the feast of sacrifice. The mother divorced Özkan's father only ten years after the family's move to Germany in the 1960s. This sets up the border crossing context for the author's account of her regular visits to see her mother in the Istanbul suburbs. Özkan's mother lives happily there with the rest of her side of the family, while the father lives permanently in Germany with his two daughters.

Regular visits from Germany to Turkey are routine for Özkan. This becomes clear in the first couple of pages of her novel. She describes her pre-flight rituals. Her habit is to pack light because her home is in Germany. She has a German husband and a Turkish German daughter, and she never stays in Turkey for more than a couple of weeks (Özkan: 3). Özkan also prepares herself mentally and physically for her Turkish relatives and the Turkish bazaars in Istanbul with meditation and hot yoga. It is a similar mindset to that of Bridget Jones, who readies herself with a baker's dozen of tequila shots for visits to her mother on the outskirts of Leeds. These measures seem unnecessarily drastic, but they are essential. Özkan assures the reader who might have never been to Istanbul or stayed with Turkish families before that one might go mad without appropriate preparations: "I once heard somebody say about Istanbul: You cannot conquer this city. It conquers you—just like my mother. If that's supposed to be a compliment about Istanbul, then it must be because of Istanbul's magical beauty. [...] Istanbul is not for the weak or for people who love their everyday routine's reliability. You have to be quite light on your feet or, better yet, you have to have multiple personalities so that Istanbul won't wear you down—just like my mother" (Özkan: 13).

Özkan rejects the notion of her novel as exotic travel writing. The reader might expect such a perspective from the native informant on orientalist images of modern Turkey (Yeşilada: 117). Instead, Özkan sets up old tropes like lifting the veil or a Western gaze into her Turkish lifeworld like a dreaded family trip to spend Christmas with one's relatives. She describes her trip to Turkey as the common practice of a German "courtesy visit" (Özkan: 4). German family satires such as Vicco von Bülow's *Papa ante Portas* (1991) have propagated these hopelessly old-fashioned German rituals since the early 1990s. *Bye Bye Süperland* falls more in line with German family comedy than with Turkish German family drama. Most importantly, it has the chick-lit feature of the overbearing parent who drives her daughter insane over the Christmas/Eid holiday. Özkan's crossing into another cultural sphere is also only temporary, which counters the tragic notion of the impossible return motif. Second-generation filmmakers like Fatih Akin (*We Forgot to Go Back*, 2001) have frequently commented on it as a source of identity trauma in Turkish German documentary films.

Özkan's novel is a light hearted entertainment comedy about family quibbles rather than a sad story about split migrant families or Turkish German female suffering. Her mother and sister are at the centre of this. The dust cover of the novel plays on the notion of geographical displacement as the norm for Turkish German writing. The image shows Özkan's mother with a mobile phone with which the doting parent is only "a phone call away" (Özkan: 4). "Many thanks, my beloved Turkish Telcom" (Özkan: 5), remarks Özkan in an ironic tone. It is a comment on her mother's ability to interfere more frequently in her daughter's life choices through texts, emails and free-to-download smartphone apps. It is actually easier for the mother to meddle in the daughter's life than if she lived next-door in Germany. Virtual connectivity further undermines the cliché of the travelling Turkish German migrant family, which German families pitied for coming to Germany in an old car and with many rest stops along the German autobahn (Berghahn, 2014). Özkan makes fun of this scene's over-use in drama films on the Turkish German diaspora with an example of anecdotal humour. She rather enjoyed it when the family forgot her annoying sister at a German autobahn service station during a toilet break. "It took a couple of kilometres before my parents discovered to their horror that the silence in the back of the car was for a good reason" (Özkan: 64).

There are many amusing family moments in *Bye Bye Süperland*. Citing them supports Berghahn's point that all family narratives about migration and diaspora "have a great deal in common" (Berghahn, 2014: 5). Özkan employs the ethnic comedy staple of the you-never-call-you-never-write Jewish mother to show that Turkish German families are no different from German families. That she is so close to her mother despite the geographical distance is the sign of a positive discourse on international movements across borders, which replaces a notion of traumatic loss over leaving the Turkish home behind. Almost every chick-lit mother drives her children mad. Özkan's mother knows how to manipulate her daughter emotionally. A good deal of the story is about how Özkan's mother has been pulling at her daughter's heartstrings for a long time. The Istanbul resident succeeds in making Özkan travel to and fro between the Bosporus and the Rhine so often that transnational travel, a regular commute, eventually becomes an essential part of the daughter's second-generation hybridity. Parallel societies are therefore no real concern for Turkish German women such as Özkan. Her simultaneous attachment to the mother in Turkey and her blood family in Germany is unproblematic. What Özkan finds more burdensome is that unlimited international talk plans are now offered by Turkish telephone providers. One of her tongue-in-cheek comments suggests that mothers around the world use that phone plan feature to tell their daughters across the borders of countries that "it wouldn't hurt to lose a bit of weight, now wouldn't it" (Özkan: 24-26).

Bye Bye Süperland illustrates how Turkish German chick-lit authors ironise dated ethno-cultural clichés about transnational travels through their connection to stereotypical gender rhetoric. Özkan suggests that kinship, cultural similarities and multiple loyalties often intersect in modern families. Whelehan confirms them as a typical chick-lit tenet in a variety of cultures. She argues that it is important to note, though, that contemporary chick-lit novels mock the concept that modern women should be able to have it all, "while nobody asks if the grass is actually greener on the other side" (Whelehan, 2005: 87). This plays out in Özkan's novel in a chapter called "Lost in Bureaucracy", in which Özkan indeed "has had it with all [sides]". The Kafkaesque red tape Turkish authorities confront Özkan with during one visit makes her yearn for Germany's "regular counter opening hours for line B" (Özkan: 44). She unexpectedly rejoices in the thought of a German "local city worker who is available every day from 9 to 5 and doesn't put much emotion into their job" (Özkan: 44). The experience confirms Özkan's suspicion that more choices between ethnicities, cultures, countries and lifestyles do not necessarily mean that one has better alternatives. Her mother's rant against Turkish handymen and a wish addressed to Allah for double-glazed German windows in the winter in Istanbul stress this point (Özkan: 18).

The reader may not be surprised by the end of the novel that Özkan's Turkish German travel experiences have left her like Aunt Semra with a decidedly pragmatic perspective on border crossings. She operates in a space between formal rules and the realities of her life as a Turk and as a non-native German. There is one occasion on which Özkan flies back to Germany in company with her German husband after a lengthy visit to Turkey. She wants to turn her life companion of 20 years into a drug mule. Her mother's home-made Turkish Mumbar sausage in her luggage, Özkan tells him, would never pass through German customs if she, as a non-EU citizen, carried it in her suitcase. But that he should smuggle filled sheep intestines instead scares the German. He puts his love for EU customs regulations on imported goods before the unique Turkishness of his wife's non-European food: "[t]here was nothing I could do. Whatever I said to my husband, he wouldn't commit to a life of crime" (Özkan: 7-8). To have to relinquish Turkish food at German customs is a sobering reminder for Özkan.[2] She realises that there are still times when she crosses borders as a liminal German while her native husband seems to relish his national privilege of unrestricted access and implicit trust. Similar moments appear in Akyün's and Akgün's novels in the clashes between German men and Turkish German women and allegedly modern German politicians and female Turkish German politicians, respectively. Özkan is as amused as Akyün and Akgün that she has the cool to react in gleeful spite to the patronising behaviour of white German men, sending the husband to sleep on the couch that night when they got home from the airport.

Kerim Pamuk: Post-colonial Narratives

Gender and sexuality have been some of the central issues in the novels of male Turkish German writers like Feridun Zaimoğlu since the early 1990s. Schmidt argues that the nexus between minority men in Germany and diverse masculinities has been to date "somewhat overlooked in scholarship in favour of issues of ethnicity" (Schmidt, 2011: 199). It is precisely this issue of ethnic minority masculinity and male Muslim identities which contemporary Turkish German dick-lit brings to the fore. I have mentioned how the genre started with the comedy novels of male Turkish Germans such as first-generation authors Osman Engin and Şinasi Dikmen. Their novels foreground the construction of a gendered Turkish German identity. Cheesman points out, though, that Engin's *Kanaken-Ghandi-The Kanak-Ghandi* (2000) and Dikmen's *Hurra, ich lebe in Deutschland-Hooray for Germany* (1996) focus much more on ethnicity as imperfect performance than on a reasonably credible notion of authentic Turkish masculinity (Cheesman: 23-24).

Yardley finds that it is a sign of progress in the debate on gender identity when male novelists tackle traditionally female issues related to "dating, jobs and life direction" (Yardley, 2013: 24). Male Turkish German authors such as Kerim Pamuk, Ihsan Acar and Murat Topal focus on these aspects in their second-generation Turkish German dick-lit novels. The stories are also autobiographical but work with different aesthetics from Turkish German chick-lit novels. Both Turkish German chick-lit and dick-lit celebrate the upwardly mobile migrant who moved from suffering to success. However, the men in Turkish German dick-lit do not follow the Bridget Jones formula. They follow Anglophone dick-lit models when they make lists and draw up rankings of popular culture trends rather than sharing their stories directly via email or diary, or in direct address to the reader. The man in Nick Hornby's dick-lit refer to and think of themselves as autonomous, whereas popular chick-lit women strive for notions of community and being relatable, according to Barry Faulk (Faulk, 2007: 153). Pamuk, Acar and Topal fall broadly into this category.

The difference in communication style is a crucial point to make because dick-lit authors are less interested in conveying intimate "confessions" to their reader than chick-lit authors who write for their "sisters" (Ferris and Young: 23). Yet, the men still want to produce with their "comic writing a male bildungsroman [about who they are], the ups and downs of a relationship, fatherhood, or their place in society in general" (Faulk: 155). These male "dicks" just write in another way. They dress up their incessant, lacerating self-analysis as a beguiling self-expressive identity like music snob Rob Fleming, a nod to *James Bond* author Ian Fleming, in Nick Hornby's *High Fidelity* (1996). Dick-lit novelists proffer "the voyeuristic charm of getting to know male psychology at its most intimate, while avoiding connotations of psychosis" (Faulk: 155). David Fincher's *Fight Club* (1999) has become an iconic dick-flick for portraying that issue in popular Anglophone cinema.

Female and male Turkish German authors of second-generation chick-lit and dick-lit share a sense of Germany as the German home. Turkish German literary scholars point out that contemporary Turkish German comedy novelists have moved on from certain features of first-generation authorship. The second-generation label refers no longer to aspects of migration itself but to post-migration scenarios (Specht, 2011: 23). Kerim Pamuk suggests in his novel *Allah verzeiht, der Hausmeister nicht-Allah Has Mercy, A German Janitor Doesn't* (2009) that second-generation Turkish German men like him were unmistakably socialised in Germany. Nevertheless, native Germans, specifically other men, question Turkish German men's identities. They doubt that their modern masculinity is equal to theirs because of a family's migration history, an exotic visual appearance or an "un-Germanic" name (Pamuk: 3).

Pamuk demonstrates how Turkish Germans make fun of their perception as lesser Germans to retaliate in a comedic pissing match between lads. In his novel he draws on the idea of promotional travel writing to present Germany to the reader as an unknown territory (Bendixen and Hamera, 2009: 1-3). The story of *Allah Has Mercy, A German Janitor Doesn't* (2011) starts out with the assumption that Germany is an exotic place which is just waiting to be discovered by non-European adventurers. The novel begins with Pamuk's invitation to an imagined Oriental reader: "[m]y dear fellow brothers and sisters in the faith who hail from the East" (Pamuk, 2011: 1). They are invited to go with him on a journey through this strangest of places called Germany. On the first page of the narrative a plane descends on Germany and aboard are Pamuk and his fellow explorers. Their travels through Germany are going to shed light on and evaluate in a mode of cultural superiority the cultural differences between German natives and non-native Muslims in the country.

Pamuk explores German society by contrasting Muslim selves with German Others. This reverses the ethnic minority perspective in Hatice Akyün's and Lale Akgün's novels. Ironically, though, the German reader is both object and addressee of Pamuk's novel. The book is written exclusively in German with a primary focus on German traditions. German social values lurk in the shadow of discourses on violent "ghetto Turks". The reader becomes aware of this when the alleged promotion of Germany quickly turns to rankings of the country's ten most racist regions and politicians most likely to bring back "the little black one". This is not about a dress but a little, black upper-lip moustache (Pamuk: 4-12). Pamuk's inversion of ethnic Otherness is significant. As Adelson points out, exploratory desires have a long history of fuelling the Germans' colonialist thinking. Them bringing their more advanced culture to pre-modern areas and people is a long-held Germany fantasy of superior Germanic culture (Adelson: 23). One could argue that the German majority population has had similar motivations to civilise members of the Turkish German minority in Germany over the course of the past 50 years. The language in the AfD's 2020 political programme would suggest as much.

Pamuk makes numerous jabs at the Germans' colonial fantasies. The cover image of *Allah Has Mercy, A German Janitor Doesn't* satirises a Eurocentric *terra incognita* notion of the unknown Other and presents the reader with a contour map of Germany. Stock image cartoons show mothers in yoga pants as they push sport buggy strollers in West Germany, while the image of a "Currywurst" or curried sausage food truck replaces Germany's capital city of Berlin in East Germany. These stereotypes about German culture, that women in active war rear their children during workouts and that Germans love their iconic sausage street food, are substitutes for actual geographies. The substitution reorders the hierarchy of allegedly superior German culture. Stock images reduce Germanness to funny tropes of food and white-people-meme lifestyles. The process is akin to other popular internet memes, which superimpose alternative messages on existing imagery. Turning the German map into a meme-like caricature alludes to the availability of clichés about other countries and cultures in the German popular imaginary.

The non-native German or integrated reader benefits from Germany's Othering. He or she may find it amusing that a Turkish German author would sell Muslim foreigners the idea of resetting and making a good life in Germany. And to do so as if no other Muslim person had ever set foot on German soil. Pamuk emphasises the Christopher Columbus-like exploratory gesture by addressing the reader directly as his fellow Muslim brothers or Muslim sisters, whose "Cattle Class flight" is about to descend upon the exotic lands of Germany (Pamuk: 2). Pamuk uses a satirical perspective on promotional literature to conjure up the historical labour migration discourse of West German politicians. I discussed this aspect in chapter two in my analysis of Şamdereli's culture clash comedy film, *Almanya*. Şamdereli revisits how West German elites invited migrant workers in the 1960s to come and share in Germany's welfare. Yet, Germany failed to make good on its gilded promises. I consider the reappearance of the same motif of broken promises in Pamuk's novel as a mocking allusion to Germany's self-promotion as cosmopolitan host country. Mandel has comprehensively commented on this topic (Mandel, 2008: 1-3).

There is a profound affirmation in *Allah Has Mercy, A German Janitor Doesn't* that Germany is compatible with Muslimness. Pamuk insists that male Muslims who journey between the Rivers Spree and Rhine will be pleased to find that Germanness is very similar to different Muslim cultures. It is basically the same. Like Toula's Greek father in Joel Zwick's *My Big Fat Greek Wedding* (2002), Pamuk traces all of Germany's cultural riches back to their origins in the Muslim world. A case in point is Pamuk's voyage to every corner of Germany to break down the boundaries between actual Germanness and an imagined Muslimised one. Several interludes along the way allow him to reflect on German dialects, traditional garments and buildings. He is certain that Bavarian gibberish sounds like ancient Turkish; that Swabian folk wear for women appears as colourful as Persian wedding gowns; and that the Brandenburg Gate's architectural design was inspired by the grand architecture of Arab mosques. In *My Big Fat Greek Wedding*, the first-generation Greek American father keeps on interrupting everybody in the film only to explain how every aspect of Western culture in America goes back to ancient Greece. Pamuk also pauses his own narration several times. He tells the reader how Germans profited from the many Arab and Turkish foods and ethnic cuisines which the first explorers brought from the Orient to the land of pork Schnitzel and overcooked cabbage, Kraut (Pamuk: 88).

Yet Pamuk also warns his readers against unadvisable behaviour as Nick Hornby's protagonists often do. The preoccupation with the most agreeable places for Muslims in Germany bears traces of Anglophone dick-lit's home-spun and commonplace wisdom and humour. There is no greater similarity between Pamuk and Hornby than in how Pamuk farcically explains that Muslim men should not think of "Easties" (Pamuk: 54) as their Eastern brethren. Muslim men may come to regret this kind of thinking and encounter Eastern German hospitals instead of Eastern hospitality. Any "Shawarma-Shiite" (Pamuk: 76) who wants to experience German health care from the inside is advised to go to Brandenburg city with a full beard and the Quran in hand. Nick Hornby's protagonist, Rob, advises the reader in *High Fidelity* not to ask true connoisseurs of music for cheap bubble-gum pop. Will Freeman warns his young male protégé in *About a Boy* that wearing his mother's handcrafted knitwear in middle school is low-hanging fruit for bullies and getting punched.

Pamuk writes in a flippant, snobbish tone. It is the trade-mark feature of dick-lick narrators. He creates for himself a superior position of alleged cultural expertise on Germany's many sub-cultures, specialising in people who wear Birkenstocks (Pamuk: 93-95). The professed knowledge sustains humorous and sometimes even quite challenging commentary on the reductive pseudo-colonial and orientalist perceptions which Western Europe's white Christians have of other ethnic communities (Benbow: 106). However, one must note that it is a facetious exaggeration of cultural difference to destabilise assumed hierarchies in everyday culture. Cheesman has shown that Turkish German comedy authors like Dikmen and Engin do not call for the Turks' isolation from the majority population. Rather, their ironical viewpoint serves them to inform the native readership about the struggles of minorities so that all communities can live together more happily (Göktürk: 177-178). This is certainly the case when

Pamuk addresses his own status as an integrated Muslim German man in modern Germany. It is easy to "bro-friend" native German men, he writes. All it takes is male bonding over urban male rituals like rooting for the same sports team, be it Galatasaray or Bayern Munich; or paying for a trip to Rio, "including intensive *female* care services for all of one's needs" (Pamuk: 20; 45).

In some places Pamuk channels the persona of a merciless German janitor to come off as satirical about self-indulgent Germanness. The theme of Germany as a pseudo "multi-culti" nation is central to his book. He criticises the Germans' need to be indistinctly the same without space for alternative forms of Germanness. Exemplary of this is the preposterous primary of German masculinity. As if German culture standards were not enough, German menswear and beauty trends had Germanified Turkish "[...] princes walk around in this country wearing leather jackets, greengrocer moustaches, and mullets" (Pamuk: 125). Imaginary Germany emerges here as a dead-end for the expression of ethnic Otherness at the cost of assimilating to fit into German society.

Allah Has Mercy, A German Janitor Doesn't extolls the pleasures of ethnic and gender clichés for better or, literally, worse for fashionable wear. The book's core is a comedic reversal of the sought-after 1990s list of do's and don'ts in popular entertainment magazines, revered by both chick-lit and dick-lit protagonists as the gospel. Pamuk's list of don'ts asks Muslim men to beware of male German caretakers. Pamuk explains that they are like Germany's local ISIS, in that "they fight with self-sacrifice against the demonic chaos of unruly humanity, seeing themselves as the final and unsurmountable line of defence for German rule of law. They are: German janitors. They can easily compete with our Taliban and Jihadis when it comes to religious fervour, test of faith, courage, and martyrdom" (Pamuk: 18). Another don't is about Muslims trying to understand native Germans: "[t]he German is a deeply fractured creature, my dear Aubergine-Osmane. He always wants to be everything at the same time. If you were to ask him for their most favourite reflection, he would give you in response a most carefully crafted advertisement online-dating profile: spontaneous, but domesticated; sturdy, but sensitive; romantic, but grounded; emotional, but reasonable" (Pamuk: 106). Pamuk projects onto Germans their own anti-modern idea of Turkishness and ethnic difference. This strategy shows how he plays Germany's cultural chauvinism for laughs. A similar ridicule of cultural authenticity is apparent in Ihsan Acar's novel. He portrays the notion of original Turkishness as a desire of German readers to reaffirm their stereotypical image of Turkish men in modern Germany.

Ihsan Acar: Ethnic Originality

Dick-lit authors frequently depict men as questioning and conflicted when they fail to fulfil oversimplified gender concepts offered by self-help manuals like John Gray's infamous 1992 publication *Men Are from Mars, Women Are from Venus*. Ihsan Acar in his second-generation dick-lit novel *Der Türke: das Original-The Real Deal Turks* (2007) questions the effects of a similarly dichotomous view of ethnic identities as exclusively German or Turkish. Acar deploys a host of ethnocultural clichés to explain his Turkish German identity. His story first depicts his childhood, then youth, and finally adulthood in the German city of Berlin. He sees himself neither as an integrated Turkish German man nor as an allegedly original Turk. This sums up Acar's approach to what Gill calls the "laid-back attitude of the new lads" (Gill, 2009: 3) in contemporary dick-lit. Gill argues that modern men depend less than the so-called traditional old boys on restrictive notions of masculinity and ethno-nationalist sentiments of societal order to feel safe when society changes around them (Gill: 5).

Acar's attitude can be described as defiant of the old ways. He dislikes predetermined concepts of The Turkish and The German man and Turkish German and German masculinities, respectively. Yet, the reader will find no outrage over religious discrimination or protesting ethnic bias in Acar's book. That was the hallmark of male Turkish German authors like Zaimoğlu and his novel *Kanak Sprak* (1995) in the 1990s. Instead, Acar mirrors Akyün's style of "irony, knowingness, and distancing [...] and sometimes he is being even deeply shallow" (Gill: 4) to make a witty point about how modern Turks do integration, namely by instructing natives in supposedly inferior ways of being Turkish. Why try to climb the ladder if others can just come sliding down is an apt summary of Acar's viewpoint: "[i]t's much more convenient that way" (Acar, 2007: 54), he explains with what I suggest here is a reformulation of Kuispers' example of pro-social American redneck humour (see chapter one). Acar embraces the stigmatisation native Germans associate inferior Turkishness with, especially when it refers to adolescent male Muslims who are categorically "unreliable, hot-headed, and emotionally unstable up to the last inch of their frosted tips" (Acar, 2007: 16).

Acar, like Pamuk, upends the clichéd images of Turkish migrants which Germans put to the ethnic minority even after 50 years. His advice to Germans is to learn from Turkish lifestyles rather than to demand like Thilo Sarrazin that Turks should assimilate to be more German and less Turkish. Acar's opinion that Germans could benefit from some Turkish passion may remind the reader of Hatice Akyün's *A Spicy Kraut*. "Having a chilled out Köfte BBQ in the city park without permission" (Acar: 43) refers to Pamuk's dismissal of the Germans' obsession with order in *Allah Has Mercy, a German Janitor Doesn't*. His anger at cultural patronisation is evident, yet again not phrased in anger when Acar writes in the final section of his novel as a direct address to the German reader, "Now you know enough about them to take part in the integration of the German Turks. Get a CD of Ferdi Tayfur or Sezen Aksu. Roll down your window when you're going for a cruise in your car and turn up the volume as soon as you spot a Turk. They'll totally dig it" (Acar: 110).

The last lines of *The Real Deal Turks* seem to encapsulate an insight into how Germans consume ethnic difference through reductive knowledge about other Germans. They are also exemplary of Gray's simple opposition of Venus and Mars. Dick-lit characters like Hornby's male heroes use black-and-white thinking first to deconstruct and subsequently to reconstruct their masculinities in line with, or against, the mainstream norm. Acar treats such mutually exclusive thinking as a self-fulfilling prophecy. He ironises the alignment of gender with ethnic identity to express his concern about the Germans' assessment of minority identities as authentic versus inauthentic males. This plays out in Acar's novel as episodic accounts of him growing up in Germany as a second-generation Turkish German, whom the locals accepted only when he behaved according to the Germans' expectations. Acar suggests that German men want to see Turkish German men as Other males who threaten both German and Turkish German women. There are stock images of Turkish German men as Islamic extremists, abusive fathers or brutal husbands who trick both unsuspecting Turkish German and German women into marriage and then show their true colours. These types are, however, nowhere to be seen in the urban German landscape Acar tells of in his book.

Turkish German men who consider themselves utterly normal bear the brunt of contemporary debates about cultural authenticity in Germany. I have shown in chapter two how they are accused of pretence if they are not visually Turkish or deemed inauthentic if they refute gendered clichés. *The Real Deal Turks* toys with the idea that Turkish German men come from a different world from German men, specifically in terms of romance. Even more revealing than a lack of problematic integration discourse is thus Acar's critical opinion on more and less desirable ethnicities in the context of romantic relationships. Love, courtship and romance appear as the central themes in his novel and most of the other novels discussed here. I explained in chapters two and three that interethnic love elicits a reaction from mainstream audiences like no other notion of cultural fusion. And again, I would point for this to the much-cited two-world paradigm which German chick-lit and dick-lit authors undermine in different scenarios in their novels.

Turkish German novelists such as Acar and Pamuk use dick-lit comedy to reclaim the right to be any kind of man and masculinity they wish to be, and they represent this confidence as part of their dick literature. The humorous appropriation exemplifies the contemporary state of Muslim German fiction and non-fiction: "The enforcement of a duty of authentic and yet at the same time essentialist depiction of suffering from Turkish Otherness leads to writers working though The Guy Turk or The Girl Turk with comedy" (El Hissy, 2012: 42). Another second-generation Turkish German comedian and author, Murat Topal, features last in this chapter. Like Pamuk and Acar, he, too, opts for comedic subversion of traditional Germanness and Turkishness. This strategy pokes fun at the Germans' obsession with foreigners to choose between authentic Turkish and authentic German masculinity.

Murat Topal: Identity Construction

Murat Topal thematises ethnicity and identity formation in his two novels *Der Bülle von Kreuzberg-Kebab Cop* (2010) and *Das Dach kommt später-Rooftop Goes Up Later* (2012). The topics manifest as acts of identification and actual construction work. When Germans doubt Topal's Germanness and his right to be in Germany, he takes this on by creating a place for himself and his family in German society. In his first autobiographical novel Topal speaks of his childhood and his first job. He was born to a first-generation migrant father from rural Turkey and a German mother. Later, he became a policeman in the migrant-heavy Kreuzberg district of Berlin. The second novel is the narrative of how Topal tries to build a house for his young family (Topal, 2012: 1). The cop-turned-comedian sets out to fulfil the manliest of man dreams in German society: "Family, I shall build us a home!" (Topal: 2). *Kebab Cop* and *Rooftop Goes Up Later* resemble Akyün's *A Spicy Kraut*, as Topal invites the reader with his novels into the private realm of a Turkish German's allegedly hybrid everyday life. That he ironises what Yeşilada terms the "look beyond the veil" (Yesilada: 117) as a "look beyond the Turko moustache" suggests a laid-back dick-lit attitude I have discussed in Acar's work.

The most urgent task for Topal in his first novel is to highlight that he is not a cliché Turk despite his physical appearance. He writes about his looks, "Tall, broad-shouldered, and by now without hair, shaved off by choice, one should say" (Topal, 2010: 6). Topal confirms on the first pages of *Kebab Cop* that underneath the bouncer-like appearance there is a softie. What he sees as more fitting for a description of his visual appearance would be a Turkish version of Mr Clean. He is all smiles and ready to scrub toilets harder than any German housewife ever has. The incongruity between Topal's self-description and his perception by Germans as Other is obvious. In a graduation photo of his trainee class at the Berlin police academy, remarks Topal, he stood out like a sore thumb in the middle of a sea of blonde, blue-eyed German men. The same is true for an old picture of his primary school class (Topal: 6). Yet, he concludes that this was a good thing, because his parents and friends and other family members always had an easy time spotting him in the crowd compared to the identical blondes (Topal: 6).

Pamuk and Acar dismiss the issue of stereotypical appearance. Topal makes it the centre of his novel, just as Akyün does in her first book. He jokes frequently in *Kebab Cop* that he has learned to enjoy the status of a German hidden in plain sight, an ethnic chameleon. This plays on the two-worlds idea and assimilation as overblown concepts which are only skin-deep. The second-generation Turkish German man has learned to capitalise on his perceived Turkishness in the same way that in chapter three I described Kaya Yanar has with his ethnic comedy. Turkish German men like Yanar and Topal speak little to no Turkish and have never lived or associated their identity with Turkey; that is, other than to play it as a joke in their stand-up routines. Instead of rallying angrily against reductive identification as Turkish Others, they express their objection to incongruous ideas about their identities by tricking people with racialised expectations.

The prime example of how Topal laughs off misidentification by German natives is the chapter called 'To protect and to swerve'. The title character, Topal's *Kebab Cop*, deals with racist attacks on his persona on a regular basis. His professional life is no exception. During the arrest of a "skinnie", as Topal refers to a German Neo-Nazi skinhead he catches red-handed in the verbal abuse of an African migrant, he puts on a fake Turkish accent close to Erkan and Stefan's performance described in chapter three. One should note that Kaya Yanar does the same in his ethnic drag performances in *Whatcha Looking At?!*. "'Ey Dude", says Topal dressed in a German police uniform, "you got's trouble ther' or whad? Do I slam you in the slamma!" (Topal: 118). The reader knows that Topal has reached his goal when the disbelieving attitude of the German skinhead who is being arrested turns to sheer shock as the scene progresses. "'I want a real German police officer! Immediately!!! I do know my right!'" (Topal: 118), he yells. Topal reacts with humour to the racist man's disregard for the police uniform and his undeniable status as a German officer of the law. He responds in jest while keeping up the ethnic charade: "'You right?'—Some low hanging fruit that was!—'You right about what? Is no problem, can also take you to jai-ail, you be right there, too'" (Topal: 118).

Topal relishes in the sudden reversal of cultural authority. He considers it a sign of actual multiculturalist progress and relief from having to do this alone when his colleagues jump on the ethnic comedy bandwagon. The co-workers add further horror to the duped Nazi's worst nightmare of being arrested by foreigners in his own country. Two female, blonde colleagues of Topal put on thick Russian accents while a male colleague answers with an Eastern European twang the plea of the racist for a real German policeman: "Whurr arr the haandcufffs?" (Topal: 119). The Germans de-escalate the drama before it even begins. According to Topal, the whole troupe laughed heartily all the way back to headquarters while the racist German was utterly puzzled by this scenario (Topal: 119).

Scenes from the day-to-day life of a German policeman with Turkish looks reveal a casual racism. Those experiences of casual racism in Germany receive sustained attention by Pamuk and Acar. The two authors write about it, like Topal, in a witty and informal tone to assure readers that Turkish German men can respond with class rather than retributive violence. Schmidt points to anger issues as the motif most problematically linked to Turkish German masculinity and literary depictions of Muslim men in German society (Schmidt: 200). Topal is aware of this. He contributes in *Rooftop Goes Up Later* thematically to the prominence of debates about non-native and Muslim German men and about domesticity. The cover page of the second novel alludes to this with a stick figure drawing. What is supposed to look like a man wearing a construction helmet is holding a baby's pushchair with the left hand. With his right hand he is doing construction work. It is a reference to both the two-world paradigm of Turkish German hybridity and the gender bind of modern women featuring so vividly in Akyün's chick-lit.

Topal is quick to assure the reader that he did not force his wife into marriage and that it was not arranged. In fact, he admits that it is hard for him even to get a word in edgeways at home. This is always true when his Swabian wife from the German Alps and Topal's German mother with a love for Prussian discipline decide what is best for him (Topal, 2012: 2). The confession ironises the cliché of the Turkish husband who locks up his wife behind bars after the wedding and separates her from the family. Nothing could be further from reality in *Rooftop Goes Up Later*. Topal's in-laws pay regular visits to "Muratle", as his wife's mother calls him in one of Germany's local Alpine dialects (Topal: 12). The visits make Topal feel more confined than usual in his small rental flat in central Berlin. The in-laws also trigger his wish to escape from the many nagging Germans in his life. The nagging motivates him to dream up a German "self-built home, the kind that makes a real man, well, real" (Topal: 19). It is not he, but German women who run his life, so he must be more proactive. Topal closes the first chapter, "Haya, Haya, Build a Home", not with a Turkish proverb as Akyün often does when she talks about her Turkish German family in *A Spicy Kraut*, but with his mother-in-law's regional wisdom of wise, German-Alps-dwelling people (Topal: 11): "Muratle, my little dearle, see reason. If you only ever live in a flatle, then you'll die in the end on rentle" (Topal: 12).

Hilarity ensues accordingly. The dick-lit counter-discourse to prevailing horror scenarios of patriarchal and bossy Turkish German men intensifies with each step of the construction, from property purchase to the finishing touches of the title's rooftop. Topal has two left thumbs when it comes to handiwork. This undermines the Turkish macho cliché as much as his Turkish father's incompetence in doing construction work. The old Topal is similarly incompetent at being a rugged, male craftsman. Father and son decide to include real German men in the construction project after several near-fatal accidents with chainsaws and diggers for hire by the hour. However, what Gill calls "instructive older masculinities in dick-lit" (Gill: 26) fail regardless of the ethno-national credentials attached to them. The 92-year-old German Gerd is as useless as Topal's father. "Building a house as per official regulations" (Topal: 43), what kind of German man making it through WWII would have ever heard of that? The response comes swiftly and with a bang as the trio try to dig a hole for the foundations of the house but hit solid rock. A colossal explosion is the direct result of two clueless Turkish German men who are handling construction-site explosives under the direction of an equally clueless German man.

German perceptions of Turkish German masculinity are ridiculed numerous times by the time construction finishes at the end of the story. All the acts of positively imbecilic males and masculine hubris shed new light on the question of who the real boss in Turkish German families is. Akyün points out that it is not the men, either German or Turkish. Topal confirms this with the perfect answer to a question raised by Akyün about German masculinity: "[s]ometimes I wonder where in the world German men left all their testosterone?" (Akyün, 2007: 146), Akyün asks. "At the local building regulations office" (Topal: 34), speculates Topal. Though neither Akyün nor Topal rejects the notion of gendered Turkishness or Germanness as such. They seem to agree instead that an attribution of gender roles to ethnicities is an everyday stereotype over which one inevitably stumbles in the domestic spheres of German society.

CHAPTER V

Funny Online Kanakism

"Jilet Ayse "Ghettobraut aus Berlin Neukölln"! Isch schwöre isch bin Türkin und raste aus, wenn mir was nicht passt! BAM! Auf die Fresse!"
"Jilet Ayse "Ghetto braud from Little Istanbul in Berlin" I tells you I's a Turk lady and I go crazy if I don't like something! WHAM! Punch you in the face!"

—Idil Baydar's introduction to her online comedy channel on YouTube, performing as her alter ego, Jilet Ayse (Baydar, 2011)

Summary

This chapter deals with the most recent phenomenon of contemporary Turkish German comedy. A new generation of Turkish German comedians republishes content like recorded live performances and televised appearances to online platforms or uses digital media to publish original work. Enormous online viewership segments and a wide range of affordable, high-resolution recording devices such as hand-held cameras and even smartphones have created a new way for comedy to circulate in and across different types of mass media. Embedded in message boards, review sites, blogs and social media apps, a digital entertainment world has flourished, often competing with, if not overtaking in its reach, the impact of traditional screen media that are television and cinema. The online world serves niche characters such as Jilet Ayse in publishing her cliché-ridden satire videos without the use of an intermediary. Several short to medium-length clips of ad hoc performances and republished content form a hyperlinked body of Turkish German online comedy, all connected through user preference algorithms and audience interactions. Sometimes fans edit or comment upon primary materials, thus creating a meta-discourse around the original performance.[1] This chapter contends that new media comedians like Jilet Ayse, a fictional persona created by Turkish German comedian Idil Baydar and the Turkish German stand-up Osan Yaran, spearhead the second-generation movement of Turkish German humour culture without filling stadiums like Bülent Ceylan or Kaya Yanar. Of the popular culture platforms these new comedians are using, YouTube has become the primary site in which Turkish German Muslim content producers and consumers can interact with global users to present a fuller spectrum of ethnic essentialism and religious bias in 21st-century Germany.

Counterhegemonic Framing of Ethnic and Cultural Diversity in YouTube Comedy

At the end of the second decade of the new century, it may not be surprising that Turkish German comedians are widely publishing their comedy on YouTube to thematise their faith, their cultural values, their ethnic identity and their kind of Germanness as part of their comedy. The online streaming portal offers them easy access to global audiences, who consume the content in German or aided by closed captions and situate it in ethno-cultural discourses through user comments and/or comedian-user interactions. YouTube was launched in 2005 as a video streaming website. It "provided a very simple, integrated interface within which users could upload, publish, and view streaming videos without high levels of technical knowledge, and within the technological constraints of standard browser software and relatively modest bandwidth" (Burgess and Green, 2009: 1). When Google bought YouTube in 2006, it added tools to facilitate copyright infringement and digital piracy, to block users who pirated content or to monetise on content via advertisement integration. This meant content producers could make money off their copyright material and, eventually, form larger and more complex YouTube channel networks (Snickars and Vonderau, 2009). Another important factor to mention here is that YouTube content is usually prone to less regulation than state-run or even private broadcasting and other mainstream media (see the educational mandate for German state-run television in chapter three), which means that comedians like Serdar Somuncu can try their hand at different and perhaps less tame content than they present to mainstream audiences on broadcast television (Bower, 2012).

Turkish German comedians have capitalised on YouTube's connection of revenue with views and clicks or hit counts. The cultural economy of YouTube as an entertainment institution sustains the development of their comedy's counter-hegemonic potential. Turkish German comedy has gained visibility for its mission to further the sense of Turkish German agency and Turkish German screen power (Yeşilada, 2008) I described in the introduction with reference to cinema and television. One can align this argument with similar claims about Afro-American, Indian American, Asian American and Muslim Canadian comedy in digital screen cultures as laid out by Bore and Bradley (Bore, 2017; Bradley, 2015).

It is the concern about contemporary representation which the Turkish German comedians discussed in this chapter echo in their recorded and republished comedy performances, developing projects and original scripted sketches. They tease out the complexities of Turkishness and Muslimness by turning normal everyday experiences about narrow definitions of what it means to be Turkish or Muslim in German society into enjoyable YouTube entertainment. In mainstream screen media and even in popular print fiction, traditional commissioning and production practices cannot compete with the ease of making content for YouTube or releasing copyrighted material there under the company's Creative Commons licence. According to Tofler, this holds true for costs of production, labour costs and adherence to cinema screen and television broadcasting regulations (Tofler, 2017: 820). Shareability is another factor. Online content is usually of shorter length, and longer, existing work can be edited down to a series of brief clips and interlinked highlight reels. Highly visible YouTube content also attracts increased sponsorship deals or funding opportunities for future commissions. In this context the online environment offers emergent comedy artists, developers and performers a potentially viral performance stage.

Stehle and Smith-Prei have proven the potential of online popularity as an effective public forum in their case studies on Turkish German rapper turned academic, Dr Reyhan Şahin/Lady Bitch Ray. "LOL likes" can draw the attention of millions to marginalised Turkish German voices like those of a "hyper-sexualized 'ghetto bitch'" (Stehle, 2012: 229). The popularity principle underlying what Smith-Prei calls Şahin's "pop-feminist aesthetic [derived from] the depiction of negatively coded female corporeality" (Smith-Prei, 2011: 1) also underpins the digital representations of what it means to be Turkish German and a woman in the age of identity politics. Like Lady Bitch Ray's Turkish German music videos, the popular entertainment genre of Turkish German comedy bears out a negatively coded ethnic Otherness, too. However, the producers of Turkish German online comedy express issues of migration, gender and assimilation explicitly through forms of pro-social ethnic humour I described in chapters one and two to elicit enjoyable user reactions. A closer look at comment threads attached to YouTube content by Idil Baydar and Osan Yaran suggests that viewers participate in this pro-social project, actively including themselves as both external and Turkish German in-group participants in the dismantling of ethnic hierarchism and allegedly improper behaviour for "Germans with Turkish immigrant background" (Tuzcu, 2013: 157).

Idil Baydar: Positioning "Jilet Ayse" as Relatable Migration Comedy on YouTube

The user comments posted in response to the landing page video on Jilet Ayse's YouTube channel frame the overdrawn Turkish "Kanak" (Mayroth, 2016) clichés she performs as relatable comedy entertainment.[2] In the video clip, which is only 42 seconds long, a half total shot shows Jilet Ayse sitting on a red velvet couch. There are colourful pillows draped neatly around her. A small pot plant stands on a knee-high coffee table. Viewers can only barely make it out in the lower half of the frame. Jilet's long hair is high, poofed-up, teased out on top and pinned back at the sides into a fauxhawk. She wears glossy, bright red lipstick and lots of makeup and rouge. She is dressed in a printed nylon windcheater, zipped open to reveal a t-shirt which reads "WALLAH! I AIN'T DONE ANYHTING".[3] It is a play on the Arab phrase for "I swear" and the pronunciation of a German phrase, meaning "It wasn't me", and said to refer to a certain Turkish German sociolect used in Turkish German comedy as a shorthand accent. This is "Germany's migration nightmare" (Mayroth, 2016) and comedy Youtuber Baydar puts it on full blast in her high-res video.

Jilet welcomes the audience with a spoof take on Turkish German girlie talk. This aspect of the performance is a remnant of Baydar's early comedy days starting around 2010. She was reportedly more "entertainment-savvy" (Mayroth, 2016) and made fun of German television events such as pop-cast act Monrose, which consisted between 2006 to 2010 of Turkish German singer Senna Guemmour, Turkish German singer Bahar Kızıl and Italian German singer and actress Mandy Capristo. Making fun of being a Mandy, who became famous for dating Turkish German soccer star Mesut Özil, eventually landed Baydar a freelance job with *Bild Zeitung*, Germany's largest daily tabloid. However, the satirical Mandy impersonation, a throwback to Baydar's early skits as a Turkish vlogger princess with a ludicrous baby voice like Gülcan Karahancı's during her days as an oversexed music channel host on German broadcasting station VIVA, disappears in a matter of seconds. Switching gears drastically, Jilet suddenly makes a face and starts yelling right into the camera with her upper body hunched forward in a menacing way and her voice switching to a baritone register, "Eyy, FUCK YOU!!

Okay?! You're on my channel! Who do you think you are? Why you think you can just come over here on my channel and step all over it?! Watch out, dude, there'll be some punches going straight to your ugly face!! What you wanna find here? Hey!? Well, lemme tell you what you'll find here: you gonna find the crime, the victims, and the perps!! Do you get my drift?! Don't get onto my channel! Because, if I'm too STRONG, you're just too WEAK!!"

Users posting in the public comment section below the video address Baydar's creative talent and her ability to pack a lot of anti-racist humour into a very short video recording:

> You totally had me after only 10 seconds :D

> I come to this channel and i see this...i can't stop laughing anymore hahaha that woman is amazing

> i love your videos jilet !! 🖤 that's why i came to your channel please don't hit me 😄😄😄😄😄😄

> Perfection. Don't let them intimidate you, ever. Solid woman of honour. If you need anything...message me. Have subscribed you.

The comments indicate that YouTube users appreciate the character of Jilet Ayse. Some seek it out specifically because her kind of relatable, short-clip or teaser-sketch content may not be available elsewhere. Certainly, the comedy standard on television and in cinema, as I described in chapters two and three, is different from Baydar's fictional character. Ayse hails from Berlin-Tempelhof, a so-called problem area. She is loud, dressed to exacerbate demands for cultural integration of ethnic Others' visual appearance, and she uses a cliché-ridden Turkish German accent while employing explicit language. All this would require censorship on television or necessitate film regulation labelling, or at least would have to go through the official route of broadcast censoring and cinema content oversight. Because of the style, tone and innovative take on ethnicity at the intersection with social class, comedy critics frequently employ comparisons between Baydar's Jilet Ayse and German stand-up comedian Illka Bessin's popular character, East German Cindy from Marzhan. Cindy hails from Berlin's notorious blue-collar sector, Marzhan. Her origins mirror Jilet's imagined origins in Berlin Tempelhof, a migrant-heavy blue-collar district. Both women are loud, uncouth and stand out among online comedians for their play on being mainstream culture's anxieties incarnate. Cindy is the nightmare of allegedly encultured high-brow Germanness. Jilet Ayse's character embodies the fears of all Germans who fantasise about non-integrated and anti-assimilation Turks, namely nasty Turkish migrant women whose bodies and personas take up uncensored media space online "without asking for permission or forgiveness" (Şahin et al., 2016: 121).

The reception of Ayse's rebellious comedy performance is overly positive in YouTube's comment section. On Twitter her handle's description reads:

> I'm budiful, my favurite designer is Adidas, I luv my dog Massacre Fatma and my 8 cell's CUZ YOLO IN THE SWAG[4]

Like most user comments on YouTube, Twitter users also showed support for Baydar's comedy persona and reacted positively when she joined the messaging service in December of 2012 with the following tweet:

> Ey ohh victim cuntz, jilet ayse is on Twitter now !!!

A fan reacted to this by tweeting:

> The only thing that really made it all worth it driving to Sava Nald [and their designer runway show at Berlin Fashion Week] was the fact that I met @jiletayse. And now, it's time for some Dürüm [Kebab wrap]!

On Instagram Baydar tends to posts 10-second shorts she tapes at home on her smartphone. While these appear less produced than her YouTube videos, and some of the videos seem to be spontaneous, unscripted improvisations, thousands of her followers appreciate the over-the-top physical comedy quality of Jilet's rants and ramblings about German politics and German popular culture.

This comment was posted in response to Jilet's video post about a soccer game in which a Brazilian player makes her want to get naked and "make love to him with her child-bearing hips":

> @so4loe 😂😂😂😂😂 Dedicated and Expressively Eloquent that woman 😊 😊

The audience feedback and direct interactions of users with Baydar's comedy content shed light on the politics of German popular culture entertainment in digital transnational media contexts. The explicit language and imagery frame the Turkish German comedian's critique of objectifying and sexualising Turkishness and Turkish women, especially when it comes to the depiction of female Turkish German bodies, language and the historic discourse on media representations of ethnic German Others in Germany (Stehle, 2012).

Baydar's comedy content turns on a mockery of Turkish German femininity ideals by her being a butch, big and unrestrained loudmouth. The way Jilet acts is in total incongruence with accepted forms of being an integrated Turkish German woman in German society, as has become apparent in the romantic clash comedies I discussed in chapter two. From a circumspect look at gender-marked usernames who post comments both in Turkish and in German on YouTube, Twitter, Tumblr and Instagram, it seems that a broad cross-section of Turkish German and native German female online users appreciates the incongruity humour of Baydar's Turkish German anti-lady. Users' largely favourable embrace of Baydar's online comedy is essential and moves her into the vicinity of female American comedy giants with relatable comedy routines. Amy Schumer and Tiffany Haddisch are two prominent contemporary examples of this.

The ironic performativity of Baydar's fictional projection from "Turkish ditz" to "Turkish mob wife" to "Twitter She Turk" and "Insta-Kanak", all identifiers Jilet Ayse uses to describe herself, points to the possibility of online media as a space for intelligent pop comedy (Goltz, 2015). Given the current climate of online trolling and Twitter abuse of comedy artists like American comedian Kevin Hart for perceived minority bias in his comedy routines about gay men (Romano, 2018), digital audience support for Jilet suggests that audiences are in on the joke with her. According to Tully, acceptance by the mainly female online audience is possible because younger female comedians have learned to turn a post-feminist logic around, thus letting women off the hook if they dare to laugh at "incongruous [identity] performance strategies: mimicking patriarchal logics, inverting the grotesque, and juxtaposing serious feminist issues with parodies of frivolous pop culture texts" (Tully, 2017: 339). Jilet is likable because she is relatable. She refrains from pseudo-satire and from reproducing the dominant ideology of anti-social ethnic humour, which would be to bash German women as anti-female or anti-Turkish, or by mocking only qualities perceived as typically female German.

However, Baydar's performances also make fun of the general integration debate in Germany. This political aspect positions her doubly as an active participant in the discussion on female voice in a patriarchal discourse and male-dominated comedy landscape (Stehle, 2012). Speaking as a female Turkish German comedian through the performative mask of a Turkish German woman is the context for the recurring thread of migrant Otherness. It features constantly in Jilet's YouTube videos. The continuity of theme and topic suggests that airing German minorities' discontents about a continually negative framing of Turkish German identities, specifically by female comedians for female audiences, has not diminished in the 21st century; on the contrary, "marginalized female comics provide particularly interesting examples of autobiographical performance. Because they represent a group marginalized by the dominant (male) culture, female comics rhetorically construct and perform their marginality onstage. In so doing, they perform both self and culture, exemplifying for audiences the inevitable interdependence between personal and social identities. [...] Their social critique is potent and, because it is offered in a comedic context, safe from retribution as well" (Gilbert, 1997: 317).

In this sense, female comedians like Baydar perform their marginality through rebel personas like Jilet Ayse. It is an act "simultaneously oppressive, by using demeaning stereotypes, and transgressive, by interrogating those very stereotypes through humorous discourse" (Gilbert, 1997: 318). Baydar's present and past work confirms that this interplay is very much deliberate. She skilfully pairs opposite identities, subverts social hierarchies. And she offers thousands of online users a brief relief from the dutiful reprimand of online users who support ethnic Turkish stereotyping; and from having to police female gender clichés. Other aliases or phrases Baydar has used to describe Jilet to German mass media outlets and in online interviews demonstrate this pop-feminist awareness. There are "migration nightmare", "Germany's Future" and "National Kanak". Though, despite the praise for her ingenuity, Baydar's work has not received universal approval. There is some criticism of the way she leaves her comedy's intended message up for interpretation, which reinforces the clichés about Turkish Germans rather than subverts them.

Some YouTube users have picked up on a sense of ambiguity in her depiction of Jilet Ayse. What I describe in chapter two as a form of misunderstood pro-social "shield" comedy is related to Turkish women as the butt of the joke and the target of her ridicule. Spielhaus picks up on this, too. She confirms in an analysis of a sketch on domestic abuse that Jilet is a smart, albeit not unproblematic pro-social ethnic comedy act, the kind which ultimately led to US comedian Dave Chappelle's initial withdrawal from comedy and him walking away from a 50 million dollar contract with Comedy Central (Haggins, 2009): "[h]ere [with

Jilet Ayse's take on domestic abuse] hides a cathartically designed incongruity within the dominant image of the Muslim woman, whose aggressive and potentially threatening exterior may hardly want to fit the image of an oppressed victim" (Spielhaus: 127). Whereas many German newspapers and culture magazines lauded Baydar's observational prowess and Jilet's sharp-tongued wit for her routine *Deutschland, wir müssen reden!-Germany, we have to have a talk!*, some YouTube users expressed their dismay in the comment section of a short video entitled *Ich bin voll sauer!!!-I am sooo mad!!!*, maybe because it was not clear who Jilet was making fun of:

> We ask ourselves if you are a comedian who makes fun of Kanaks or of the Germans, who still think that that's what Turks are like

One could argue that this issue highlights the weak point of the comedic mode in popular culture. I described it in chapter one with reference to Göktürk's interrogation of audience taste and comedic subjectivity. Online comedy entertainment's simultaneous strength and weakness is contextual breadth, making for imprecise notions of certain members of the audience as an indistinct mass of subjects and/or objects of humour. It blurs the line between the sword and shield functions in ethnic comedy. The pro-feminist attitude of Baydar's fantasy figure as Thilo Sarrazin's worst nightmare illustrates this. Jielt Ayse is evil personified according to Sarrzin's theses about Turkish Muslim migration to Germany. She is a model of female Turkish self-determination Baydar said was created in direct response to Sarrazin's demagogic hallucinations of Turkish German Muslims as hostile, parasitical enemies to native German culture (Kloë, 2016: 210). "At the same time, Jilet's statements take Thilo Sarrazin's points to the extreme" (Kloë: 210), which flies in the face of German idealism about feminist "multi-culti" sisterhood. In *Germany, we have to have a talk!*, Jilet calls her Turkish German sister an integration whore. Jilet also rejects any notion of German female independence in response to the question whether her boyfriend is allowed to hit her in the face. He is. "I does then so deserve this! After all, he [Ayak, Jilet's boyfriend], buys me my clothes, all Adidas, and he's also wanting some kiddos sometime, too. Eight or nine units, but, sometimes, you gotta put a woman in her place, ey, you get me, just like a dog" (Baydar, November 2017).

It is hard to draw the line here between association and dissociation and pro-social and anti-social. The ethnic identity Baydar performs and her goal to affirm Turkish clichés as an outlet for reactionary racism depend on the audience's active engagement in critical entertainment. Most viewers indicate on social media and in their YouTube comments that they align themselves with Baydar's agenda. They laugh because they allow and fully buy into the comedian's carnivalesque transgression, which is to depict Turkish women in an unflattering light. It is clearly a performative comedy mask, but a small number of viewers voice their concerns about criticising anti-Turkish bias in Germany with a carnevalesque line of counter-hegemonic humour. This has prompted YouTube users in support of Baydar's content to engage more critically with the material and offer interpretations of her videos to other, more sceptical viewers. Some of those videos manage to get 1,500,000 views:[5]

> This is critical social satire, I can still cannot believe that some would even think about taking this acting for real. It's genius work ! Idil Baydar taekes on the role of Jilet Ayse and talks about things that are being stereotyped in public, the good think about all of this is, that one should also turn on their brains phps while watching, the whole thing serves not just to entertain, there's a lot more in there by far.

> Well if you take this too seriously and you feel like you're being attached then you really missed out on what's goin on big time xD

> It is sad how many people didn't read the small phrase "critical social satire"... folx, when will you finally get it: This is NOT meant to be bone dead serious! "Satire is a form of poetic mockery, which bemoans societal issues or points to a lack of virtue. Historically, it has also been referred to as Mock Writing, Needling Words and Pasquill (a mocking social satire expressed in writing about a certain group of people)" When I read your (mostly misspelled) hate-comments, it's ME who gets mad!

> And me just like: ulan is he a girl?! hahahahahahahaha laughflash oh maii god xD I am a lady Turk too :D you have to have a sense of humour about this ;D

From this perspective, Turkish German online comedy consumed through platforms like YouTube appears to be a powerful mainstream culture discourse in which to reframe anti-Muslim sentiments and Turkish bias. Yet, Critchley admits that one cannot attribute this critical effect to humour as such, since not all humour is the same and some jokes are quite reactionary or, at best, serve simply to reinforce social consensus (Critchley, 2013). Despite the intention that it work as a form of pro-social ethnic comedy, audiences may understand Baydar's Jilet comedy act as a tool to reinforce dominant ideologies or to reproduce stereotypes. Therefore, it is vital to acknowledge that mass mediated humour always carries the potential to achieve its opposite in terms of consent and dissent, building in-group coherence and the formation of inter-communal alliances.

It is important to consider Baydar's wider comedy repertoire against this backdrop. Her line of characters shows that cases of well-received inter-ethnic and transcultural comedy mostly work because their incongruities reveal the stupidity of racists and the ineffectiveness of political correctness. Gerda Grischke, a German retiree and shameless blue-collar xenophobe, is a case in point. Baydar describes in an interview with RENK Magazine for Theatre and Stage Performance how she developed Grischke's character at the same time as the figure of Jilet Ayse around Christmas 2011: "They were created at the same time. I had developed Gerda for a smaller theatre play and I just found Jilet on the street. Back then I was working in a few [Berlin] schools so I could observe a lot" (Karakus/RENK 2017). In the interview Baydar explains what some perceive as hurtful mockery in her characters and how they embody ethnic differences. Some viewers think of it as improper while others see it as a much-needed intervention in politically correct and hence futile discussions about how communities in German society relate to each other and why that is the case.

> **Currently, Gerda is in Jilet's shadow. [RENK]**
> True, but I think it has to be like that. They both tell the same story, actually. Maybe I can just convey it more authentically with Jilet. What many people don't know is that the lives of the two figures overlap. Aside from the whole other stuff that she spouts off, Jilet also talks about her sister who has a boyfriend—the son of Gerda Grischke. [BAYDAR]
>
> **Can you describe Gerda and Jilet for us? [RENK]**
> The German Gerda hurts to listen to. The whole subtext that you hear from old grandmas: Should we be scared of foreigners now? Maybe we should just let the Indians in? Gerda expresses quite directly. "They don't mean nothin' bad by it. I ain't got nothin' against foreigners in foreign countries, you know. But you can't 'ave them here, too, innit? That's why they call them foreigners, darlin'. Cos they ain't here!" Jilet is angrier and is more associated with being funny. It's a little like the small, always angry Frenchman Louis

de Funès. The angry tells a story that is so funny that you almost forget the pain in it.

You can find them both in the same socio-cultural milieu. Both are poor, both are losers of the system. On paper, Gerda did everything right: She worked hard her whole life but now receives such little pension that she has to turn tricks behind Bellevue Palace. And because someone has to get blamed, it's the foreigner. [BAYDAR]

There is a paradoxical interplay of conflict and commonality between Jilet and Gerda. It is a remarkable complexity. Neither character contains the full truth about the lived realities of everyday life in Germany. Yet, both turn on the same overloaded popular comedy elements with trashy talk and nasty behaviour unbecoming of German middle-class women. One could argue that Baydar appropriates the best of both worlds, deliberately mixing a theatrical feminist performance logic with many "well-known features of German ethno-comedy: similar to characters of typical 'culture-clash'-comedians such as Kayar Yanar or Bülent Ceylan" (Bens et al., 2019: 77):

Do Jilet and Gerda bother you sometimes? [RENK]
They've completely occupied me, and because Idil is such a wuss, it doesn't bother her. In reality, Idil is a German hidden in the body of a Turk! [BAYDAR]

So you don't separate them and say, "It's six o'clock, Jilet's clocking out!"? [RENK]
No way! It's 24/7 craziness. Sometimes it gets on my nerves so much that I just play Farmville excessively and tell people I'm really busy. [BAYDAR]

The participatory online culture of YouTube has helped Baydar achieve what she set out to do. It is to construct a Turkish German comedy identity, which is meant to ask of both Turkish Germans and Germans a degree of reflective involvement in the consumption of her online comedy. The political dimensions of this effort seem obvious.

But to what extent does Jilet's role benefit these people? Doesn't it just stir up more prefabricated images in people's minds, in this case of teachers? [RENK]

If you are a teacher and claim that all your students are like Jilet and don't reflect at all about what is being disassembled on stage, then that's irresponsible. It is their job to question why Jilet is the way she is. [BAYDAR]

Baydar's character inventory, and the dialogue she puts Gerda and Jilet in with each other and with the audience watching them and reacting to them, indicates how YouTube online content can be a space for collective critical comedy experiences. It refers to the ongoing distinctions and polemic projections within the general German public, who may connect the screen culture discourse to the dangers of a political right-wing upswing in actual reality.

That means your wish is that people begin questioning things when you are on stage? [RENK]
People should think about whether or not it is actually reality. [BAYDAR]

Having countered the claim that Baydar's online comedy could potentially facilitate a certain bourgeois intellectual superiority over a social class which allegedly never participates in anti-racist discourse, I move on to the comedy practice of another popular, contemporary Turkish German comedian. I discuss in the final section of this book how republished Turkish German comedy content on YouTube produces a kind of second-hand curation of ethnic comedy. I suggest that the question of how Turkish German comedy travels across media is indispensable from questions of social pragmatics of humour and the different spheres of popular entertainment culture and ethnic identity debates.

Osan Yaran: Breaking Down Walls between TV Screening and YouTube Streaming

The online presence of Turkish German comedian Osan Yaran's comedy performances on YouTube has surged over a very short period. Yaran's most viewed live performance recordings to-date are live performances of televised stand-up comedy contests or appearances on German public television. The republished content on YouTube has been seen by millions of users. I discuss his most popular comedy content published since 2015. *Bitches und Beispiele-Bitches and Examples* went on YouTube in November 2015, followed by *The Walking Rentner-The Walking Retiree* in December 2017. *Mein Sohn-My Son* was posted to YouTube in March 2018; *Manchmal ist Deutschland ein bisschen zu Deutsch-Sometimes, Germany is a bit too German* went online in August 2019, then came *Deutsche Pünktlichkeit auf türkischer Hochzeit-German Punctuality at a Turkish Wedding* in October 2019.

In 2010, Yaran had started to cut his teeth on "Kleinkunst" or local art performance at small-scale poetry slams in East Berlin's migrant-heavy area of Spandau-Staaken. He had moved there with his family from Berlin's West German Wedding district. Yaran mentions the consequences of this move for his Turkish German identity formation on his website: "[t]hat's why one could say I'm basically an East-Turk, a Turkish Eastie Germanian, an Eastmanian!" (Yaran, 2019). While a full-time employee at German grocery discount store LIDL, he managed to book paid comedy gigs in stand-up clubs in Berlin and appeared at the famed Quatsch, or Nonsense, Comedy Club. The Quatsch/Nonense Comedy Club became famous in the 1990s for televising stand-up comedy on the private German broadcasting channel, ProSieben. Thanks to the free-to-air broadcast screenings of the Comedy Club's live performance acts, many German comedians managed to break into mainstream entertainment with Anglophile comedy formulas, as described in chapter three.

Yaran talks about his career moves as part of the info copy on his personal website's landing page: "I started working for LIDL when I was nineteen to pay for my wedding—Turkish weddings are not cheap! I started out as a cashier, then associate assistant manager, then deputy manager, and finally store manager. 2014 was when the comedy thing began" (Yaran, 2019). He broke into larger regional and finally national comedy circuits shortly after that and began looking at comedy as a full-time career in 2016.

The analysis of Yaran's comedy requires what Bore calls an understanding of the current trend in mainstream comedy's articulation as the "multi-sited phenomenon" (Bore, 2019: 7), which is modern multi-screen comedy. Technologically mediated communication challenges traditional contexts of screen study. The separation between television screens and computer screens has been radically erased two decades into the new century. Hine notes that mainstream comedy and popular mass culture studies research need to move with the times, tastes and technologies to deliver relevant findings on what this means for comedy entertainment: "[i]n a contemporary society within which the concept of context appears to have spiralled beyond comprehension with the advent of diverse forms of technologically mediated communication, the challenge of choosing appropriate contexts to study, and reflecting on the consequences of those choices for our ability to theorise adequately, seems greater than ever" (Hine, 2011: 567). It is for this reason that I consider the re-publishing of Yaran's award-winning comedy content (Hamburg Comedy Award 2017, Northern Germany Comedy Broadcast Winner 2017, Stuttgart Comedy Clash Winner 2019) conducive to the question about how Turkish German comedy travels between audiences and across different media types. There is then also the question of what kind of original comedy content YouTube users decide to reshare and how they react to it.

By resharing and commenting, the online community of YouTube users contributes actively to the anti-racist humour discourse of Turkish German Muslim artists such as Baydar and Yaran, who are the primary content producers. According to Haridakis and Hanson, this makes reshared Turkish German comedy part of an active social connection culture. Its participants are highly motivated to share, critique the content and connect with each other and even the primary producers. This is "consistent with uses and gratifications assumptions, motives and individual differences, differentially predicted viewing and sharing behaviors" in social media humour (Haridakis and Hanson, 2009: 317). Unlike television audiences, however, YouTube viewers seek out and watch in self-designed order online comedy videos because of a distinctly social aspect. YouTube as a social networking platform rewards pro-social behaviour, as users connect to each other through comments on the streaming content in the comment section. All this aligns the viewers' interpersonal motives such as inclusion, affection and control with Baydar's and Yaran's motivation for producing their ethnic comedy content in the first place. It is to include as many people as possible in the mainstream representation of cultural identities and belonging; to affect stability and positive developments in comedic genres; and to interrogate who controls the meanings, pleasures and displeasures one receives from transcultural comedy content.

Like Baydar's work, Yaran's comedy revolves around ethnic identity issues in contemporary German society. However, his focus on ethnicities in multicultural Germany is less antagonistic than Baydar's. He performs as himself, talking in his routines about everyday situations and personal experiences in Berlin. Much like Murat Topal's dick-lit comedy, he draws on his youth and upbringing and his work and personal life for content. Yaran's comedy elicits amusement by shifting the perception of quotidian issues in Germany from native German to Turkish German perspectives or the viewpoints of ethnic Others. This harks back to a less complicated American comedy act. Limon described it in his seminal work on stand-up comedy in the United States (Limon, 2000). It is driven by a form of relatability, in which meanings arise from nuanced though mostly light-hearted stances on current politics or debates about gender, racism and religious bias. Unlike Baydar, Yaran does not mobilise outrage or offence in the audience to put his message about cosmopolitan Germany to those attending his stand-up acts. One could call him more mainstream-minded. Jilet Ayse's provocative character works by positing that there is a kind of pro-social ethnic comedy which is most effective if it produces an uneasy coproduction of humour between content and viewer. Yaran's comedy reconciles that critical strand with more comfortable subjects without losing sight of enough reflexivity to point out that anti-Muslim bias and Turkish Othering have real implications for people's lives.

In *The Walking Retiree*, Yaran discusses slice-of-life observations in a sequence of loosely related events. He explores the intersection of multiple layers of daily life in Berlin. He moves from who-smelt-it-dealt-it fart jokes to welcoming a Dutch audience member by saying, "Ey, dude, this is such a relief! You guys, you know, I'm a Turk! It's so good to know that there's an even more Kanak person than me here tonight!". He then jumps immediately and without transition to a bit about Jehovah's Witnesses, framing the set-up by saying, "Ey, you know folks, I live in Berlin and I respect every faith we have here. But: my favourite religion by far are Jehovah's Witnesses. Ey, you must admit folks, it's not easy to place yourself in front of somebody's front door and then go: heyyyyy, you are wrong. WE are the chosen ones". He closes the bit with a short punchline, "Try this in the Turkish Quarter in Berlin, won't ya. Then you'll see for how much longer you're going to be the chosen one".

This bit, like other ethnic comedy bits in *The Walking Retiree*, puts recurring emphasis on cultural diversity rather than cultural difference. Yaran explains that he called the act *The Walking Retiree* to hint at the hit television series *The Walking Dead*, and for his love of watching zombieesque, shelf browsing senior citizens at LIDL. Yaran's live audience appreciates all jokes with equal bravado. It cheers for toilet humour and jokes about mistaking a couple of Jehovah's Witnesses as sex tourists. It cheers as loudly for his jokes about an imagined couple of Jihadi's Witnesses or a transsexual friend of Yaran's, calling herself Bayi-on-ceee after the sex change operation. "You know folks, so she says to me, 'Oh, I was afraid how you'd react, you know, because you're such a Muslim!'. And I go: Come on Bayi-on-ceee, where's the problem? It's all good—as long as you wear a headscarf now!".

Yaran's original performance intersperses the comedic thematisation of Muslim minority culture with somewhat critical goals. For one, there are efforts to correct misinformed views that he feels distort contemporary Turkish German identities. The audience laughs throughout his act, clapping and even whistling enthusiastically as he closes the act with an Other's take on Germanness: "You know folks, I love Germany, it's the best country ever, really. But sometimes it's a bit, you know, too German. Like when you drive on the Autobahn, and all of a sudden, there's a sign that says, CAREFUL! ROAD MARKINGS MISSING IN FOUR KILOMETRES! Dude, what's that all about?? I mean, what?? Like, do even the deer and the wildlife know about this when they cross the street? Really?? Do they?! Are they German deer? You'll have one tell another: 'Hey, Rudolph, we cannot cross the street here, because: there are no markings!'". The audience applauds loudly.

Yaran promotes social cohesion while encouraging the enjoyment of situational humour in incongruous culture swap scenarios. He addresses cultural attitudes held about Muslims from the inside, and attitudes held about German majority society as part of their community from the inside, too. The live audience seems to welcome his critical social message, as do hundreds of thousands of YouTube viewers. Most viewers comments favourably on Yaran's hybrid position as an equal-opportunity-butt-of-the-joke comedian. Users appear to like the fact that he defies the native-versus-Other logic of traditional ethnic comedy entertainment in favour of a non-regressive comedy to attack negative social attitudes rather than to reinforce them. The top post in the YouTube comment section of *The Walking Retiree* received 1,300 likes and zero dislikes or thumbs-downs for referring to this aspect of Yaran's work:

> This is the weapon which we can use to get rid of racism. If everybody could laugh like this about Muslims, Christians, Jews and all other religions, then we will all be closer to each other. We are all human and that should remain the most important thing. Just have some love for each other. :)

Other users continued their discussion of the re-published comedy act and the audience reactions in the live recording of *The Walking Retiree* by posting replies to the comment above as a meta-thread:

> You are right! ♥

> The only weapon there is to bring those people together. Unite the true and goodhearted people and show the Dummies (Nazis, Antifas, criminal foreigners, religious extremists) that there is a peaceful way to live together!
>
> Does he really work for a Lidl? 😊
>
> Haha I (muslim) had two or so years ago 3 bearded muslim men standing in front of my door, who wanted to teach me on Islam, and I didn't let them come inside 😊

Even Yaran participates in the second-hand curation of his content by posting to this sub-comment thread from his verified YouTube account:

> Yes, folks, I know, I got a little extra here in my act, but hey, the programme is really good!

Yaran takes on less of a burden than Baydar to situate his comedic meanings in relation to critical performance art or audience reception. Yet, he is still concerned primarily with owning racist attitudes in German society as an inclusive comedy act and having a diverse audience own them with him. This suggests that in large parts of his programmes there is a social cohesion element to his observational ethnic comedy. It is also present in the audience's responses.

My Son has Yaran tell the live audience what has happened to his life after becoming a father for the first time. His son, as the short routine is called, turns on Yaran's life as a parent and on the stereotype of absent Turkish fathers. The plot of *Kebab Connection* picks up on this topic, too. Yaran goes from being a member of a Turkish heavy battle rap group to being part of an arts and crafts group with a German woman named "Gudrun". "I used to bring weed, now I bring along cheese sandwiches (audience laughs) with weed (audience laughs louder and claps)", he confesses in a self-deprecatory manner. He can even deal with self-censorship to avoid potty talk in front of his toddler, but cannot stand parent-teacher association meetings where he is being singled out by German teachers as the father of a Turkish boy named Burak: "[t]here's only two foreign children in the whole of the kindergarten group. Two! My son Burak, and the little, black, African boy called Lokombo Ombo. Ey teacher dude, guess whose father you reckon I am, won't you!". And while "German parents are always waiting patiently to take notes and for the most proper ones to take the minutes of the meeting (audience laughs again)", "Turkish parents are ready to go, that's why they're always wearing their jackets. And you know how you can spot the Arab parents? Easy! They're not there! (audience laughs and cheers intermittently)".

Here, Yaran appraises the conditions of his existence as a Turkish German male and as a dad. As a measure of social tolerance and light-hearted self-critique, he arranges German next to allegedly Arab and stereotyped Turkish parenting styles. He mocks them all and thus ensures that none is perceived as better or worse than the others or considered an actual representation of factual reality. It is, as Holms points out, a trend in contemporary mainstream stand-up comedy to cater to a liberal entertainment policy, affirming difference and the culture of "us" (Holm, 2017: 29). Again, YouTube's video streaming audience seems to validate this interpretation. With unanimous consent, user feedback in the comment section supports the routine as a cool, funny or hilarious entertainment event.

> heard this so many times but. thas dude isabsolutely awesome

> really fresh due smooth humour :) Top

> I watched this so many times already, but I think it's still so totally funny haha 😄😄😄

> Soooo nice

This is not to say that Yaran's comedy strictly follows an inoffensive and easy multiculture comedy agenda to play solely on likeability. In *Bitches and Examples*, he goes straight to the issue of ethnic stereotyping without appearing too agreeable or well-mannered. Central to this routine is the opening joke to which Yaran leads up in a perceptively angry tone before getting to the actual joke: "[y]ou know I really can't stand these prejudices." He then goes on to tell the actual joke about the mismatched reality of Turkish German women and men and German perceptions of reductive visual appearances and behaviours. "All those people tell me, it's like, with you Muslims, all the women are wearing a headscarf and all the mean have a beard. Yeah! Total nonsense, dude, just complete BULLSHIT!" It is a loaded attack against the essentialist representation of Turkishness in German society and the tension building up in the live audience is noticeable. There is some snickering and the recording picks up subdued laughs, but no claps or cheers. It is in this moment that Yaran reroutes a potentially anti-social ethnic comedy moment in a pro-social one by adding a quick twist of relief humour at the expense of narrow-minded, racist subjects in German society: "I mean, yeah, well, ok, SOME women DO HAVE a beard, too! Ok, I'll admit that. And, what's more, in my family, most people wear a headscarf. Even my grandfather. Cool, I mean, he's got dementia and thinks he's actually a pirate: CAPTAIN SÜLAYMAN SPARROW!!".

The live audience breaks into a collective reaction of visible relief. Some laugh loudly and most members of the audience applaud. However, some can be seen turning around to other audience members, looking somewhat clueless or asking for clarification. It seems as if some of the audience members are checking in with each other about the intention of this sudden change. One could argue that they are reassuring themselves of the appropriateness of their laughter when the Turkish German comedian switches from accusatory tension to relaxed enjoyment. More jokes like this come up throughout the performance. Yaran addresses the issue of having to explain his need for a prayer room at work; or alleged Turkish sexism for adding "BITCH" at the end of sentences to make his speech more evocative: "[l]ike when I say at the bank counter 'Hey, I need to make a payment…BIIIITCHHH!', and then the guy working there gets it and straight away goes along with it when he says 'Of course, I got you, SIIISSS!'". There is a provocative opener, followed by a relief humour punchline. It takes the audience a couple of minutes to figure out this comedic strategy of raising sensitive political topics without accusing anyone in the room of being complicit in their hegemonic dominance.

It is with this video that YouTube users are more actively and more critically involved than with other content of Yaran's republished live stand-up performances. Some users who seem to identify in their profile names as Muslim or Turkish or Turkish German repeat some of the salient political messages about ethnic diversity and respect:

> How do you know if someone is a Muslim who actually practices their faith ? He will tell you at some point for sure.

Other users pick up on specific audience members and their real-time reactions to the probing setups Yaran uses before diverting tension into funny punchlines:

> 2:10 Emogirl is not amused

Again, a larger number of users who either identify as Swabian or hint at their sympathies for this German community in south-western Germany relate their commentary to Yaran's punchline about "German minorities having a go at each other". The "Swabians being, oh dude, yeah, they are some of the most brutal ones":

> Osan: "Above all else, we have in Berlin…an ethnic minority, marginalised community, and it is much more strange and aggressive and dangerous than anything else." Me: "Swabians?" Osan: "The Swabians!"

> Heya, I am a lady from Swabia and we are not brutal at all 😄
> who here is also Swabian😄✋

> Ey no bashin Swabs best people ♥

Even YouTube viewers who critique, as distinct from criticise, Yaran for repeating some of his jokes in different performances, attest readily that this kind of ethnic comedy resonates with them. This is an important aspect of Yaran's work, especially with him raising the issue of Jewishness and Turkishness in *Sometimes, Germany is a bit too German* in the cold opener to a recorded live performance on national public television: "[h]i Stuttgart, so I'm a practising and devoted Muslim, right, and you, I'm very cosmopolitan and very tolerant. One of my best friends is a Jew, and I will admit, Stuttgart, right, we do have lots of discussions, right? I say: 'Mohammed is the best', and he says: 'Moses is the best', 'Mohammed is the best', 'Moses is the best'…I mean, oh well, now we agreed that Batman is the best".

> Osan Yaran is really very funny! Shame he just always uses the same jokes…

> Osan Yaran, I love the Jehovah's Witnesses as Muslims?😄 Welldone. German sense of order and signs everywhere confuse foreigners. So funny. 💕

Religious diversity among non-Christian communities in Germany is a joke that comes up frequently in Yaran's work. He has managed to sustain the topic by combining it with popular culture tropes as a comedy relief. Citing the comic character of Batman is part of an incongruous comedy strategy which allows the audience to admit that religious identities in Germany may conflict with each other. Yaran thereby hints at the moral, cultural and political context of mainstream humour before directing the answer of which religion is the "best" to an apolitical topic of nerdish fandom for American comic books. Referring to transnational popular culture is, however, not an escape route. The joke about non-Christian religions' hierarchy in Germany is an attempt to expound the politics of German culture. It does, quite literally, ask about the positioning of minority religion in mainstream society. This is a politicised and controversial topic. It highlights such contemporary issues as religion, Germany's past dealings with Jewish Germans and present discrimination against Muslims, and the clash between Jews and Muslims on a geopolitical scale. For the most part, this reveals that the politics of Turkish German stand-up comedy are neither overly trivialising nor inherently subversive (Spielhaus, 2014: 322).

Yaran, like Baydar, contributes to an energising of civic culture. He engages the audience with topics steeped in the political. The counter-hegemonic elements in his routines add to rather than drain German entertainment culture of serious content, as argued by Postman in his general critique of modern entertainment comedy culture (Postman, 2006). In terms of shared content and viewer networking around his streamed republished performances, Yaran's viewers gravitate towards content which makes Turkishness and Turkish identities in Germany appear more ordinary than German attitudes and cultural values. That much becomes clear when one watches his stand-up routine, *German Punctuality at a Turkish Wedding*. The live performance attracted almost half a million views on YouTube within two months. Ten thousand viewers liked the video, whereas only 536 viewers gave it a thumbs down. The routine turns on commonplace rituals most audience members in the live recording event and YouTube users can relate to while watching. Its climax is the "Turkish wedding complex": "Hey folks, I had a Turkish wedding myself! You know about Turkish weddings? At my wedding, there were nine hundred Turks! Dude, nine hundred Turks in a big function room! That looked like the opening of a new job services office for the unemployed, dude, let me tell you that. And with my four German colleagues in there. I'll tell you what, they looked like they were working there. And the best thing is, on the invitation for Turkish weddings, it always says 5pm. But, hey, they NEVER start at 5pm. Ey folks, my co-workers stood there at the door at five to five, trying to get in. I'm telling you, not even my parents were that early. And they were the hosts! So, then my mother comes up and asks them who they are for ten minutes and then, then she tells them to help her carry the chairs inside. HAAAAAAAA!".

Yaran closes this part of his routine with a description of how his German boss tried to dance at the wedding. Yet, for hours on end, the German only managed to stand there stationary and pump his hand up into the air. "This", Yaran concludes, "looked like he was waving people goodbye, and then he started to turn in a circle, and it was like he was pointing to people, like, 'You are all being deported, the boat is full now'". Yaran conducts all his current routines in this jokingly subversive way. The live audience cheers for all the jokes, both those talking about how ordinary German rituals seem outlandish to Others and those making light of Turkish German culture. However, some of the online users whose names suggest that they identify as "bio-Deutsch" or historically German express negative viewpoints. Their comments on the specific nature of Yaran's ethnic comedy jokes suggest that this specific performance reproduces reductive and event racist knowledge about ethnic identities instead of subverting them:

> Not mean to be a downer, but I think it's really surprising that since what feels like 30 years, Kaya Yanar and "Watcha Looking at?"etc, use the same jokes about "Germanness" and that people find them funny.

> This guy is so unfunny. And he crosses a line. He's also a subtle racist. I know a lot of Turks who are like this. A lot of them don't say things like that not just in jest. Folks, they hate us germans. They also vote in Germany for a Turkish President. I say everyone who does that should go back to turkey.

> He makes fun of us, and none of those idiots [in the live audience] understands that this is not about jokes anymore..., I would have left. This stuff should be banned...these people should be banned and deported. For me this is hidden discrimination.

Only one comment expresses a sense of gratitude for being taught about the ins and outs of a Muslim wedding and takes it with a sense of comedic mockery:

> But the thing about the weddings is totally true in real life 😂😂😂 I have experienced this myself. I was invited to an Arab birthday party. Times was given, begin 14:00 o'clock. And well, what can I tell you...I was the first one to get there. The other guests only arrived after about 15:30 😂😂😂 From 14:00 o'clock to 15:30 o'clock people changed their clothes, put on makeup, and put food on the tables... 🙂 I'll know better for next time now

TURKISH GERMAN MUSLIMS AND COMEDY ENTERTAINMENT

Staging stereotypes remains an ambivalent entertainment business despite recognisable progress. YouTube user reactions confirm the funny qualities of Yaran's work as well as the serious reception and pessimistic views spelled out on the notion of standstill or cheap shots at the expense of one ethnic identity for the amusement of another. Idil Baydar has addressed this issue by staging her Turkishness and her Germanness as equally imaginary stage characters. Osan Yaran collapses his stage persona and personal identity. Seasoned Turkish German comedians and cabaret performers such as Serdar Somuncu welcome the former technique (Spielhaus: 332). Of the latter they grow increasingly weary as there is a danger of reproducing a Turkishness or Germanness beyond any reality, even that of the lived realities of the Turkish German comedy performers.

CHAPTER VI

Settling into "Post-Migrant" Mainstream Culture

"Die Kunst aus der Hand zu lesen, war ein Angebot, das Wahrsagerinnen machen konnten. Dieses Angebot hat sich inzwischen erübrigt. Inzwischen kannst du selber aus der Hand lesen, mehr noch, du kannst aus deiner Hand sehen. Du kannst sehen, wie die Zukunft aussehen wird. Du kannst sie gestalten. Eine Möglichkeit deine Zukunft zu gestalten, wäre zum Beispiel in Stuttgart. Bei der Türkisch-Deutschen Kabarettwoche. Vom 12. bis zum 21. April läuft sie. Und da sind sie alle. Also, viele! Also, Jilet Ayse ist da. Und Özgür Cebe ist da. Und Serhat Doğan ist da. Muhsin Omurca ist da. Und Ozan Akhan und Jilet Ayse und ich, wir machen den Comedy Orient Express. Ich bin natürlich auch da, solo. Mein Programm, Fatih Morgana, kannst du kommen und dir das anschauen. Und jetzt, hast du die Möglichkeit, deine Zukunft zu gestalten. Oder anders gesagt: Du hast es in der Hand! Wir sehen uns!"

"Reading someone's palm used to be an offer only fortune tellers could make. This offer is no longer needed. Today, you can read your own palm. In fact, you can actually "see" in your palm. You can see what the future will hold. You can shape it. In Stuttgart, there is a way to do just that. There is the Turkish German Comedy week. It runs from 12 to 21 April. And everyone is going to be there. Well, really everyone! So, Jilet Ayse will be there. And Özgür Cebe will be there. And Serhat Doğan will be there. Muhsin Omurca will be there. And Ozan Akhan and Jilet Ayse and I, we are going to do the Comedy Orient Express. Of course, I will be there doing my solo programme, too. My programme, Fatih Morgana, you can come and watch it. And now you have the opportunity to shape your future. Or let's say: it is in your hand! I'll see you there!"

—Facebook video announcement posted by Turkish German comedian Fatih Çevikkollu on behalf of the organisers of German-Turkish Comedy Week in Stuttgart, Germany, to promote the event (Facebook, 2019)[1]

Summary

The final chapter of this book discusses some of the most current issues in Turkish German culture and comedy entertainment in the 21st century, especially in relation to its future in the third decade of the new millennium. I also offer very brief reflections on the assessment of the idea of post-migrant culture production. This label has in recent years been attached to productions in contemporary Turkish German culture, serving to indicate the most current phase in its long history. I end by referring to three major trends associated with Turkish German comedy and German mainstream culture entertainment: 1) Islam and religion 2) women in Turkish German comedy 3) streaming and social media. This section features contributions from the field's most prolific comedy performers, writers, actresses and other comedy artists, and new up-and-coming individuals, cultural production techniques, social media platforms and online video streaming channels.

The 2020s: A (Post-) Migration Context for Turkish German Comedy Entertainment?

"More recently", writes Göktürk (2020) in revisiting cultural paternalism in Turkish German Cinema in the updated and revised edition of *The German Cinema Book*, "Shermin Langhoff and her team at Ballhaus Naunynstraße and subsequently the Gorki Theatre in Berlin have popularized 'post-migrant theatre,' a term they see as countering ostracism with an insistence on settlement" (Göktürk, 2020: 502). Referring, however, to El-Tayeb's caution against purely rhetorical claims to the overcoming of cultural bias against migrants much like the proclaimed post-racial era of post-Obama America, she adds, "I for my part am not convinced that 'post-migrant' is a productive label to add to our list of categories. It suggests a transcendence that does not fit the ongoing complex reality of migrations. The emphasis on having arrived and settled is surely an important point to make but categorizations need to remain flexible to accommodate those who keep coming—otherwise they will just perpetuate the logic of national containers where some can claim rights to belong and stay and other cannot" (Göktürk, 2020: 502).

This resistance to supporting the notion of a post-migration Turkish German culture context points to its own distinct issue in the study of Turkish German Muslimness. The analysis of Turkish German cultural participation in German society has historically been focused on the logic of the national and of containment of ethnic Others and minority cultures, as I have detailed in the preceding chapters. And by bypassing their rigid borders, social boundaries and imaginary ethno-cultural restrictions, as I have explained in the main chapters, too, Turkish German comedy entertainment in the new century gestures towards a project to expand Germanness. It seeks to complicate binary identity politics, which still pit Muslims against non-Muslims, and to entangle the history of Germany with that of other countries and cultures. It shows the continuities between flows of migration and identity as an organic, intergenerational whole, rather than a narrative of interrupted life stories and a perpetual state of disconnect with one's culture(s) and sense(s) of belonging. This extols the actual gains of Turkish German migrant culture from the alleged post-migration stresses like culture shock and conflict, both of which may lead to a sense of cultural confusion, feelings of displacement and isolation.

The creative work of Turkish Germans, and more specifically their gains around mainstream comedy as illustrated in the quotation at the beginning of this chapter are increasingly visible in German mainstream culture. More importantly, their easy availability and widespread popularity with Turkish speaking and German-speaking audiences suggests that they have created a plurality of opportunities from which to derive the pleasure of humour based on the lived realities of Turkish Germans in Germany: on cinema screens, on television and other small screens, in books, on stage, live or recorded, streamed and re-shared and framed para-textually by user comments on social media. In all of this, though, as Post and Schramm remark, ethnic humour does not reproduce the Euro-pudding logic of strongly national motifs of belonging, assuming them as pre-given homogenous communities which can be bonded in artifice only in overly simplistic integration fictions (Post and Schramm, 2019: 113-115). Instead, contemporary Turkish German comedy works to reappraise the meaning and roles of concepts like diversity, Othering and integration, which are changing as post-migrant perspectives and analyses beget new aesthetic redefinitions of the historically German "we" group's claim to normativity. The latter, in El Tayeb's assessment, is no longer perceived as a homogenous entity in which "an essentialisitically defined, white, Christian Europe always and necessarily remains the norm" (El Tayeb, 2016: 19). An while I do not label my work here as such, I do suggest that this book, like other current works on transnational Turkish German culture by scholars such as Ela Gezen and Elizabeth Stewart, takes some of its cues from the concept of "post-migrant". The term has inspired me to discuss a distinctive phase in Turkish German cultural production and reception and reflect on its potential for future scholarship.

However, and here I fully agree with Göktürk, this should not mean that one simply closes the book on the problematisation of Germany's struggle to come to terms with its status as a migration nation by applying the term "post-migrant" to the discussion of Turkish German culture and Muslimness in Germany in the new century. Spielhaus emphasises that the tensions between non-Muslim and Muslim Germany persist, as do certain clichés and long-rehearsed tropes related to Islam and Turkish Germanness (Spielhaus, 2017: 118-120). I made this clear in chapter two. As well, reductive knowledge about the Muslim and Turkish German Other has affected and certainly still does affect the conditions of production for contemporary Turkish German humour entertainment in the new century. Yet, as Spielhaus also concedes, it will be impractical, if not impossible, to keep up the categorisation and theoretical attribution of certain terms like Turkish German, Arab German or ethnic in the analysis of comedy in German-culture contexts. Even the most established German satire shows, television companies and cinema comedy productions, and cabaret and local stage play producers, are increasingly more open to all kinds of Germanness and collaborations among the producers of humour related to its attending themes: race, ethnicity, religion, class and gender.

Trends in Turkish German Comedy Entertainment

Turkish German comedy entertainment in German mainstream culture through the first two decades of the 21st century has increasingly exhibited voices and issues previously relegated to niche audiences and independent productions. Encouraged by the burgeoning of these voices and issues in recent years, and a growing awareness of certain innovations around consumer behaviour of mainstream comedy culture consumers and technology, I present here several trends which have, at least at this time, gained notable prominence and may attract more scholarly attention in future.

Islam and Religion
The recent focus on European Islam and Muslimness has sparked renewed interest in both representatives and representations of Muslimness. In Germany's case, the increased focus on a Muslim presence in the wake of the global 2015 refugee crisis (see chapter two) has evolved as a question about the relationship between politics and religion. While secularism, as it has traditionally been seen in German culture as an issue of relations between church and state, has evolved to encompass a more generalised notion of religiosity itself, the discourse around Islam has re-initiated a debate about religious and political authority (Kahn,

2013: 216). Turkish German comedy in the 21st century, in this respect, provides a unique framework for the furthering of a conversation about Islam, religion and politics. However, as I have indicated as well throughout this book, this debate has proved to be a challenge in German society, not least due to the wider German public's disinterest in national postulations of religious diversity and the notably diverse array of religious and political thought throughout the Muslim world. One can argue that this context makes it easier for Turkish German comedians like Fatih Çevikkollu to present in their comedy routines a more generalised version of Muslimness, which may seem somewhat reductive yet is not dominated by outsider-imposed categorisations of Islam (Kahn, 2013: 216).

This is not to say that the topic of Islam in German society has flourished as a widespread theme in Turkish German comedy entertainment, informing audiences about idiosyncratic identity development processes of Muslim minority communities or making them aware of the cultural depths of Islamic traditions. Yet, insofar as it creates a very visible space for a certain level of discourse around these questions and the topic of Islam in German popular culture and arguments about a so-called moderate Islam, Turkish German comedians have been able to touch on recognisable reference points. Framed by 9/11, some of the most relevant examples here are to be found in the works of Fatih Çevikkollu. One of the most established Turkish German comedy artists, who rose to fame in German mainstream culture for his regular appearances as the character of Murat Günaydin in the popular sitcom, *Alles Atze-That's So Atze* (RTL, 2000-2007), Çevikkollu's comedy has a history of highlighting majority society attitudes to domesticating and securitising Muslimness in mainstream Germany. The opener to one of his most popular stand-up comedy routines, *Moslem TÜV-German State Regulations Authority for Muslimness*, is directed explicitly at the German notion of Islam as an anti-humorous and hence anti-secular religion and form of identity:

> Good evening. (audience applauds) Thank you. So, I hope you allow me to introduce myself: My name is Fatih Çevikkollu. Yes, that's Turkish. If you wanted to translate that into German, it'd be something like ... Fatih Çevikkollu. (audience laughs) Oh yes, I'm Muslim. (pauses for effect) Well, can you tell? Like, just now? I said Muslim and immediately the room got really tense. (Çevikkollu, 2008; see also Çevikkollu and Mysorekar, 2008)

Here, as other Turkish German comedians who identify as Muslim and perform in Germany have been illustrating with their comedy performances (see chapter five), Turkish German comedy takes aim at the mechanism of how German mainstream news, press and other entertainment media mediate and represent Muslimness and Turkishness. Rather than claim to ridicule self-representations of their diverse community and its attitudes towards Islam, this kind of incongruity humour calls out German mainstream culture's allegedly liberal understandings of Muslims in the country while grouping them into essentialist categories of "we" and "them". Yet, as in the previous chapters, it is not always clear whether this kind of comedy revolving around Muslimness only straddles a larger critique of anti-essentialism in contemporary German identity politics, or whether it is more related to the anti-racist comedy agenda as exemplified in Mutlu Ergün-Hamaz's *Kara Günlük: Die geheimen Tagebücher des Sesperado* (2016). One could also argue that it actually seeks to move into an area of uncomfortable silence and even taboos around the repercussions faced by some Muslim comedians for joking about Islam in Muslim majority countries like Egypt.[2]

Women in Turkish German Comedy

A new wave of female Turkish German comedy artists, stand-up performers, writers, directors and YouTubers has gained attention over the past two decades for its creative innovations and artistic contributions. Among them are Yasemin Şamdereli (*Alles getürkt!-Fake as a Turk!*, 2002; *Sextasy*, 2004; *Ich Chef Du Nix-Me Boss, You Not*, 2007), who directed *Almanya-Welcome to Germany* (2011) in close collaboration with her sister, Nesrin Şamdereli. Scholars of Turkish German cinema, first and foremost Göktürk, attest to the Şamdereli sisters' creative potential to give new energy to the representation of Turkish German history in film by comedically intervening in the fossilisation of Turkish labour migrants' stories. "The opening sequence of Almanya", Götürk writes, "is a good example of how popular comedy is breathing new life into the archives of migrant lives" (Göktürk, 2020: 502). By assembling collective memory through a collection of different kinds of footage, styles and works of earlier Turkish German generations, the Şamdereli sisters make a point about intergenerational relations, connections and the misguided assumption that Turkish labour migration is necessarily an exercise in historicisation of memory rather than making it porous and thus multi-temporal.

There are also Turkish German actresses who have made a name for themselves by appearing repeatedly and to critical acclaim in Turkish German comedy entertainment films. The most prominent among them are Aylin Tezel, Demet Gül, Mandala Tayde, İdil Üner and Sibel Kekilli, while actresses like Sesede Terziyan have also starred live on stage in plays such as *Verrücktes Blut-Crazy Blood*, an intense integration comedy play written by Jens Hillje and directed by Nurkan Erpulat.

In the specific context of Turkish German stand-up comedy, Idil Baydar (see chapter five) has risen to considerable popularity in recent years (Spielhaus, 2017). This is despite the fact that women in stand-up across the globe account for just 10 per cent of comedians and male comics continue to earn more than their female counterparts, with women of colour earning generally less than all others (Tomsett, 2017). Many of the female comedians also continue to battle against the idea that women are not funny, seeing that television comedy panel shows, comedy clubs and international comedy slam events overwhelmingly bill men. However, female comedians, and especially those with non-historically German identities, are beginning to explore other avenues to get their feet in the door, as I explain in the next section. In 2020, the relative absence of Turkish German women in mainstream entertainment comedy is blatantly obvious. To the small group of diverse female comedians booked more regularly and billed as primary acts in German mainstream culture comedy entertainment belong Senay Duzcu and Meltem Kaptan, both Turkish Germans, the Iranian German comedian Enissa Amani and the Russian German comedian Liza Kos. And while the overall number of female stand-up comedians in German-language entertainment has grown over the past 20 years, there is still little representation compared to the large number of male comedians dominating the profession, and even less when it comes to the representation of diverse German female, trans or LGBTQI identities, and women of colour.

Perhaps the most female-driven field of cultural production to date, Turkish German comedy literature remains the stronghold of female writers. Next to the better-known names I have discussed here, namely those of Hatice Akyün, Lale Akgün and Hülya Özkan, there are Ayşegül Acevit (*Was lebst Du?-Whatcha Livin' At?*, 2005; *Zu Hause in Almanya-At Home in Almanya*, 2008), Sibel Susann Teoman (Der Teufel ist blond-*The Devil is a Blonde*, 2006; *Türkischer Mokka mit Schuss-Spiked Turkish Coffee*, 2007; Der Teufel sieht rot-*Mad as Hell*, 2008; Flitterwochen auf Türkisch-*Turkish Honeymooning*, 2008) and Meltem Kaptan (*Verliebt, Verlobt, Verbockt-He Loves Me, He Loves Me Not*, 2016). This comes as no surprise. Historically, female writers of Turkish German comedy fictions, specifically those dealing with transnational genres coded as female like chick-lit (Yeşilada, 2009), travel writing (Benbow, 2019) and romantic comedy styled as "pop autobiographies (Weber, 2013), have always had a broader fan and female consumer base.

Streaming and Social Media

Perhaps the most viable financial path for Turkish German comedians is to translate their acts into broader success and develop a larger fan base via rather new, digital formats and platforms. They allow in particular female Turkish German comedians like Baydar to have their material streamed and shared and downloaded directly by audiences onto personal computers and handheld screen and audio devices. According to Donian, many comedians could survive on the advertisement sold "for popular comedy podcasts such as *WFT with Marc Maron*, or Scott Aukerman's *Comedy Bang! Bang!*" (Donian, 2019: 20). At a rough estimate, comedy podcasters with approximately 40,000 downloads per episode in the United States can make well over US$75,000 a year. Shows in the range of 100,000 downloads can gross somewhere between US$250,000 and 500,000. Many comedians in America, Donian notes, "have also heralded a new trend—the podcast-turned-TV series—parlaying successful podcasts into larger earning (cable) TV shows. [...] More recently, HBO's adaptation of *2 Dope Queens* (2018) featuring Jessica Williams and Phoebe Robinson" (Donian, 2019: 20) and the runaway success of the comedy series proved that female producers with ethnically diverse backgrounds stand to gain most from immediate producer-to-audience mainstream productions.

This is not an American comedy culture phenomenon. The creation of podcasts, websites devoted to ethnic comedy, social media apps like Twitter, Facebook and Instagram, and the instantaneous streaming services available for free or at low cost across television, internet (YouTube), tablets and other kinds of mobile or hand-held screen devices has also enabled Turkish German comedy to progress past physical venues and regulatory or other production limitations due to costs, in television and cinema. In fact, one can speak of a 21st century comedy wave, which signals a new, global digital period after the transnational Anglophone comedy culture boom of the 1980s/1990s. That first boom was sustained by physical comedy club scenes and international entertainment products being imported on the big and small screen across the world. The second renaissance of a much more inclusive mainstream comedy culture is fuelled by technology and more artistic and creative liberties compared to those of traditional venues. Never before has so much original material for comedy, both family friendly and more edgy, come from a more extensive and diverse group of comedy artists, writers, directors and performers than today at the beginning of the third decade of the new millennium. Indeed, one does not have to look too far to find exciting new materials and Turkish German comedy routines online. Just a quick search on the most popular outlets like YouTube, Instagram and Twitter, as I indicated in chapter five, leads to a comedy which crosses over into different genres and forms, and in doing so is producing a new kind of cultural artifact.

CONCLUSION
European Muslims' Issues: Turkish German Comedy in a Global Entertainment and Identity Politics Framework

This book appears in a series dedicated to *Current Issues in Islam*. That breadth is necessary to capture the global realities of Muslim identities and their lived experiences in relation to Islam and a surge in anti-Muslim sentiments. Also, it indicates that one cannot tell the story of Turkish German comedy entertainment in Germany without telling the story of popular Muslim comedy in the global West. It is a political narrative of crisis management, which was born from the need of Muslims to address the impact of 9/11 or Danish cartoons about the Prophet on non-Muslim majority cultures in America and Europe respectively. My scholarship on demographic changes in traditionally Christian majority countries, in tandem with popular culture studies, details how Turkish German interventions have taken shape around counter-discursive comedy cultures in different mass media types. In the 21st century these interventions serve to debunk neo-nationalist fantasies of Islamic separatism (Nielsen, 2014: 12). Evidence of this being a necessity rather than a choice for Muslim individuals and the community has emerged in the works of scholars such as Spielhaus and Hirzalla and van Zoonen. They argue that non-Muslim majority societies must spread the message: the Muslims are not coming. They are already here. They have been for quite some time. And they will not force you to eat halal, follow Sharia law, lose your foreskin or renounce Jesus (Spielhaus, 2014; Hirzalla and von Zoonen, 2015).

In 2020, Muslim entertainment comedy increasingly engages the anxiety around Islamic beliefs and the mere presence of Muslims as the reality of being

Other in non-Muslim majority countries. Whether a film or television comedy plays in Munich or New York, the "random" selection by airport security of passengers believed to be Muslim is a widespread plot point. The 2019 pilot for Aatif Nawaz's British comedy sketch show on BBC Three, *Muzlamic*, drives this point home with visceral detail. Goofy and sometimes overtly reminiscent of Ali G-ish performances, British comedians Ali Shahalom and Aatif Nawaz propose to millions of viewers in the United Kingdom "a sketch show exploring life from the perspective of two Muslim comedians or, rather, two comedians who happen to be Muslim" (BBC "Muzlamic", 2019). *Muzlamic*'s pilot episode opens with a sketch about a pair of Muslim holidaymakers, caps on backwards and beards neatly manicured, being questioned by airport security. When asked if they have ever had any trouble with the police, they offer PDFs and printed copies of their answers to standard questions such as: "Do you know ISIS?" When taking their leave and walking out of the interrogation room, they offer to send in "the next brown boys, yeah?" "I didn't say brown. He said it," the white security officer who had interrogated them says nervously, head turned to the CCTV cameras and tiny beads of sweat gathering on his forehead.

Muzlamic is one of numerous European Muslim comedies turning on the premise of hidden yet systemic racism against Muslims, especially Muslim men. Productions based on this premise first rose to popular culture acclaim in the early 2000s with *Allah Made Me Funny*, an American stand-up comedy troupe consisting of Bryant "Preacher" Moss, Azhar Usman and Azeem Muhammad. In Canada, the serial comedy *Little Mosque on the Prairie* was a hit with audiences from 2007 to 2012. It, too, deals with the framework of Muslim alienation despite Canada's self-proclaimed identity as cosmopolitan multi-culture. The longevity of certain themes in Muslim comedy around the world shows that Islam has become deeply entrenched in debates about securitisation in mainstream cultures across Europe and North America. In Australia and New Zealand, comedians Aamer Rahman and Nazeem Hussain tackle the tropes of Islamist terror in their 2007 sell-out comedy festival show, *Fear of a Brown Planet*. Body searches by customs officials and police also appear in the stand-up comedy of female European comedians such as Sadia Azmat, a British native, and Ellie Jokar, an Iranian-born Dane. While Jokar focuses on anti-immigrant sentiments in continental Europe, Azmat works through the Brits' public perception of Muslims as threats to everyone's safety on stage and in her comedy podcast, *No Country for Young Women*. In part, one can argue, the female comedians do double duty. Azmat and Jokar also engage the gendered cliché triad reserved exclusively for female Muslim comedy artists: headscarf, burka and domestic abuse.

Proponents of Islamophobia have been pushing for populist and state-sanctioned rejections of Islam since the rise of Islamist terrorism in Europe over the past decade. US President Donald Trump proposed during his election campaign in 2016 a register of all Muslims in America. In 2018, the US Supreme Court upheld Trump's so-called Muslim travel ban, while right-wing politicians in France and the United Kingdom as well as Sweden and Denmark discussed the sourcing of personal profile data on social media platforms as means to prevent acts of Muslim extremism. In Germany, the attacks of 2016 in Berlin have fuelled discussions about a halt to forced migration from Muslim majority countries such as Syria and Afghanistan. All the while, debates about the ban on or restriction of the hijab, headscarf and burka are still current across Europe and North America, with Austria's controversial 2017 ban testing Western legal opinions on face-covering clothing in public spaces and official institutions.

I write all of this as the focus of German politics has shifted more and more towards a vilification of Muslim men as potential perpetrators of acts of violence while the actual violent attacks on them by German neo-Nazis thrive seemingly unhindered. Fatih Akin's film, *In the Fade,* warned of these issues two years before the East German city of Dresden declared a "Nazi emergency" in 2019.

Since 2016, the new-fangled political party of the AfD, which promotes itself as an Alternative for Germany, has shaped the core of its political agenda around a rigorous plan to deport Muslim Asylum seekers, especially if they are young, unattended and male. The political arm of the anti-Muslim PEGIDA movement hit a protectionist nerve with German voters with this plan. This became apparent when AfD representatives entered German state governments in Eastern Germany in large numbers and gained more than 8 per cent of the vote in the 2017 federal elections.

Summary of Findings and Outlook: Where Do We Go from Here?

I end *Turkish German Muslims and Comedy Entertainment* with an overview of current trends in German, Austrian, American, Canadian, Danish, Swedish, British and Australian comedy culture and real-life political contexts. I do this to highlight the argument I have made throughout this book: that the different types of mainstream comedy entertainment (film, television, literature, online) react in unison and on a transnationally interconnected scale to Muslim stereotyping and the complex issues faced by minority communities in countries across the globe. These issues are real and require effective interventions on a global scale. I contend that current issues in Islam in the new century should be studied not solely through the national context of one country's entertainment productions. Neither should we discuss only national inventories of creative, humour-driven messages about living in a Western majority society while Muslim.

My study of Turkish German identity issues through the lens of the social pragmatics of humour has also led me to pay close attention to the many layers of understanding one requires to examine comedy. There are intended and unintended messages; there is the risk of reproducing negative, anti-social messages about ethnic identity and about who may belong to a group and who shall be excluded from it because of religion, gender, sexual orientation or citizenship status. It is very easy to turn "Shield" into "Sword".

The study of popular entertainment culture is also often criticised for neglecting the political dimensions of films, books, television series or content produced originally or republished for audience consumption via online platforms like YouTube.

This is a short-sighted perspective. And it does not hold water. I have emphasised throughout this book and based on a socio-historical background provided in chapter one that Turkish German comedy culture is profoundly political. Its politics revolve around presence and persistence. The strategies it employs stem from a post-modern entertainment culture which has come to play a central role in our everyday lives. From how mainstream audiences consume their news through a new wave of political satire shows on television to late night comedy hosts making pleas for civic discourse to return to ideals of courtesy and respect, the rules have changed. At the beginning of the third decade of the 21st century, our information society no longer operates under the same linguistic or epistemological guidelines previous generations have accepted. They accepted them as the normative rule in discussing serious issues such as identity politics, ethnicity, racism, migration and national belonging.

Instead, comedy culture has started to react to a post-truth world dominated by neo-nationalist forces. It has kicked in like an immune response. In German society it reacts to regressive identity discourses plaguing the country for centuries. Anti-semitism and ethnic Othering paved the way for an intricate bias against Muslimness to take a firm hold in German-speaking cultures and, later, the German nation state. The alleged political truths about Muslim Germans, and Turkish Muslim Germans above all, are a systemic construct based on insidious cultural mechanisms: alienation, disassociation, minoritising, de-historicising and, finally, ghettoisation. Jewish German history is clear on where this leads to, namely termination.

I demonstrated in chapter two that Turkish German culture clash comedy films are critical of social strata and identity labels imposed by majority society on minority Others. They contradict the widespread media buzz around Muslims as terrorist threats to Germany's social stability and internal security. Laced with humour to offer the representation of personal culture clash experiences in romantic relationships and diasporic families as refreshingly amusing takes on social incongruity and hierarchical groupthink, they model common sense transformation as personal choices. They represent diverse characters and multiple ways of being Muslim, German, a woman, a man or queer. Their stimulating wit dismisses the idea of incongruous identity markers. There are impassioned mockeries of monolithic nationalism where Turks and other non-native Germans intrude and usurp Germanness' status as prime culture. In the end, their happy endings reveal that everybody is better off for letting go of an internalised spectrum of bias, from mean-spirited bigotry to micro-aggressions in daily interactions with different parts of German society.

I have studied comedy films representative of 20 years of Turkish German comedy cinema. And while certainly not all of them could be included here, I realised while working on *Turkish German Muslims and Comedy Entertainment* that more and more people outside the academy recognise films which I mention to them. They enjoy them for their humour and appreciate the issues they present to audiences. At public screenings, audience members enjoy these films for the levity they bring to conversations entrenched in Turkishness as problem and Islam as something too deviant ever truly to be part of the Western European identity complex.

Chapter three outlined how an ethnic sitcom subverts skewed perceptions of multicultural co-existence as necessarily segregated. The narrowest of my case studies and discussions based on a close reading, I approached *Turkish for Beginners* as an exercise in specificity. I detailed the series' specific production conditions, the transnational origins of the sitcom genre and its hybridisation when it became wedded to German highbrow broadcast. There is the history of public and private German television channels and a contextual reference to the Americanisation of German popular culture through the mass medium of television. This approach frames my discussion of how a particular slice of television programming is a contributor to the overall political climate in German society. Again, detail and specificity reflect just how much creative ingenuity Turkish German comedy producers and screenwriters expend to enter the cultural arena of public television, which in Germany often comes after and not before consensus in the wider population on a political issue or the course of political action.

I detailed in chapter four how Turkish German chick-lit and dick-lit authors explore the ethnicisation of their protagonists' identities through mechanisms of gendering, so readers see that both are constructed under specific conditions and for certain purposes. That would be to overstate the importance of such books as narratives of critical value although a good number of critics dismiss them as entertainment fluff. However, they are part of a comedy wave of politically and socially aware popular culture books. They may directly invoke the popularity of Sex and the City, the mass-culture appeal of Bridget Jones or Nick Hornby's dick-lit lads, but this is not the main reason they are successful.

Readers were hungry for alternative forms of gendered pop fiction. The Turkish German authors I discussed use their lived experiences to tell tales of love, life and family from an outsider position, which turns out to be not much of a cultural outside after all. The use of funny Turkish German men and women as protagonists counteracts the fact that they are under-represented in other entertainment and media sectors. Analysing the relationship between gender, humour and ethnicity more generally reveals that female and male Turkishness has long been considered incompatible with the power, and right, to be funny *literarti* in Germany's cultural apparatus. Their arrival on the bookshelves of Germany and continuous ranking at the top of bestseller lists in the world's largest literary economy constitute a turning point in the association of Turkish German male and female writers with humour. They use popularity gained from literary texts to tackle common gender stereotypes, which is a valid point in underlining the importance of their perception as culture professionals and, what is more, their proficiency in German culture.

I suggested in chapter five that scripted online comedy content and the journey of republished performance acts from television to computer screens with global user audiences adds to an exciting and evolving geography of Turkish German identity in online worlds. Turkish German comedy available for free on YouTube is part of a social realignment trend in the production and consumption of ethnic comedy materials. For a long time, content producers have determined the discursive framing of Turkishness and engaged viewers directly through live-event screenings in the cinema and on television. However, now online audience users also play an active part in the second-hand curation of primary producers' stand-up routines or their home-made videos. Digital screen streaming on sites like YouTube and social media platforms like Instagram takes Turkish German comedy entertainment and its humour to a place of both ultra-high visibility and interactivity. The comedic mode becomes a heightened commodity value, for humour and fun are the common elements underlying most of the popular content across several traditional and newer experimental channels on Google-owned YouTube.

Shareable, convenient, consumable pro-social ethnic comedy delivered to taste and with the ease of a click is the result of a long evolution of Turkish German comedy as described in the interlinked developments of cinema, television and literature. Its fuller dimensions, as I have pointed out with the examples of Idil Baydar and Osan Yaran, is an impactful Turkish German comedy world, where primary and secondary creators invoke, play with and mock national identity frames and what it is like to be Muslim and German in German society in 2020. It is a rich and promising field just waiting to be explored further.

Finally, in chapter six, I reflected on the state of Turkish German comedy in the 21st century in a German-specific, national context, situating it in a possible (post-)migration world of humour in Germany's mainstream entertainment culture and outlining current and potential future trends.

All this makes mainstream comedy a productive locus for studying inter- and intra-communal identity negotiations and to ask why that appeals to millions of viewers, readers and online users at this time and in this global environment.

One would also hope for more academic inquiry to take hold in an area, which requires further examination of the relationship between humour, comedy, entertainment and racism. New book series such as *Islam of the Global West* (Bloomsbury) and more established series such as *Current Issues in Islam* (KU Leuven University Press) suggest that supra-regional and multilingual studies into anti-Muslim sentiments are much needed. We need them, and more of them, to assess through multiple research models where we are headed in a millennium marked by xenophobic state governance and the devaluation of any identity we consider different from ours.

Notes

Preface

1 The Turkish German community is internally diverse and not all its members are Muslim, though the majority are. Approximately 2,000 of Germany's 3,000 mosques are Turkish and a small number of them are financially supported by the Turkish government. According to the 2011 German Census's very limited information on religion in German society, about 40 per cent of Turkish Germans described themselves as religiously unaffiliated, while 3 per cent were Christian and 44 per cent said they belonged to another religion, mainly Islam (Zensus, 211). Historically, "two thirds of Germany's Muslims are of Turkish origin, and the rest come from countries in the Middle East, South Asia, the Balkans, and the former Soviet Union. Thus, Islam in Germany has a largely Turkish character" (Goldberg, 2002: 29). For a historical overview of the Turkish diaspora in Germany see Chapin (1996), and for a discussion of Turkish Muslims in Germany from a diasporic viewpoint see Pratt Ewing (2003) and Thomson Vierra (2018).

2 I use the terms majority and minority culture and community to indicate the demographic ratio between self-identified members of the Turkish German community and the dominant ethnic group in society. This follows a use of terminology of social majority and minority groups as applied in Enes Bayraklı's and Farid Hafez's edited volume, *Islamophobia in Muslim Majority Societies* (2018), and relates also to the origins of the terms as laid out by Richard Schaefer in *Encyclopaedia of Race, Ethnicity, and Society – Volume 1* (2008) to denote inequalities in social, political and economic power.

Introduction: Finding a Voice of Their Own

1 This part of the Turkish German community is commonly referred to as the so-called second generation of Turkish German labour migrants. Mostly born in the 1970s in Germany or having come to the country as small children, these filmmakers, screenwriters and authors "reflect their own cultural background in a far more relaxed way than the generation before them did. [...] And even despite the increased xenophobia of the post-unification era, these young filmmakers [as well as screenwriters and authors] make a point of being German and Turkish at the same time. Yet in doing so, they do not operate with traditional binary oppositions, but with transcultural characters and storylines" (Yeşilada, 2008: 74). With a nod to internationalisation, globalism and the blurring of

national boundaries, they rely on the generic Hollywood conventions of a more universally accessible comedy and wave the serious discourse of German humour goodbye. The work of the new generation is different for Yeşilada in comparison to preceding films, television shows and novels. She typifies Turkish German comedy as a new genre in Turkish German cultural production, which has grown out of the cultural changes of the late 1980s and early 1990s. In this genre, especially films and television series about bi-cultural identities playfully foreground inclusion instead of difference. Yeşilada points out that is simply a matter of "offering Turkish German stories without telling migrant tales" (Yeşilada: 78) of the ethnic stereotype staples of 1970s and 1980s Turkish German visual culture. Prominent examples of the latter are the aggressive Turkish macho and the veiled and domestically abused Muslima (Yeşilada: 74-78).

2   It is easy to measure the commercial success, critical acclaim and popularity of Turkish German cinema, literature and online content via impact and reception metrics like views, clicks, downloads, licences granted or tickets and books sold, and awards received both in Germany and internationally. The films, books and online materials I have compiled here all received hundreds of thousands of views, awards or ticket sales. However, the notion of success requires some more nuance in relation to the television series I discuss in chapter three, *Turkish for Beginners*. Viewer numbers were relatively low when season one first aired. It was when German culture critics loaded season one with praise that a fan following started to build online with parts of the show playing on YouTube as fans pasted clips and sometimes complete episodes. By the time season two and, later, season three aired, and with DVD sales and re-runs of season one drawing in more prime-time audiences, the series had truly earned the status of mainstream success and was also sold internationally for broadcast.

3   The process of German culture products being *Turked* or re-formulated by Turkish German culture creatives through their specific perspectives has been well documented for its counter-discourse usage. Most visible as an example of this is the literary genre of chick-lit a la Turka (Yeşilada, 2009) I discuss in chapter four. *Turked* is a pun to reflect on the German verb "to turk", which implies that something is fake or inauthentic. Repurposing the term reflects a self-deprecatory attitude. It underpins the cultural strategies I present in this book.

4   In chapter one, I put the social history of Jewish Germans in dialogue with Turkish Germans and East Germans. With a more differentiated scholarship on ethnic German identity discourse underway, I suggest here a productive continuance of Leslie Adelson's groundbreaking work, which put 1990s tales of "Turks, German, and Jews" in touch with each other (Adelson, 2000: 93). While this book is not the place for a longer treatment of intersectional comedy culture discourse, it still informs my scholarship in the dialogic

interplay between genre, media and entertainment culture that constitutes transnational Turkish German entertainment comedy.

5   Yeşilada describes the directors and screenwriters of Turkish German comedy as innovators of a new migrant aesthetic. They have moved to the other side of foreignness, changing from butts of stereotypical jokes about Turks to the ones who tell them. For instance, filmmakers such as Yasemin Şamdereli deconstruct the reductive image of the Turkish German migrant by reconstructing it with the gloves of publicly correct speech off and the hat of the ethno-cultural professional on (Yeşilada, 2008: 73-74).

6   There is a long-running discussion about the danger inherent in ethnic comedy. Ethnic comedy can work to reinforce the clichés it seeks to subvert or reject. In the United States, Dave Chapelle's stand-up comedy and his televised comedy series, which ran on Comedy Central from 2003 to 2006, have been heavily scrutinised for this reason. Ultimately, the controversy surrounding the ethnic comedy skits and characters prompted Chapelle to leave the show at its pinnacle of popularity in 2006 despite Comedy Central offering him US$50 million to continue. See more on this point in my discussion of ethno-racist humour and its potential social effects in chapter one.

7   Berghahn confirms that the Turkish German comedy phenomenon paved the way for such innovative feel-good integration comedies as *Almanya – Welcome to Germany*. About the film's success she writes, "With 1.4 million admissions in Germany alone, is to date the commercially most successful Turkish German film, surpassing Fatih Akin's critically acclaimed *Gegen die Wand-Head-On* (2004) and *Auf der anderen Seite-The Edge of Heaven* (2007), which boasted audiences between half a million and 700,000" (Berghahn, 2013: 41).

8   I elaborate more on this concept in chapter one.

9   I rely here on Northrop Frye's broader classification of comedy and tragedy as thematic themes of fiction, and the classing of mass culture or popular entertainment comedy as "low social" or "popular mimetic" aspects of the "comedic mode" (Frye, 2002: 4). Frye's essay collection, *Anatomy of Criticism*, was first published in 1957 and groups all manifestations of literature into one of four archetypes. The comic, the romantic, the tragic and the ironic, which he associates with the four seasons: spring, summer, autumn and winter, respectively. Alternatively, he also uses the idea of the three modes, the comic, the tragic and the thematic, to categorise fictions. Each of these modes, again, manifests itself in a variety of forms: mythic, romantic, ironic, high mimetic and low mimetic. Frye thought that the low mimetic would commonly follow the high mimetic in historical order, which again pits the national (historical Germanness) against the local (Turkish Germanness) and the elite (native, majority) against the ordinary (migrant, minority).

10 See chapter one for more detailed definitions of the concept of pro-social and anti-social ethnic comedy.
11 Humour artist Serdar Somuncu, a former Turkish and now German national, has become actively involved and decidedly vocal in widening the debate about how German culture has pushed migrants into a space of national silence. Somuncu has risen to fame in the German comedy scene as a racy stand-up comedian. He humorously attacks multiculturalism by asking the Federal Republic to let go of its utopian and unproductive belief in a homogenised society. His 2011 *Hassprediger-Preaching Hate* programme became famous for Somuncu's public readings of Hitler's *Mein Kampf*. Somuncu has stressed repeatedly in interviews and on his website that Germany needs to deal with its socio-ethnic problems by facing them head on and re-visioning integration as a process to include both majority and minority society (Bower, 2012: 195-197).

Chapter I: Germanness, Othering and Ethnic Comedy

1 On the rich and innovative scholarship related to German minority culture and the expansionist desires closely attached to the German Home see Tiffany Florvil's and Vanessa Plumly's excellent collection of curated essays, *Rethinking German Studies* (2018). While it is not the focus of this book, the close link between Turkish German and Black German Studies offers additional productive intersections to address Germany's expansive and fluctuating colonial history and the consequences of it for West Germany and East Germany, and contemporary German society in the new century.
2 See my discussion in the introduction of how Günter Wallraff used this centuries-old trope of the lazy, dumb Turk in his sensationalist ethnic masquerade pieces.

Chapter II: Clash Films

1 All translations are mine.
2 See, for example, Leslie Howard's and Anthony Asquith's *Pygmalion* (1938), William Keighley's *The Man Who Came to Dinner* (1942), Vincente Minnelli's *The Reluctant Debutante* (1958), Jules Dassin's *Never on Sunday* (1960), Arthur Penn's *Little Big Man* (1970), Jamie Uys' *The Gods Must Be Crazy* (1980), John Carpenter's *Big Trouble in Little China* (1986), Peter Faiman's *Crocodile Dundee* (1986), Spike Lee's *Do the Right Thing* (1989) and Garry Marshall's *Pretty Woman* (1990).
3 There are six major clash scenarios. There is the clash of socio-economic status, the clash of distinctive and seemingly incompatible personality types, the clash between a sub-culture and a mainstream culture or another sub-culture, the clash in geographically informed lifestyles, the clash involving a fantasy figure as the non-human counter-perspective,

and the switch films where characters walk in each other's shoes for a while (Fuller and Loukides: 170).

4 The location is certainly not a coincidence. The Schanzenviertel, also called Sternschanze by Hamburg locals, was once famous for being a leftist hotspot for alternative art and experimental theatre in the 1980s. The area has transformed into one of Hamburg's most cosmopolitan quarters and affluent neighbourhoods over the past four decades. There is now a wide variety of ethnic communities and different social classes.

5 See my discussion in the introduction of Fatih Akin's work on cultural remixing through image and sound in film.

6 Döner kebab is a type of kebab meat sandwich, made of meat cooked on a vertical rotisserie spit. The Döner ranked high as a quintessential Turkish food in the 1980s. Originally served on a plate, it became a popular street food in Germany after Turkish immigrants invented a sandwich version in Berlin-Kreuzberg in the early 1970s. It is now considered a quintessential German food, which Turks in Germany created as a hybrid product for the German market. The Döner has become iconic for its success story of culinary culture mixing (Henderson, 2015).

7 There is a realisation that true integration in German society and recognition of the differences in multi-ethnic coexistence are not as easy as the vision of multicultural togetherness promoted during the 1980s in Germany. This has been the topic of many political discussions about facing up to the reality of continued racism in German society and its cultural segregation between Muslim and other communities, as expressed by former German MP Mehment Gürcan Daimagüler in the foreword to his novel *Kein schönes Land in dieser Zeit: Das Märchen von der gescheiterten Integration-No Nice Country At This Time: The Myth of Failed Integration*: "[i]t starts with a kind of matter-of-fact attitude that this country uses when it talks about 'We' and 'You'. 'We' Germans. 'You' foreigners. It's been almost 50 years since my mother went on her way to Germany. I was born here, and I grew up here. I dream in German. I have no other Home and I don't want any other. I like being German—well, mostly. ... But I still get asked by well-intentioned Germans how my home country is doing and if I have ever thought about going back. By 'Home' they mean Turkey. And there are others, with less benevolent voices, who are happy by just yelling out: 'All Turks out'. [...] After 9/11, everything only got worse. These were some single shots fired before, but now I experience this kind of siege and heavy bombardment daily. The language has changed too: instead of *you foreigners* or *you Turks*, now it's *you Muslims*. *You* oppress women, you are terrorists, you are anti-democratic. Back in the day I had to take the blame for Turkish extremists trying to topple the government; now it's about Al-Qaida terrorism. A great development. Old racism dressed up in a new coat" (Daimagüler, 2011: 2).

8 "43. Adolf-Grimme-Preis 2007: Wettbewerb Fiktion – Begründung der Jury". *Grimme-Institut*, n.d. Web. 4 December 2014.
9 The satellite image is iconic. Deniz Göktürk, David Gramling and Anton Kaes write of it, "Every night, more than a. They allow migrants to view 24-hour programming in their native languages but cause anxiety among German media experts about the ostensible failure of national integration" (Göktürk, Gramling and Kaes, 2007: 332).
10 As noted in the introduction, references to creative arts like film and music have become a popular inclusion in Turkish German culture clash comedy and romantic comedies. See Gueneli's discussion of European sounds in Fatih Akin's *Im July-In July*. They complement on the acoustic level our understanding of the spatial construction of a filmic multicultural community (Gueneli, 2019).
11 The naming of Aylin's Turkish fiancé is no coincidence. At the time the film was produced and released, the fame of Tarkan, a Turkish pop superstar, had reached German mainstream culture. One of Tarkan's 1997 Turkish pop songs called Şımarık, also known as "Kiss Kiss", entered the German top 100 radio charts in 2001 and was well known to German audiences.
12 *Evet, I do* explicitly addresses ethnic and religious diversity within the Turkish German community. The plot also features some wedding rituals and traditions alleged on the diegetic level of the film to be part of Turkish everyday culture. As Coşkun's father tells his son, kidnapping the bride was part of the wedding ceremonies in his rural village in Turkey. This is somewhat unusual for a Turkish German comedy film with broader mainstream appeal. Overall, Turkish German comedy entertainment in the new century takes a more implicit approach to the problematisation of identity politics. Sometimes, as I discuss with the example of Kaya Yanar and his television sketch show in chapter three, these comedies reference the notion of the "political correctness gone mad" argument put forward by Dave Chappelle, Ricky Gervais and Steve Coogan (Brasset, 2019). Turkish German comedy entertainment does not support essentialism, but it does endorse it as the terrain on which its popular fictions can play out and are being seen by millions of viewers and audience members (Berghahn, 2020). This is important as some topics like gay Turkishness/Turkish homosexuality are less common in mainstream media, as is illustrated by the recent cancellation of the Turkish Netflix show *If Only* (2020). With the script produced by one of Turkey's most successful screenwriters, Ece Yorenc, the show was cancelled by the Turkish government because it included a gay character. Yorenc told this to Turkish film website Altyazi Fasikul, which illustrates Berghahn's argument that mainstream visibility is effective in bringing niche or less visible topics to the mainstream audience, albeit with reduced detail.
13 I revisit this ritual in chapter four. Hatice Akyün mentions it in her book for comedic effect.

Chapter III: Television Narratives of Ottoman Invasion and Cohabitation

1. "Bora Dagtekin über 'Fack ju Göhte': Ich arbeite für die Zuschauer." *Kino.de*, 11 December 2010.
2. My textual analysis of *Turkish for Beginners* is character-driven and based on the interactions between the different cultural poles and generations of the show, for example Turkish and German and first, second and third generations. The approach builds on a similar approach introduced by Erjavec and Kovacic (2009: 149-152). This chapter also owes much to one of the first structuralist readings of media texts in television and cultural communications studies, namely John Fiske's dialectic approach to the British sci-fi sitcom *Dr Who* (Fiske, 1984: 165-189).
3. Sieg argues that Germans have a long and complex history regarding ethnic performance and especially Jewishness on the theatre stage and in German-language film. Her case study of the popularity of Karl May's *Winnetou* adaptations for German television and cinema in the 1970s and 1980s suggests that German audiences saw in the appropriation of Native American culture a way to escape the debate about national guilt in the post-war discourse (Sieg, 2004: 23-24). Benbow contends that Germans consumed Afro-German and Turkish German ethnicity especially during the comedy wave of the 1990s as a way to prove to other nation states their society's cultural progress (Benbow, 2007: 26-27).
4. The increasing trend towards an internationalisation of German television since the late 1960s is the subject of Hans Magnus Enzensberger's continued critique of the medium. In "Das Nullmedium oder warum alle Klagen über das Fernsehen gegenstandslos sind- The Zero-Sum Game Media or Why All Complaints about Television Are Immaterial", Enzensberger outlines the increased "emptiness" of Germany's television programming. From the perspective of a cultural pessimist he argues that the public channels have not met the pedagogic goals as laid out in the German federal government's educational mandate, the so-called educational mandate [do we need this repetition?]. To follow that mandate, Alexander Kluge initially sought to install a certain level of political gravitas and art style in German broadcast via political talk shows and art magazines. However, Forrest describes how Kluge eventually conceded defeat in mainstreaming cultural niche products in the 1990s. His programmes did not attract enough viewers and Kluge later became a pronounced sceptic of mainstream television (Forrest, 2012: 21-39).
5. The series has won a great number of prestigious awards at national as well as international comedy festivals and award ceremonies. Apart from the German Adolf-Grimme-Preis for "Best Entertainment Show" in 2007, the show received the Italian Prix Italia for "Best Drama-Show or Serial" in 2006 and the French Nymphe d'Or at the Festival de Télévision de Monte-Carlo for "Best European Producer for a Comedy Show" in 2006.

Turkish for Beginners also received nominations for the Prix Europe in 2006 and the widely recognised Rose d'Or in the "Sitcom" and "Social Awareness" categories in the same year. A film version related to the series was released in 2012. It was popular with audiences as well.

6   Struppert and Keding wrote the first monograph on Yanar's *Was Guckst Du?!-Whatcha Looking At?!* They used an intercultural communications theory approach. Theirs is among the few but thorough engagements with ethnic comedy and mainstream humour in German television. Kotthoff (2004: 186-187) analyses Yanar's show with a greater focus on cultural studies.

7   The sitcom had a total run of 52 episodes. Topics covered included typical problems of teenagers and parents. The series also focused on cross-cultural experiences. Due to popular demand, season three was continued on public television despite the producers' plans to create a commercial film adaptation of the show. This happened in 2011, two years after the series' finale. The third and final season consists of 16 episodes. All of them aired in the autumn of 2008. This was mostly due to the show's popular reception, especially with younger audiences. The sitcom did, and still does, cause reaction in fan forums, fan sites and on the internet and in social media.

8   Peterson and Benbow argue that the series' title, "Turkish for Beginners", points to the idea of instructing the German audience in Turkishness. They derive from a close reading of the title a "multi-culti" agenda and that it would follow that Germans need to re-learn what they think they know about the majority of Turkish Germans with whom they share a country (Benbow: 238; Peterson: 97).

9   The *Ekel* or "Nasty" Alfred Tetzlaff is a commercial clerk. He was born as a Sudeten German, formerly known as Bohemian or German Bohemian. This was a community of approximately 3,000,000 ethnic Germans living the Czech lands of the Bohemian Crown, which later became part of Czechoslovakia. After the WWII, the remainder of the German-speaking community, mainly located in Czech Silesia, was expelled and forced to migrate to Germany and Austria. Alfred is the undeniable star of the West German comedy series, *A Perfect Match*. The series is characterised by its setting in 1970s Wattenscheid. Tetzlaff, a man in his late forties, is small in appearance. His physical stature, small black moustache and side-parted dark hair, along with his raging temper and loud manner of speaking, reference him as Adolf Hitler. A declared opponent of social reform and especially the Turkish German labour migration agreement, the reactionary patriarch could be seen as the earlier version of Grandfather Schneider, who also makes extensive use of historical references and political upheavals initiated by the German student movement era of 1968.

Chapter IV: Bridget Jones's Halal Diary

1. Hatice Akyün opens *A Spicy Kraut* with her clichéd self-description as a dark-haired, exotic beauty, who does not mind a good push-up bra (Akyün: 1).
2. Göktürk has addressed the issue of culture-specific foods, which accompany individuals like ethnic signifiers across borders and cultures and never quite fade or lose their importance as reminders of cultural authenticity (Göktürk, 2003: 177-180).

Chapter V: Funny Online Kanakism

1. I omit identifiable YouTube user profile and/or channel names for data privacy reasons and out of concerns for ethical research practices, and because of impracticalities in seeking users' informed consent for identifiable publication of their online comments.
2. https://www.youtube.com/watch?v=zw5X3ACaThw.
3. "Wallah! Ich Hab Nix Gemacht". One could also infer that "Wallah" is used to suggest a contraction, alluding to the German phrase "Wow, Alter! or "Whoa, dude!". The phrase "Wallah" has been used by the two founders of a German clothing label, the so-called Wallah Bro's, who are marketing it like a brand design. Wallah merchandise is available via their Facebook and other online marketplace platforms (https://wallahbros.bigcartel.com/). The label is popular with younger consumers and the phrase is used more and more often in memes outside its original context, too.
4. https://twitter.com/jiletayse?lang=en.
5. https://www.youtube.com/watch?v=EkdO9bVLohk.

Chapter VI: Settling into "Post-Migrant" Mainstream Culture

1. https://www.facebook.com/DeutschTuerkischeKabarettwocheStuttgart/videos/266471347640021/?ref=tahoe.
2. https://edition.cnn.com/2012/05/01/opinion/egypt-convicted-actor-adel-imam-khalil/index.html.

References

Primary Sources

Acar, Ihsan. *Der Türke: Das Original*. Munich: Deutscher Taschenbuch Verlag, 2007.
Ade, Maren. *Toni Erdman*. Cologne: Soda Pictures, 2017.
Ahadi, Ali. *Salami Aleikum*. Munich: Zorro Medien GmbH, 2009.
Akgün, Lale. *Tante Semra im Leberkäseland: Geschichten aus meiner türkisch-deutschen Familie*. Frankfurt am Main: Krüger, 2009.
Akgün, Lale. *Der getürkte Reichstag: Tante Semras Sippe macht Politik*. Frankfurt am Main: Krüger, 2010.
Akin, Fatih. *Im Juli*. New York: Koch Lorber Films, 2000.
Akin, Fatih. *Solino*. Berlin: Warner, 2002.
Akin, Fatih. *Auf der anderen Seite*. Cologne: Pandora Film, 2007.
Akkuş, Sinan. *Evet, ich will!: Verliebt, verlobt...denkste!* Munich: Cinemendo, 2010.
Akyün, Hatice. *Einmal Hans mit scharfer Soße: Leben in zwei Welten*. Munich: Goldmann, 2007.
Akyün, Hatice. *Ali zum Dessert: Leben in einer neuen Welt*. Munich: Goldmann, 2010.
Aladag, Feo. *Die Fremde: When We Leave*. St. Charles, Illinois: Olive Films, 2011.
Baydar, Idil. "Jilet Ayse." Idil Baydar, 1 August 2011, https://www.youtube.com/user/IdilBaydar/about.
Baydar, Idil. "Deutschland, wir müssen reden!" Idil Baydar, November 2017, https://www.youtube.com/watch?v=gLcpZfyTGQA.
Benjamin, Richard. *Made in America*. Los Angeles, California: Warner Brothers, 1994.
Çevikkollu, Fatih and Sheila Mysorekar. *Der Moslem-TÜV: Deutschland, einig Fatihland*. Hamburg: Rowohlt, 2008.
Daimagüler, Mehmet Gürcan. *Kein schönes Land in dieser Zeit: Das Märchen von der gescheiterten Integration*. Berlin: Gütersloher Verlagshaus, 2011.
Dikmen, Şinasi. *Wir werden das Knoblauchkind schon schaukeln: Satiren*. Berlin: Express Edition, 1983.
Dikmen, Şinasi. *Hurra, ich lebe in Deutschland: Satiren*. Munich: Piper, 1995.
Dikmen, Şinasi. *Integrier dich, Opa!: Stories vom Erfinder des deutsch-türkischen Kabaretts*. Saarbrücken: Conte, 2008.
Ein Herz und eine Seele. Season 1 & 2. Television Series. ARD Video. Publishing Date: May 2005. Year of Production: 1973-1976.

Engin, Osman. *Kanaken-Gandhi: Ein satirischer Roman*. Munich: Deutscher Taschenbuch Verlag, 2011.

Ergün, Mutlu. *Kara Günlük: Die Geheimen Tagebücher Des Sesperado*. Münster: Unrast, 2016.

Gray, John. *Men Are from Mars, Women Are from Venus: A Practical Guide for Improving Communication and Getting What You Want in Your Relationships*. New York: HarperCollins, 1992.

Holtz, Stefan. *Meine verrückte türkische Hochzeit*. Münster: RatPack Filmproductions, 2006.

Özkan, Hülya. *Güle Güle Süperland: Eine Reise zu Meiner Schrecklich Netten Türkischen Familie*. Munich: Knaur-Taschenbuch-Verlag, 2011.

Pamuk, Kerim. *Allah verzeiht, der Hausmeister nicht*. Frankfurt: Eichborn, 2009.

Şamdereli, Yasemin. *Almanya: Willkommen in Deutschland*. Grünwald: Concorde Home Entertainment, 2011.

Sanders-Brahms, Helma. *Shirins Hochzeit*. Frankfurt am Main: Zweitausendeins, 2012.

Sarrazin, Thilo. *Deutschland schafft sich ab: Wie wir unser Land aufs Spiel setzen*. Munich: DVA, 2010.

Saul, Anno. *Kebab Connection*. Los Angeles, California: Lifesize Entertainment, 2006.

Şenocak, Zafer. *Atlas Des Tropischen Deutschland: Essays*. Berlin: Babel, 1993.

Topal, Murat. *Der Bülle von Kreuzberg: Aus dem Leben eines deutsch-türkischen Polizisten*. Berlin: Ullstein, 2010.

Topal, Murat. *Das Dach kommt später: Roman*. Berlin: Aufbau Taschenbuch, 2012.

Türkisch für Anfänger. Season 1 & 2. Television Series. Universum Film Ltd. Publishing Date: 27 March 2006. Year of Production: 2005. Duration: 269 minutes.

Türkisch für Anfänger. Season 3. Television Series. Universum Film Ltd. Publishing Date: 14 May 2007. Year of Production: 2006. Duration: 358 minutes.

Von Bülow, Vicco. *Papa Ante Portas*. Munich: Rialto Film, 1991.

Was Guckst Du?! 120 Episodes. Sat.1/Bonito. Publishing Date: 2005. Year of Production: 2001-2005. Duration 3000 minutes.

Wnendt, David. *Er ist wieder da*. USA: Netflix, 2015.

Yaran, Osan. "Bitches und Beispiele." Osan Yaran, November 2015, https://www.youtube.com/watch?v=kGtHV9w1HXs.

Yaran, Osan. "The Walking Rentner." Osan Yaran, December 2017, https://www.youtube.com/watch?v=tamSXK75Y54.

Yaran, Osan. "Mein Sohn." Yaran, Osan, March 2018, https://www.youtube.com/watch?v=oQPc-bWhSXM Yaran, Osan. "Manchmal ist Deutschland ein bisschen zu Deutsch." Osan Yaran, August 2019, https://www.youtube.com/watch?v=BA2XR7QK5Vs.

Yaran, Osan. "Deutsche Pünktlichkeit auf türkischer Hochzeit." Osan Yaran, October 2019, https://www.youtube.com/watch?v=lnOrzgFcSaU.

Zaimoglu, Feridun. *Kanak Sprak: 24 Misstöne vom Rande der Gesellschaft*. Hamburg: Rotbuch-Verlag, 1995.

Zaimoglu, Feridun. *Leyla: Roman*. Cologne: Kiepenheuer & Witsch, 2006.

Zwick, Joel. *My Big Fat Greek Wedding*. New York: HBO Home Video, 2003.

Secondary Sources

Adelson, Leslie. "Touching Tales of Turks, Germans, and Jews: Cultural Alterity, Historical Narrative, and Literary Riddles for the 1990s." *New German Critique* 80 (2000): 93-124.

Adelson, Leslie. *The Turkish Turn in Contemporary German Literature: Towards a New Critical Grammar of Migration*. New York: Palgrave Macmillan, 2005.

Allrath, Gaby, Marion Gymnich and Carola Surkamp. "Introduction: Towards a Narratology of TV Series." *Narrative Strategies in Television Series*. Gaby Allrath and Marion Gymnich (eds). New York: Palgrave Macmillan, 2005: 1-45.

Androutsopoulos, Jannis. "Repertoires, Characters and Scenes: Sociolinguistic Difference in Turkish-German Comedy." *Multilingua - Journal of Cross-Cultural and Interlanguage Communication* (2012): 301-326.

Appadurai, Arjun. *Modernity at Large: Cultural Dimensions of Globalization*. Minneapolis, Minnesota: University of Minnesota Press, 1996.

Bachrach, Susan, Edward Phillips, and Steven Luckert. *State of Deception: The Power of Nazi Propaganda*. Washington, D.C: United States Holocaust Memorial Museum, 2009.

Banerjee, Mita. "Queer laughter." *Cheeky Fictions: Laughter and the Postcolonial*. Susanne Reich and Mark Stein (eds). Amsterdam and New York: Rodopi, 2005: 149-160.

Bayraklı, Enes, and Farid Hafez. "Introduction." *Islamophobia in Muslim Majority Societies*. Enes Bayraklı and Farid Hafez (eds). New York: Routledge, 2019: 1-14.

BBC "Muzlamic." *BBC Three*, BBC, 13 August 2019, https://www.bbc.co.uk/programmes/p07goj3p.

Benbow, Heather. *Marriage in Turkish German Popular Culture: Styles of Matrimony in the New Millennium*. Lanham, New Jersey: Lexington Books, 2015.

Benbow, Heather. "Transnational Turkish German Travelogues: Turkish German Women Writers' Millennial Travel Narratives." *Anxious Journeys: Twenty-First Century Travel Writing in German*. Karin Baumgartner and Monika Shafi (eds). New York: Camden House, 2019: 90-106.

Bendixen, Alfred, and Judith Hamera. *The Cambridge Companion to American Travel Writing*. Cambridge: Cambridge University Press, 2009.

Bens, Jonas, Aletta Diefenbach, Thomas John, Antje Kahl, Hauke Lehmann, Matthias Lüthjohann, Friederike Oberkrome et al. *The Politics of Affective Societies: An Interdisciplinary Essay*. Wetzlar: transcript Verlag, 2019.

Berghahn, Daniela. "My Big Fat Turkish Wedding: From Culture Clash to Romcom." *Turkish German Cinema in the New Millennium: Sites, Sounds, and Screens*. Sabine Hake and Barbara Mennel (eds). New York and Oxford: Berghahn Books, 2012: 19-31.

Berghahn, Daniela. *Far-Flung Families in Film*. Edinburgh: Edinburgh University Press, 2014.

Berghahn, Daniela. "Das Mainstreaming des diasporischen europäischen Kinos aus der ethnischen Nische zum populären Kino". *Cosmopolitan Cinema Kunst und Politik in der Zweiten Moderne*. Matthias Christen and Kathrin Rothemund (eds). Marburg: Schüren, 2020: 305-326.

Berman, Nina. *German Literature on the Middle East: Discourses and Practices, 1000-1989*. Ann Arbor, Michigan: University of Michigan Press, 2011.

Biendarra, Anke. *Germans Going Global: Contemporary Literature and Cultural Globalization*. Berlin: De Gruyter, 2012.

Bilici, Mucahit. "Muslim Ethnic Comedy: Inversions of Islamophobia". *Islamophobia/Islamophilia: Beyond the Politics of Enemy and Friend*. Andrew Shyrock (ed.). Bloomington, Indiana: Indiana University Press, 2010: 195-208.

Bizeul, Yves. *Rekonstruktion des Nationalmythos?: Frankreich, Deutschland und die Ukraine im Vergleich*. Göttingen: V&R Unipress, 2013.

Blickle, Peter. *Heimat: A Critical Theory of the German Idea of Homeland*. New York: Camden House, 2004.

Boran, Erol. *Eine Geschichte des türkisch-deutschen Theaters und Kabaretts*. Dissertation Repository: Ohio State University, 2004.

Boran, Erol. "Faces of Contemporary Turkish-German Kabarett." *Text & Presentation*. Stratos Constantinidis (ed.). Jefferson, North Carolina: McFarland Press. 2005: 172-186.

Bore, Inger-Lise Kalviknes. *Screen Comedy and Online Audiences*. London: Routledge, 2017.

Boss, Johannes. "Parallelgesellschaft sanft." *DWDL*, 19 January 2019, https://www.dwdl.de/archiv/5224/parallelgesellschaft_sanft/.

Bower, Kathrin. "Minority Identity as German Identity in the Conscious Rap and Gangsta Rap: Pushing the Margins, Redefining the Center." *German Studies Review* 43.2 (May 2011): 377-398.

Bower, Kathrin. "Serdar Somuncu: Turkish German Comedy as Transnational Intervention." *Transit 7.1* – eScholarship: University of California, 2011.

Bower, Kathrin. "Serdar Somuncu: Turkish German Comedy as Transnational Intervention." *TRANSIT: A Journal of Travel, Migration, and Multiculturalism in the German-speaking World* 7.1 (2011).

Bower, Kathrin. "Serdar Somuncu: Reframing Integration through a Transnational Politics of Satire." *The German Quarterly* 85.2 (2012): 193-213.

Bower, Kathrin. "Made in Germany: Integration as Inside Joke in the Ethno-Comedy of Kaya Yanar and Bülent Ceylan." *German Studies Review* 37.2 (2014): 357-376.

Bradley, Regina. "Awkwardly Hysterical: Theorizing Black Firl Awkwardness and Humor in Social Media." *Comedy Studies* 6.2 (2015): 148-153.

Brasset, James. "British Comedy and the Politics of Resistance: The Liminality of Right-Wing Comedy." *The Joke is On Us: Political Comedy in (Late) Neoliberal Times*. Julie Webber (ed.). New York and London: Lexington Books, 2019: 177-192.

Brubaker, Rogers. *Nationalism Reframed: Nationhood and the National Question in the New Europe*. Cambridge: Cambridge University Press, 1996.

Brummett, Barry. *Techniques of Close Reading*. Los Angeles, California: SAGE, 2010.

Brunow, Dagmar. "Film als kulturelles Gedächtnis der Arbeitsmigration: Fatih Akıns *Wir haben vergessen zurückzukehren*." *50 Jahre türkische Arbeitsmigration in Deutschland*. Seyda Özil, Michael Hofmann and Yasemin Dayioglu-Yücel (eds). Göttingen: V&R Unipress, 2011: 183-2004.

Burgess, Jean, and Joshua Green. *Online Video and Participatory Culture*. Oxford: Polity Press, 2009.

Burns, Rob. "The Politics of Cultural Representation: Turkish-German Encounters." *German Politics* 16.3 (2007): 358-378.

Butler, Pamela, and Jigna Desai. "Manolos, Marriage, and Mantras: Chick-Lit Criticism and Transnational Feminism." *Meridians: Feminism, Race, Transnationalism*. 8.2 (2008): 1-31.

Celik, Ipek. *In Permanent Crisis: Ethnicity in Contemporary European Media and Cinema*. Ann Arbour, Michigan: Michigan University Press, 2015.

Chapin, Wesley. "The Turkish Diaspora in Germany." *Diaspora* 5.2 (1996): 273-301.

Chapman, James. "The Power of Propaganda." *Journal of Contemporary History* 35.4 (2000): 679-688.

Charney. "Introduction". *Comedy: A Geographic and Historical Guide. Volume One*. Maurice Charney (ed). Westport, Connecticut: Praeger, 2005: 1-8.

Chin, Rita. *The Guest Worker Question in Postwar Germany*. Cambridge: Cambridge University Press, 2009.

Critchley, Simon. *Humor*. London and New York: Routledge, 2013.

Davies, Christie. "Ethnic Jokes, Moral Values and Social Boundaries." *The British Journal of Sociology* 33.3 (1982): 383-403.

Davies, Christie. *The Mirth of Nations*. New Brunswick, New Jersey: Transaction Publishers, 2002. Print.

Davis, Jessica Milner, and Sharyn Roach Anleu. "Thinking About Judges, Judging and Humour: The Intersection of Opposites." *Judges, Judging and Humour*. Cham: Palgrave Macmillan, 2018: 1-38.

Desmarais, Claude. *A Different Germany: Pop and the Negotiation of German Culture*. Newcastle upon Tyne: Cambridge Scholars Publishing, 2014.

Donian, Jennalee. Taking Comedy Seriously: Stand-Up's Dissident Potential in Mass Culture. Lanham, Maryland: Lexington Books, 2019.

Dundes, Alan, and Thomas Hauschild. "Auschwitz Jokes." *Humour in Society*. George Powell and Chris Paton (eds). London: Palgrave Macmillan, 1988, 56-66.

Eigler, Friederike, and Jens Kugele. "Introduction: *Heimat* at the Intersection of Memory and Space". *'Heimat': At the Intersection of Memory and Space*. Friederike Eigler and Jens Kugele (eds). Vol. 14. Berlin: Walter de Gruyter, 2012: 1-14.

El Hissy, Maha. *Getürkte Türken: Karnevaleske Stilmittel im Theater, Kabarett und Film Deutsch-Türkischer Künstlerinnen und Künstler*. Bielefeld: Transcript Verlag, 2012.

El-Tayeb, Fatima. *Undeutsch: Die Konstruktion des Anderen in the postmigrantischen Gesellschaft*. Bielefeld: Transcript, 2016.

Erdoğan, Murat. *Yurtdışındaki Türkler: 50. Yılında Göç Ve Uyum = Turks Abroad: Migration and Integration in Its 50th Year = Türken Im Ausland: 50 Jahre Migration und Integration: 21-23 Mayıs, May, Mai 2009, Ankara*. Kızılay, Ankara: Orion, 2009.

Erjavec, Karmen, and Melita Poler Kovacic. "A Discursive Approach to Genre." *European Journal of Communication* 24.2 (2009): 147-164.

Faas, Daniel. "Reconsidering Identity: The Ethnic and Political Dimensions of Hybridity among Majority and Turkish Youth in Germany and England." *The British Journal of Sociology* 60.2 (2009): 299-320.

Fachinger, Petra. *Rewriting Germany from the Margins: "Other" German Literature of the 1980s and 1990s*. Montreal and Ithaca, New York: McGill-Queen's University Press, 2001.

Faulk, Barry. "Love and Lists in Nick Hornby's High Fidelity." *Cultural Critique*. 66.1 (2007): 153-176.

Fenner, Angelica. *Race Under Reconstruction in German Cinema: Robert Stemmle's Toxi*. Toronto: University of Toronto Press, 2011.

Ferree, Myra. *Varieties of Feminism: German Gender Politics in Global Perspective*. Palo Alto, California: Stanford University Press, 2012.

Ferris, Suzanne, and Mallory Young. *Chick Flicks: Contemporary Women at the Movies*. New York: Routledge, 2006.

Fiske, John. "Popularity and Ideology: A Structural Reading of Dr Who." *Interpreting Television: Current Research Perspectives*. Willard Rowland and Bruce Watkins (eds). Beverly Hills, California: Sage, 1984.

Florvil, Tiffany, and Vanessa Plumly. *Rethinking Black German Studies: Approaches, Interventions and Histories*. Oxford: Peter Lang, 2018.

Foroutan, Naika. "Identity and (Muslim) Integration in Germany." *Washington, DC: Migration Policy Institute* (2013) (March): 1-22.

Forrest, Tara. *Alexander Kluge: Raw Materials for the Imagination*. Amsterdam: Amsterdam University Press, 2012.

Frye, Northrop, and Robert Denham. *Northrop Frye on Literature and Society, 1936-1989: Unpublished Papers*. Toronto: University of Toronto Press, 2002.

Fuller, Linda, and Paul Loukides. *Beyond the Stars: Studies in American Popular Film*. Bowling Green, Ohio: Bowling Green University Popular Press, 1990.

Geller, Jay, and Leslie Morris. "Introduction." *Three-Way Street: Jews, Germans, and the Transnational*. Jay Geller and Leslie Morris (eds). Ann Arbor, Michigan: University of Michigan Press, 2016: 1-20.

Gesemann, Frank, and Roland Roth. *Lokale Integrationspolitik in der Einwanderungsgesellschaft: Migration und Integration als Herausforderung von Kommunen*. Wiesbaden: VS Verlag für Sozialwissenschaften, 2008.

Gezen, Ela. *Brecht, Turkish Theater, and Turkish-German Literature: Reception, Adaptation, and Innovation after 1960*. Rochester, New York: Camden House, 2018.

Gilbert, Joanne. "Performing Marginality: Comedy, Identity, and Cultural Critique." *Text and Performance Quarterly*. 17.4 (1997): 317-330.

Gill, Rosalind. "Lad Lit as Mediated Intimacy: A Postfeminist Tale of Female Power, Male Vulnerability and Toast." *Working Papers on the Web* 13 (2009).

Gillota, David. *Ethnic Humor in Multiethnic America*. Princeton, New Jersey: Rutgers University Press, 2013.

Gilman, Sander. "Thilo Sarrazin and the Politics of Race in the Twenty-First Century". *New German Critique* 39.3 (2012): 47-59.

Glick Schiller, Nina, Linda Basch and Cristina Szanton Blanc. "From Immigrant to Transmigrant: Theorizing Transnational Migration." *Anthropological Quarterly* (1995): 48-63.

Göktürk, Deniz. *Turkish Delight-German Fright: Migrant Identities in Transnational Cinema*. University of Oxford: Transnational Communities Programme, 1999: 1-14.

Göktürk, Deniz. "Strangers in Disguise: Role-Play Beyond Identity Politics in Anarchic Film Comedy." *New German Critique* 92 (2004): 100-122.

Göktürk, Deniz. David Gramling and Anton Kaes. *Germany in Transit: Nation and Migration, 1955-2005*. Berkeley, California: University of California Press, 2007.

Göktürk, Deniz. "Paternalism Revisited: Turkish German Traffic in Cinema". Tim Bergfelder, Erica Carter, Deniz Göktürk and Claudia Sandberg (eds). London: BFI, 2020: 494-516.

Goldberg, Andreas. "Islam in Germany". *ISLAM, Europe's Second Religion: The New Social, Cultural, and Political Landscape*. Shireen Hunter (ed). London: Praeger, 2002: 29-50.

Goltz, Dustin Bradley. "Ironic Performativity: Amy Schumer's Big (White) Balls." *Text and Performance Quarterly* 35.4 (2015): 266-285.

Gramling, David. "The Caravanserai Turns Twenty: Or, Rethinking New German Literature - in Turkish?" *Alman Dili ve Edebiyatı Dergisi-Studien zur deutschen Sprache und Literatur* 2.24 (2011): 55-83.

Gray, Herman. *Watching Race: Television and the Struggle for Blackness*. Minneapolis, Minnesota: University of Minnesota Press, 2004.

Gueneli, Berna. *Fatih Akin's Cinema and the New Sound of Europe*. Bloomington, Indiana: Indiana University Press, 2019.

Gupta, Akhil, and James Ferguson (eds). *Culture, Power, Place: Explorations in Critical Anthropology*. Durham, North Carolina, and London: Duke University Press, 1997.

Habermas, Jürgen. "Historical Consciousness and Post-Traditional Identity: Remarks on the Federal Republic's Orientation to the West." *Acta Sociologica* 31.1 (1988): 3-13.

Haggins, Bambi. "Laughing Mad: The Black Comedian's Place in American Comedy of the Post-Civil Rights Era." *Hollywood Comedians: The Film Reader*. Frank Krutnik (ed.). London: Routledge, 1995: 171-186.

Haggins, Bambi. "In the Wake of 'The Nigger Pixie': Dave Chappelle and the politics of crossover comedy." *Satire TV: Politics and Comedy in the Post-Network Era* (2009): 233-251.

Hake, Sabine, and Barbara Mennel. "Introduction." *Turkish German Cinema in the New Millennium: Sites, Sounds, and Screens*. Sabine Hake and Barbara Mennel (eds). New York and London: Berghahn Books, 2012: 1-18.

Hake, Sabine. *German National Cinema*. New York: Routledge, 2013.

Hall, Stuart. *Representation: Cultural Representations and Signifying Practices*. Thousand Oaks, California: SAGE, 1997.

Halle, Randall. "German Film: Transnational". Tim Bergfelder, Erica Carter, Deniz Göktürk and Claudia Sandberg (eds). London: BFI, 2020: 517-526.

Halle, Randall. *German Film after Germany: Toward a Transnational Aesthetic*. Urbana and Chicago, Illinois: University of Illinois Press, 2008.

Halle, Randall. "Experiments in Turkish-German Film-Making: Ayşe Polat, Kutluğ Ataman, Neco Çelik, Aysun Bademsoy and Kanak Attak." *New Cinemas: Journal of Contemporary Film* 7.1 (2009): 39-53.

Haridakis, Paul, and Gary Hanson. "Social Interaction and Co-Viewing with YouTube: Blending Mass Communication Reception and Social Connection." *Journal of Broadcasting & Electronic Media* 53.2 (2009): 317-335.

Henderson, Heike. "Kebab in London: Transnational Experiences and the Role of Food in Yadé Kara's *Cafe Cyprus.*" *Rocky Mountain Review* 69.2 (2015): 182-199.

Herbert, Ulrich. *A History of Foreign Labor in Germany, 1880-1980: Seasonal Workers, Forced Laborers, Guest Workers.* Ann Arbor, Michigan: University of Michigan Press, 1990.

Higbee, Will, and Song Hwee Lim. "Concepts of Transnational Cinema: Towards a Critical Transnationalism in Film Studies." *Transnational Cinemas* 1.1 (2010): 7-21.

Hillman, Roger, and Vivien Silvey. "Remixing Hamburg: Transnationalism in Fatih Akin's *Soul Kitchen.* Turkish German Cinema in the New Millennium: Sites, Sounds, and Screens.* Sabine Hake and Barbara Mennel. New York: Berghahn Books, 2012: 186-197.

Hine, Christine. "Towards Ethnography of Television on the Internet: A Mobile Strategy for Exploring Mundane Interpretive Activities." *Media, Culture & Society* 33.4 (2011): 567-582.

Hirzalla, Fadi, and Liesbet van Zoonen. "'The Muslims Are Coming': The Enactment of Morality in Activist Muslim Comedy." *HUMOR* 29.2 (2016): 261-278.

Hollows, Joanne. *Feminism, Femininity and Popular Culture.* Manchester: Manchester University Press, 2000.

Holm, Nicholas. *Humour as Politics: The Political Aesthetics of Contemporary Comedy.* Cham: Palgrave Macmillan, 2017.

Holmes, Janet. "Politeness, Power and Provocation: How Humour Functions in the Workplace." *Discourse Studies* 2 (2000): 159-185.

Ickstadt, Heinz. "Appropriating Difference: Turkish-German Rap." *Amerikastudien / American Studies* 44.4 (1999): 571-578.

Jackson, Melissa. *Comedy and Feminist Interpretation of the Hebrew Bible: A Subversive Collaboration.* Oxford: Oxford University Press, 2012.

James, David. "Introduction." *Modernism and Close Reading.* David James (ed.). Oxford: Oxford University Press, 2020: 1-18.

Jeffers McDonald, Tamar. *Romantic Comedy: Boy Meets Girl Meets Genre.* London and New York: Columbia University Press, 2007.

Jenkins, Jennifer. "German Orientalism: Introduction." *Comparative Studies of South Asia, Africa and the Middle East* 24.2 (2004): 97-100.

Jorgensen, Julia. "The Functions of Sarcastic Irony in Speech." *Journal of Pragmatics* 26.5 (1996): 613-634.

Kahn, Adil Hussain. "Creating the Image of European Islam: The European Council for Fatwa and Research and Ireland." *Muslim Political Participation in Europe.* Jørgen Nielsen (ed.). Edinburgh: The University of Edinburgh Press, 2013: 215-238.

Karakus, Melisa. "The German Hidden in the Body of a Turk: Visiting Jilet Ayse." *Renk* 29 July 2017, https://renk-magazin.de/en/german-hidden-body-turk/.

Kaya, Ayhan. "German-Turkish Transnational Space: A Separate Space of Their Own." *German Studies Review* 30.3 (2007): 483-502.

Kaya, Ayhan. *Europeanization and Tolerance in Turkey: The Myth of Toleration*. Basingstoke and New York: Palgrave Macmillan, 2013.

Kermani, Navid. *Wer ist Wir?: Deutschland und seine Muslime*. Munich: Beck, 2009.

King, Geoff. *Film Comedy*. London: Wallflower Press, 2002.

Kloë, Christopher. *Komik als Kommunikation der Kulturen: Beispiele von türkischstämmigen und muslimischen Gruppen in Deutschland*. Wiesbaden: Springer, 2017.

Kontje, Todd. *Imperial Fictions: German Literature Before and Beyond the Nation-State*. [place of publication], Michigan, University of Michigan Press, 2018.

Kopp, Kristin. "If Your Car Is Stolen it Will Soon Be in Poland: Criminal Representations of Poland and the Poles in German Fictional Film of the 1990s." *Postcolonial Approaches to Eastern European Cinema: Portraying Neighbours On-Screen*. Ewa Mazierska, Lars Kristensen and Eva Näripea (eds). London: Tauris, 2014: 41-66.

Kosnick, Kira. *Migrant Media: Turkish Broadcasting and Multicultural Politics in Berlin*. Bloomington, Indiana: Indiana University Press, 2007.

Kuipers, Giselinde. *Good Humor, Bad Taste: A Sociology of the Joke*. Berlin: Mouton de Gruyter, 2006.

Ladd, Brian. *The Ghosts of Berlin: Confronting German History in the Urban Landscape*. Chicago, Illinois: University of Chicago Press, 2008.

Landfester, Petra. "How Should a Body Move: Turkish German Claims to Recognition in Architecture, Film and Literature." Dissertation. University of Colorado at Boulder: ProQuest Dissertations Publishing, 2013.

Limon, John. *Stand-Up Comedy in Theory, or, Abjection in America*. Durham, North Carolina, and London: Duke University Press, 2000.

Lippitt, John. "Humour and Incongruity." *Cogito* 8.2 (1994): 147-153.

Lischke, Ute. "Berlin as a *New* Metropolis? Tom Tykwer's *Lola Rennt*." *A Different Germany: Pop and the Negotiation of German Culture*. Claude Desmarais (ed). Newcastle upon Tyne: Cambridge Scholars Publishing, 2014: 91-104.

Lockyer, Sharon, and Michael Pickering. "You Must Be Joking: The Sociological Critique of Humour and Comic Media." *Sociology Compass* 2.3 (2008): 808-820.

Lowe, John. "Theories of Ethnic Humor: How to Enter, Laughing." *American Quarterly* 38.3 (1986): 439-460.

Mack, Michael. *German Idealism and the Jew: The Inner Anti-Semitism of Philosophy and German Jewish Responses*. Chicago, Illinois: University of Chicago Press, 2003.

Mahar, William John. *Behind the Burnt Cork Mask: Early Blackface Minstrelsy and Antebellum American Popular Culture*. Vol. 501. Urbana and Chicago, Illinois: University of Illinois Press, 1999.

Mandel, Ruth. *Cosmopolitan Anxieties*. Durham, North Carolina, and London: Duke University Press, 2008.

Marchand, Suzanne. *German Orientalism in the Age of Empire: Religion, Race and Scholarship*. Cambridge and Washington, DC: Cambridge University Press and German Historical Institute, 2009.

Martin, Rod. *The Psychology of Humor: An Integrative Approach*. Burlington, Massachusetts: Elsevier Academic Press, 2018.

Mather, Nigel. *Tears of Laughter: Comedy-Drama in 1990s British Cinema*. Manchester: Manchester University Press, 2005.

Matthes, Frauke. "'"Was deutsch ist, bestimmen wir"': Definitions of (Turkish-) Germanness in Feridun Zaimoglu's Kanak Sprak and Koppstoff." *Focus on German Studies* (2007): 19-35.

Mayroth, Nathalie. "Nicht Jugendfreie Sprache." Natalie Mayroth, 2016, http://natalie mayroth.de/text/jilet_ayse/.

McCarthy, Margaret. "Introduction." *German Pop Literature: A Companion*. Margaret McCarthy (ed.) Berlin: De Gruyter, 2015: 1-30.

Meir, Ephraim. "Moses Mendelssohn's Jerusalem from Levina's Perspective." Melvyn New, Robert Bernasconi and Richard Cohen (eds). *Proximity: Emmanuel Levinas and the Eighteenth Century*. Lubbock, Texas: Texas Tech University Press, 2001: 243-260.

Montoro, Rocío. *Chick Lit: The Stylistics of Cappuccino Fiction*. London: Continuum International Publisher, 2012.

Morey, Peter. "Introduction: Muslims, Trust and Multiculturalism." *Muslims, Trust and Multiculturalism: New Directions*. Amina Yaqin, Peter Morey and Asmaa Soliman (eds). Cham: Palgrave Macmillan, 2019: 1-24.

Morreall, John. *Comic Relief: A Comprehensive Philosophy of Humor*. Malden, Massachusetts: Wiley-Blackwell, 2009.

Müller, Jan-Werner. *Another Country: German Intellectuals, Unification and National Identity*. New Haven, Connecticut: Yale University Press, 2000.

Murti, Kamakshi. *India: The Seductive and Seduced "Other"*. Westport, Connecticut: Greenwood Publishing Group, 2001.

Mushaben, Joyce Marie. *The Changing Faces of Citizenship: Integration and Mobilization among Ethnic Minorities in Germany*. Vol. 21. New York and Oxford: Berghahn Books, 2008.

Naiboglu, Gozde. *Post-Unification Turkish German Cinema: Work, Globalisation and Politics Beyond Representation*. Basingstoke: Palgrave Macmillan, 2019.

Nielsen, Jørgen. "Introduction." *Muslim Political Participation in Europe*. Jørgen Nielsen (ed.). Edinburgh: Edinburgh University Press, 2014: 1-16.

Nouripour, Omid. *Kleines Lexikon für MiMiMis und Bio-Deutsche.* Munich: DTV, 2014.

Ommundsen, Wenche. "Sex and the Global City: Chick Lit with a Difference." *Contemporary Women's Writing* 5.2 (2011): 107-124.

Pankoke, Eckart, and Karl Rohe. "Der deutsche Kulturstaat." *50 Jahre Bundesrepublik Deutschland*. Wiesbaden: VS Verlag für Sozialwissenschaften, 1999: 168-180.

Pautz, Hartwig. "The Politics of Identity in Germany: the Leitkultur Debate." *Race & Class* 46.4 (2005): 39-52.

Pearce, Lynne. *Romance Writing*. Malden, Massachusetts: Polity Press, 2007.

Peterson, Brent. "*Turkish for Beginners*: Teaching Cosmopolitanism to Germans." *Turkish German Cinema in the New Millennium: Sites, Sounds, and Screens*. Sabine Hake and Barbara Mennel (eds). New York and Oxford: Berghahn Books, 2012: 96-108.

Pirro, Robert. *The Politics of Tragedy and Democratic Citizenship*. New York: Continuum, 2011.

Post, Hans Christian, and Moritz Schramm. "Expanding the Concept of Heimat: A Postmigrant Perspective on Fatih Akin's *Soul Kitchen*." *Reframing Migration, Diversity and the Arts: The Postmigrant Condition*. Moritz Schramm, Sten Pultz Moslund and Anne Ring Petersen (eds). New York: Routledge, 2019: 113-132.

Postman, Neil. *Amusing Ourselves to Death: Public Discourse in the Age of Show Business*. New York: Penguin, 2006.

Pratt Ewing, Katherine. "Between Turkey and Germany: Living Islam in the Diaspora." *South Atlantic Quarterly* 102 (2003): 405-431.

Pulzer, Peter. *The Rise of Political Anti-Semitism in Germany & Austria*. Cambridge, Massachusetts: Harvard University Press, 1988.

Radway, Janice. *Reading the Romance: Women, Patriarchy, and Popular Literature*. Chapel Hill, North Carolina: The University of North Carolina Press, 2006.

Rappoport, Leon. *Punchlines: The Case for Racial, Ethnic, and Gender Humor*. Westport, Connecticut: Praeger, 2005.

Reimer, Robert, Reinhard Zachau and Margit Sinka. *German Culture through Film: An Introduction to German Cinema*. Indianapolis, Indiana: Hackett, 2017.

Risse, Thomas. *A Community of Europeans? Transnational Identities and Public Spheres*. Ithaca, New York, and London: Cornell University Press, 2015.

Romano, Aja. "Kevin Hart and the Myth of the Internet Mob." *Vox*, 5 January 2019, https://www.vox.com/culture/2018/12/10/18130260/kevin-hart-oscars-homophobic-comedy-backlash-public-shaming-ellen-degeneres.

Roy, Olivier. *Globalized Islam: The Search for a New Ummah*. New York: Columbia University Press, 2013.

Şahin, Reyhan, et al. "Riot Grrrls, Bitchsm, and Pussy Power: Interview with Reyhan Şahin/ Lady Bitch Ray." *Feminist Media Studies* 16.1 (2016): 117-127.

Sarrazin, Thilo. *Deutschland schafft sich ab: Wie wir unser Land aufs Spiel setzen*. Stuttgart: Deutsche Verlags-Anstalt, 2010.

Sarrazin, Thilo. *Der Neue Tugendterror: Über Die Grenzen Der Meinungsfreiheit in Deutschland*. Munich: Deutsche Verlags-Anstalt, 2014.

Sarrazin, Thilo. *Feindliche Übernahme: wie der Islam den Fortschritt behindert und die Gesellschaft bedroht*. Munich: FinanzBuch Verlag, 2018.

Saucier, Donald, Conor O'Dea and Megan Strain. "The Bad, the Good, the Misunderstood: The Social Effects of Racial Humor." *Translational Issues in Psychological Science*, 2.1 (2016), 75-85.

Schaefer, Richard. *Encyclopedia of Race, Ethnicity, and Society – Volume 1*. Los Angeles, California: SAGE Publications, 2008.

Schmidt, Gary. "Feridun Zaimoğlu's Performance of Gender and Authorship." *German Literature in a New Century: Trends, Traditions, Transitions, Transformations*. Katharina Gerstenberger and Patricia Herminghouse (eds). Oxford: Berghahn, 2011: 196-214.

Schneider, Jens. "Discourses of Exclusion: Dominant Self-Definitions and 'The Other' in German Society." *Journal of the Society for the Anthropology of Europe* 2.1 (2002): 13-21.

Seyhan, Azade. "From Minor Literature, Across Border Culture, to Hyphenated Criticisms." *Reading the Shape of the World: Toward and International Cultural Studies*. Henry Schwarz and Richard Dienst (eds). Boulder, Colorado: Westview, 1996: 15-29.

Shary, Timothy. "Introduction." *Millennial Masculinity: Men in Contemporary American Cinema*. Timothy Shary (ed.). Detroit, Michigan: Wayne State University Press, 2013: 1-18.

Sieg, Katrin. *Ethnic Drag: Performing Race, Nation, Sexuality in West Germany*. Ann Arbor, Michigan: University of Michigan Press, 2009.

Skolnik, Jonathan. *Jewish Pasts, German Fictions: History, Memory, and Minority Culture in Germany, 1824-1955*. Stanford, California: Stanford University Press, 2014.

Smith-Prei, Carrie. "'*Knaller-Sex für alle*': Popfeminist Body Politics in Lady Bitch Ray, Charlotte Roche, and Sarah Kuttner." *Studies in 20th & 21st Century Literature* 35.1 (2011), article 3: 1-22

Smyczyńska, Katarzyna. *The World According to Bridget Jones: Discourses of Identity in Chicklit Fictions*. Frankfurt am Main: Peter Lang, 2007.

Snickars, Pelle, and Patrick Vonderau. *The YouTube Reader*. Stockholm: National Library of Sweden, 2009.

Soller, Werner. *Beyond Ethnicity: Consent and Descent in American Culture.* New York: Oxford University Press, 1986.

Specht, Theresa. *Transkultureller Humor in der Türkisch-Deutschen Literatur.* Würzburg: Königshausen & Neumann, 2011.

Spielhaus, Riem. "Clichés Are Funny as Long as They Happen on Stage: Comedy as Political Criticism." *Muslim Political Participation in Europe.* Jørgen Nielsen (ed). Edinburgh: Edinburgh University Press, 2014: 322-338.

Spielhaus, Riem. "'Deutschland, wir müssen reden!' Integrationsdebatten in der kabarettistischen und stand-up Performance von Humoristen muslimischer Herkunft." *(Un)komische Wirklichkeiten: Komik und Satire in (Post)Migrations und Kulturkontexten.* Halyna Leontiy (ed). Wiesbaden: Springer Fachmedien Wiesbaden, 2017: 113-131.

Stehle, Maria. "Pop, Porn, and Rebellious Speech: Feminist Politics and the Multi-Media Performances of Elfriede Jelinek, Charlotte Roche, and Lady Bitch Ray." *Feminist Media Studies* 12.2 (2012): 229-247.

Stehle, Maria. *Ghetto Voices in Contemporary German Culture: Textscapes, Filmscapes, Soundscapes.* Rochester, New York: Camden House, 2012.

Stewart, Lizzie. "'The Future Market and the Current Reality': Zaimoğlu/Senkel's Black Virgins and Interculturalism in the German Context." *Interculturalism and Performance Now: New Directions?* Charlotte McIvor and Jason King (eds). Cham: Palgrave Macmillan, 2019. 311-342.

Taberner, Stuart. *Transnationalism and German-Language Literature in the Twenty-First Century.* Cham: Springer International Publishing, 2018.

Thomson Vierra, Sarah. *Turkish Germans in the Federal Republic of Germany: Immigration, Space, and Belonging, 1961-1990.* Cambridge: Cambridge University Press, 2018.

Tofler, Marilyn. "Australian Made Comedy Online: Laughs, Shock, Surprise and Anger." *Continuum* 31.6 (2017): 820-832.

Tomsett, Eleanor. "21st Century Fumerist: Bridget Christie and the Backlash against Female Comedy." *Comedy Studies* 8(1) (2017): 57-67.

Tully, Meg. "'Clear Eyes, Full Hearts, Don't Rape': Subverting Postfeminist Logics on Inside Amy Schumer." *Women's Studies in Communication* 40.4 (2017): 339-358.

Tuzcu, Pinar. "Performing Female 'Kanackness'—Transcultural Perspectives on Lady Bitch Ray." *Körper Geschlecht Affekt.* Birgit Bütow, Ramona Kahl and Anna Stach (eds). Wiesbaden: Springer VS, 2013: 157-171.

Twist, Joseph. *Mystical Islam and Cosmopolitanism in Contemporary German Literature: Openness to Alterity.* Rochester, New York: Camden House, 2018.

Venkat, Mani. *Cosmopolitical Claims: Turkish-German Literatures from Nadolny to Pamuk.* Iowa City, Iowa: University of Iowa Press, 2007.

Vieten, Ulrike. "Notions of Conflict and *New* Citizens' Inclusion: Post-Cosmopolitan Contestations in Germany." *Cartographies of Differences*. Ulrike Vieten and Gill Valentine (eds). Oxford: Peter Lang, 2016: 109-133.

Vieten, Ulrike, and Gill Valentine. "Counter-Mappings: Cartography and Difference." *Cartographies of Differences*. Ulrike Vieten and Gill Valentine (eds). Oxford: Peter Lang, 2016: 1-12.

Virchow, Fabian. "PEGIDA: Understanding the Emergence and Essence of Nativist Protest in Dresden." *Journal of Intercultural Studies* 37.6 (2016): 541-555.

Von Moltke, Johannes. *No Place like Home: Locations of Heimat in German Cinema*. Vol. 36. Berkeley and Los Angeles, California: University of California Press, 2005.

Weber, Beverly. *Violence and Gender in the 'New' Europe: Islam in German Culture*. New York: Palgrave Macmillan, 2013.

Weber, Beverly. "We Must Talk about Cologne: Race, Gender, and Reconfigurations of Europe". *German Politics and Society* 34.4 (2016): 68-86.

Weinstein, Valerie. *Antisemitism in Film Comedy in Nazi Germany*. Bloomington, Indiana: Indiana University Press, 2019.

Wellgraf, Stefan. *Migration und Medien: Wie Fernsehen, Radio und Print auf die anderen blicken*. Berlin: Lit, 2008.

Whelehan, Imelda. *The Feminist Bestseller: From Sex and the Single Girl to Sex and the City*. Basingstoke: Palgrave Macmillan, 2005.

White, Jenny. "Turks in the New Germany." *American Anthropologist* 99/4 (1997): 754-769.

Yaran, Osan. "OSTMANE – Integration Gelungen!" *Osan Yaran*, 22 February 2019, https://osanyaran.de.

Yardley, Cathy. *Will Write for Shoes: How to Write a Chick Lit Novel*. New York: Thomas Dunne, 2013.

Yeşilada, Karin. "Turkish-German Screen Power—The Impact of Young Turkish Immigrants on German TV and Film." *German as a Foreign Language* 9.1 (2008): 73-99.

Yeşilada, Karin. "'Nette Türkinnen von nebenan' – Die neue deutsch-türkische Harmlosigkeit als literarischer Trend." *Von der nationalen zur internationalen Literatur*. Helmut Schmitz (ed). Leiden: Brill Rodopi, 2009: 117-142.

Zambon, Kate. "Negotiating New German Identities: Transcultural Comedy and the Construction of Pluralistic Unity." *Media, Culture & Society* 39.4 (2017): 552-567.

www.ingramcontent.com/pod-product-compliance
Ingram Content Group UK Ltd.
Pitfield, Milton Keynes, MK11 3LW, UK
UKHW021835140426
5217IPUK00021B/1459